Understanding Gnosis

Inside *and* Outside
the
Gnostic Gospels

Also By Lee & Steven Hager

The Beginning of Fearlessness:
Quantum Prodigal Son

The Gospel of Thomas:
Where Science Meets Spirituality

Fearless Spirituality:
What Sages knew and Science Discovered

Religious or Spiritual:
How the Difference Can Affect
Your Happiness

Available in print and eBook formats at online and local retailers

For more information, please visit:

thebeginningoffearlessness.com

Lee & Steven Hager

Understanding Gnosis

Inside
and
Outside
the
Gnostic Gospels

Oroborus
Books

Understanding Gnosis
Inside and Outside the Gnostic Gospels

Copyright © 2015 by Lee & Steven Hager

Published by **Oroborus Books**

The Beginning of Fearlessness/Oroborus Books website:
thebeginningoffearlessness.com

ISBN: 978-0-9785261-9-1
LCCN: 2015915430

This book is dedicated to everyone who feels certain there must be something greater than what the eye sees, the ear hears or the hand touches.

It cannot be given boundaries. It is ineffable and beyond thought. It is indefinable. It is known only by becoming it—Isha Upanishad

Those who have realized Gnosis know the source and the destination. They have set themselves free—The Gospel of Truth

Table of Contents

Table of Contents

Understanding Gnosis

Introduction

Idols...are our beliefs, our cherished preconceptions of the truth which block the unreserved opening of mind and heart to Reality. The truth is revealed by removing things that stand in its light, an art not unlike sculpture...Truth is revealed...not by building, but by hacking away—Alan Watts

Since a collection of ancient manuscripts now known as The Gnostic Gospels was discovered in an earthenware jar at Nag Hammadi, Egypt in 1945, gnosis has become a popular spiritual subject. But like many other fashionable topics, the word gnosis was quickly picked up and applied to many concepts and practices that have very little, if anything, to do with the original meaning. Even the most superficial exploration of the internet demonstrates that gnosis is currently being associated with everything from astral travel to video games. Based on the Nag Hammadi discovery, many also mistakenly assume that gnosis is merely an unconventional interpretation of Jesus' teachings that lost out to mainstream Christianity, or they may associate the word with 'new age' or esoteric teachings. But in fact, the roots of gnosis reach so far back into history, it's impossible to know how or when it originally came to light.

Why should you care? When you understand what gnosis actually is, you'll see that it offers you a time-tested approach to the Divine, an approach that's simple, free and available to anyone that's willing to hear what the Divine wants to tell them. What more could the sincere seeker ask for? But we all know it's impossible to use a tool effectively if we don't know what it's meant to do or how it operates; the same is true of gnosis. Before we can use this priceless 'spiritual tool' we need to understand exactly what it is, and what it isn't.

Gnosis was first described in written form twenty-five centuries ago in texts that contain a group of spiritual concepts known as the perennial philosophy. Although many of the links currently made with gnosis are tenuous at best, gnosis and the perennial philosophy retain a solid connection throughout their lengthy history. This golden thread of spiritual thought has existed within virtually all cultures, eras and areas of the globe and can be found in so-called 'primitive' and pagan belief systems as well as the mystical branches of the world's organized religions.

In a world of continuous change and insecurity, we can ill afford to reject a message, or the means used to discover it, that has remained constant for so long. Gnosis (the means) and the perennial philosophy (the 'knowing' received through gnosis) have transcended all boundaries, uniting the healing messages of the world's spiritual masters into a satisfying whole. Currently, both the means and the message are finding powerful support in the field of quantum physics. While quantum research will inevitably rock the foundation of many of the world's seemingly impregnable belief systems, it explains and supports both the why and how of the gnostic experience.

Given the current interest in gnosis in both the academic world and in popular culture, sincere spiritual seekers can easily find themselves in a predicament: How can we tell the difference between the pseudo-gnosis popular today, the gnosis defined by scholars, and the pure practice of spiritual masters? Since the answer to that question is crucial, we chose to write this book in a 'backwards' fashion. Most nonfiction books begin by posing a problem and end by presenting a solution and outlining the tools needed to implement that solution. Instead, we'll be sharing the tools first. Why? Gnosis is, at is most elemental, a firsthand, experiential process. Instead of just reading what we present, these tools will enable you to begin, without delay, discerning for yourself which gnosis is which.

In this book we'll:

» Explore opposing definitions of gnosis and demonstrate why it's vital to understand the differences between them.

» Discover the amazing connection between gnosis and quantum research that verifies the accuracy of the gnostic experience.

» Uncover the reasons why many writings labeled gnostic aren't, and why many gnosis based writings are not recognized as such.

» Survey the surprising history of gnosis inside and outside the gnostic gospels.

» Reveal why Jesus' gnostic and apocalyptic followers understood and wrote about him in completely different ways.

» Learn how countless men and women throughout history have used gnosis to successfully approach and experience the Divine.

» Examine the basic concepts of the perennial philosophy that establish why we cannot afford to ignore them.

» Demonstrate how gnosis can bring about profound, positive changes in your understanding of the Divine, the universe and yourself.

Understanding Gnosis

Part I:
Which Gnosis is Which?

However deep one's knowledge of abstruse philosophy, it is like a piece of hair flying in the vastness of space; however important one's experience of things worldly, it is like a drop of water thrown into an unfathomable abyss—Te-shan (Tokusan) China (780-865)_

The word *gnosis* originated as a Greek noun meaning knowledge or knowing. Reasonably, it's opposite, agnostic, which literally means no-gnosis, stands for something that cannot be known or is ultimately unknowable. In its earliest Greek usage, gnosis described the type of knowledge gained through personal experience rather than the theoretical knowledge that results from the accumulation of information. The great Taoist master, Chuang Tzu (369-268 BCE) related a parable known as the "Duke Hwan and the Wheelwright" that illustrates this point:

P'ien had practiced his trade as a wheelwright for seventy years. His superb craftsmanship had put him in the employ of a fierce and short-tempered warrior, the Duke of Huan. One day, as he worked at his trade, P'ien noticed the Duke sitting nearby intently concentrating on a book. P'ien boldly approached the Duke and asked what he was reading. Several translations of the story tell us the Duke proudly told P'ien that was "taking in the words of sages, experts and authorities." Not a man who lived in fear, P'ien asked the Duke if those writers were dead or alive. When the Duke replied that they were dead, P'ien ventured even further by saying, "Then what you are reading is nothing more than the dregs and sediment, the dirt those old men left behind."

P'ien was risking his life by making that comment, and true to form, the Duke's temper flared. He shouted, "You are only a wheelwright. How dare you say anything about what I read! Explain yourself or you must die." P'ien knew that the Duke's sword was swift and he could be relied on to carry out his threat. Instead of making a hasty apology, P'ien calmly described what he had learned through his craft, "If I work too gently, the parts of the wheel will not fit, if I work too vigorously, the wheel will fall apart. If my work is not too gentle or too violent, my goal is achieved. But knowing what touch is exactly right is not something that can be taught. It must be experienced." P'ien explained that he was making wheels long into his old age because he found it impossible to pass on his balanced, intuitive 'touch' to anyone else, not even his own son.

Chuang Tzu didn't say whether the Duke accepted P'ien's explanation or not, but the point of the story is clear. P'ien didn't 'know' his craft because he had watched someone else make wheels or had read a book about it, he 'knew' because he had experienced the work directly, and in a sense, he *became* the work. For this reason, it was impossible for him to transfer his wheelwright 'gnosis/knowing' to anyone else, no matter how interested or intelligent they were. Similarly, the Duke could not gain the wisdom of firsthand experience from his books, no matter how wise the sages or experts who had written them.

The word gnosis could still be appropriately used to describe anything that requires our own experience to 'know,' such as riding a bicycle or playing a musical instrument, but few would understand what we meant. Why? We've all been affected by the fact that language is dynamic and constantly changes in response to those who use it. Sometimes a change comes about very quickly, especially when a word is popularized as slang, for example: gay, cool, bad, neat, sick or chill, which all have current meanings that have moved far from the original. At other times a word meaning changes so subtly and slowly over time, the change is absorbed by society without being noticed. In the case of gnosis, the word was co-opted to describe something new, and the original meaning was quickly forgotten by the majority who embraced the new meaning.

Like most modern dictionaries, *Merriam Webster's Collegiate Dictionary*, 10th Edition, defines gnosis as, "Esoteric knowledge of spiritual truth held by the ancient Gnostics to be essential to salvation." As you can see, this definition has nothing to do with the concept of experiential 'knowing.' The title of T*he Brill Dictionary of Gnosis and Western Esotericism*, also testifies to the fact that gnosis is currently classified with the esoteric subjects it lists, such as astrology, alchemy, magic, Rosicrucianism, Christian Theosophy, Freemasonry, Illuminism, the occult and contemporary New Age movements. To discover how this drastic change in meaning took place, we must travel back in time to the Greek Hellenistic period around 323-30 BCE.

For the Greeks and the emerging Roman Empire, church and state were virtually indistinguishable. As a revolt against state religion, which leaned heavily toward public spectacle and the veneration of deified political leaders, mystery religions began to pop up throughout the Mediterranean area. While the state religions operated as a form of propaganda and indoctrination, the mystery religions offered deeply personal meaning and experience. In their book, *The Jesus Mysteries*, authors Timothy Freke and Peter Gandy explain that "Each mystery tradition had esoteric Outer Mysteries, consisting of myths, which were common knowledge, and rituals, which were open to anyone." But more importantly, "There were also esoteric Inner Mysteries, which were a sacred secret."

Rather than the empty pomp and ceremony employed by the state, the mystery schools promised spiritual treasures for each individual who entered the group through initiation. Once involved, initiates learned that a series of steps and/or rituals were a necessary part of a process meant to eventually reunite their 'lower self' with a 'higher self,' a prerequisite of enlightenment. The so-called 'sacred knowledge/gnosis' of the Inner Mysteries was a series of carefully guarded secrets that were shared only with initiates who proved their 'worthiness' by successfully completing each step required by the group. To protect these secrets from any who had not earned the right to understand them, the heads of these schools usually employed myths that were drenched in symbolic language. As an initiate took each step, the 'knowing/gnosis' that was given to them became increasingly esoteric, and the circle of worthies they entered became smaller and smaller. Because the mystery schools applied the word gnosis to the knowledge gained through the passing on of "secret spiritual mysteries" gnosis took on an esoteric flavor. The meaning no longer defined "a direct, *personal experience available to all*" but rather "*secret information* that could only be obtained by *an elect few*." When you compare the two meanings it quickly becomes obvious that they are diametrically opposed.

Although the 'mystery religion' style of gnosis has undergone many outer incarnations, the basic structure of initiation and secret knowledge has continued to hold up the system into the present day.

Author John Moffitt coined the term "paperback shamanism," to describe a progressive interest in a trendy, trashy, kitsch variety of occultism that began with the founding of Theosophy in 1875 and has culminated in a pseudo-religious/self-help/ mysticism of New Age spirituality that includes numerous forms of mystery religion style groups. In its new age replication, the earliest meaning of gnosis, as well as its original potency, has been lost. Instead, the meaning has been diluted and manipulated to the point that it's become entertainment for the masses. It's safe to assume that current mystery school type groups embrace the esoteric meaning when they label themselves gnostic. Although each group may guard very different types of secrets and ultimate goals, they all take initiates through a series of steps, formulas, methods, rites or rituals intended to lead to the attainment of the 'ultimate secret' and eventual acceptance into a privileged 'inner circle.' While it's difficult to learn much past the 'outer mysteries' without becoming an initiate, many hint at alchemy, clairvoyance, astral travel, out of body experiences, levitation, alien encounters, the occult, magic and sexual rites etc. as part of the 'direct experience' they offer. Some disgruntled ex-initiates also complain about ever increasing financial offerings required to receive the 'higher' teachings.'

So far we've defined the original Greek meaning of gnosis as "knowing through direct, personal experience," and discovered how that meaning was coopted by the mystery schools to define "special knowledge of spiritual mysteries passed from one person to another via a series of steps or rituals." Now let's reach further back in time, long before the Greeks coined the word, to discover a third definition of gnosis. Some of the earliest writings that describe this form of gnosis are found in a collection of poems and dialogues called the Upanishads. Some scholars believe several of these Sanskrit writings may date back as far as 6000 BCE.

Regardless of the exact date they were written, it's accepted that the *Upanishads* were composed by both male and female sages over a period of several hundred years. The writings originated in 'forest academies' located on the banks of the upper Ganges River in India. These academies came into being for the express purpose of coming into contact with the Divine. The Sanskrit word Upanishad is loosely translated as "sitting down near," and brings to mind the image of students sitting at the feet of a teacher. But in this case, the purpose was not so much instruction as inspiration since each participant was encouraged to 'know' the Divine through his or her own direct, personal experience. A verse found in the *Mundaka Upanishad* explains, "Not through discourse, not through the intellect, not even through study of the scriptures can the [Divine] be realized." In other words, these spiritual seekers chose to bypass secondhand spiritual information, secrets, methods or mediators and instead 'know' the Divine directly and personally. Although the *Upanishads* demonstrate that the personal experience of the Divine was known long before the Greek word was coined, the original meaning meshed so perfectly with 'knowing' the Divine experientially, it also became associated with this 'mediator-free' spiritual approach.

The gnosis outlined in the *Upanishads* also fits beautifully with the gnosis illustrated by Chuang

Tzu's story of P'ien and the Duke of Hwan, a parable that was specifically designed to impart a potent spiritual lesson. Chuang Tzu's tale informed the discerning listener that no matter how humble the wheelwright's work or station in life might be P'ien was also a spiritual master, a sage. After using his work as a wheelwright to illustrate his point, P'ien concluded his argument by telling the Duke that the words of the sages work in exactly the same way. While the written words of a sage can demonstrate that inner awakening is possible, those words are also dead because they can't convey that awakening *itself* to anyone else. Just as P'ien had learned his trade by *doing* and *being* rather than studying, he came to know the Divine through a personal experience *of* the Divine rather than by collecting secondhand information *about* the Divine. Likewise, although P'ien could not transfer his own experience to the Duke or even his own son, his words and example could open the Duke's mind and heart to the prospect of experiencing the Divine for himself. Chuang Tzu also used the story to demonstrate that this Divine experience is available to all, from a poor wheelwright to a powerful and learned Duke.

We now have two basic definitions of gnosis that are vital to the spiritual seeker, but they have opposite meanings:

» Special and/or esoteric knowledge of spiritual mysteries passed from one 'worthy' person to another via steps or rituals.

» Knowing the Divine through direct, personal experience, a free experience that's open to all.

The irreconcilable differences inherent in these two

definitions may appear to confuse and frustrate our goal of understanding gnosis, but you'll find that these concepts hold the keys we need to unlock the truth. Like a medical examiner, we'll use these definitions as surgical tools to expose what lies below the surface of the texts we'll examine. Before we move on to our 'dissection,' we'll take a moment to understand these 'tools' on a deeper level. For the sake of clarity, we'll label the first definition listed above as 'separation gnosis,' and the second, 'oneness gnosis.'

I. Separation Gnosis

Separation gnosis is appealing simply because it matches our perception of the universe. What do we mean by that? The American psychologist William James' widely accepted hypothesis on infant development explains that we're each born with a 'global self-concept.' In other words, we begin life by assuming everything that exists is interconnected, or one thing. But around 9-12 months of age, we have not only developed an inner sense of self-awareness, we also begin to realize that parents and other family members are separate entities that continue to exist when we can't see them. A game like peek-a-boo might appear to be meaningless entertainment, but the 'hiding and reappearing person' begins our education/conditioning in the concept of separation.

As we begin taking separation for granted, we also realize that the apparent division between objects (both animate and inanimate) also means that each object exists in its own individual location. That location may shift, but we recognize that an individual location is never shared by two people or objects. (This is called 'locality,' an important subject that will come up again later in our discussion.) Our own observations and experiences also teach us that each human is a unique individual that acts autonomously, entertains their own private thoughts and displays their own distinct personality. We see countless stars, plants, animals, rocks, shells, etc. that also affirm that we live in a universe of separation. As author and lecturer Alan Watts (1915-1973) explained:

> In the process of our upbringing, and particularly in our education, our parents and teachers are very careful to teach us not to rely on our spontaneous abilities. We are taught to figure things out, and our first task is to learn the different names for everything. In this way we learn to treat all of the things of the world as separate objects.

Naming, which instantly turns everything we name into 'not me,' supports the sweeping change we undergo as our thinking shifts from a global to a separate/independent self-concept. Naming also forces the brain to express itself with language, which in turn supports analytical analysis while also diminishing our ability to experience spontaneous, intuitive knowing. Because it becomes so ingrained in us at such an early age to trust and value sense perception, logic and language, we quickly dismiss the possibility that we also have to ability to experience things the senses cannot detect, the brain cannot measure or analyze and language cannot describe.

As we go off to school, we're taught that separate 'parts' of the universe that appeared to be whole, such as the human body, can also be separated into smaller parts, such as systems, organs and cells. And yes, some of the separate things we observe throughout the universe can be broken down, recombined with other parts and reassembled into something new in a process known as 'reverse engineering.' Because the work of early scientists such as Rene Descartes (1596-1650) and Sir Isaac Newton (1642-1727) pointed toward the universe as a collection of separate parts, it has often been compared to a vast mechanism or clockwork whose components work together while retaining their own separate identity and location. Considering how our environment and senses bombard us with the concept of separation, is it any surprise that the global self-concept (oneness of all things) perceived by the infant quickly gives way to the assumption that separation is our incontestable universal reality? And in turn, this view also led to the concept of God as "The Great Clockmaker," a creator who is separate and aloof from the creation he set in motion.

Most of the gods that have been worshiped throughout human history have not only been described as separate from their creations, they're also said to live in a separate realm that exists outside of human senses; a place humans may only enter under special circumstances. Looking from that point of view, it follows that most religions agree with the words attributed to the God of the *Bible*'s *Old Testament* who proclaims, "For my thoughts are not your thoughts, neither are your ways my ways, says the Lord. For as the heavens are higher than the earth, so are my ways higher than your ways and my thoughts than your thoughts." (Isaiah 55:8, 9) These verses reinforce the idea that God possesses secret knowledge that humans are not privy to. And in fact, religion came into being as humanity's attempt to bridge the apparent physical, mental and spiritual separation between creator and creation.

II. Duality

While separation may appear to be an evident and undeniable reality of the material universe, there is another component necessary to separation gnosis that is not so obvious: dualistic thinking. Duality is a thought system comprised of opposites that cannot exist without separation. Dualism asserts that reality consists of two irreducible modes that oppose one another such as day/night, hot/cold, high/low, right/wrong or good/bad. While duality also appears to be part of the structure of the universe, it's actually no more than a mental construct based on sense perception that we have been conditioned to accept. And although we can feel overwhelmed by this pervasive mode of thinking, it's not the only way to understand the universe. Like our unwitting acceptance of separation, dualistic thinking is so ingrained we're caught up in it with little realization of how negatively it affects us. In fact, language itself, and therefore the brain's mode of reasoning, is constructed on a dualistic foundation that is uniquely conducive to separating, comparing and labeling. Duality in its most extreme form, polarization, has caused untold suffering. Let's find out why.

If you've read any of our other books, you're probably familiar with the following analogy. We continue to repeat it because it's fundamental to understanding the innate problems of polarized dualistic thinking. Please imagine an artist constructing a value scale. Begin by visualizing a line of ten equally sized empty boxes drawn on a piece of paper. In the box on one end of the line, the artist drops a blob of white paint; in the box on the opposite end she drops a blob of black paint. On the value scale, the black and white paint will represent extreme/polar opposites. The scale itself is a continuum so to complete it, the artist adds a large amount of white paint to the box nearest the white blob and a tiny drop of black. When she mixes the two, the color is very close to white, but not white. As she moves down the line of empty boxes toward the black box, she progressively mixes less white and more black in each box. As she moves closer to the black box, each box becomes darker in value until the box nearest the black box is almost black, but not black.

As you'll see when we delve into the quantum world, the universe is actually a continuum rather than a duality. Ancient sages illustrated this continuum using the yin/yang symbol, a circle that's divided by equal parts of black and white. The white area also contains a black dot, and the black area a white dot. This widely known symbol exemplifies All within One. As Chuang Tzu explained, "When there is no more separation between 'this' and 'that,' it is called the still-point of the Tao. At the still point in the center of the circle one can see the infinite in all things." (Tao: the unconditional and unknowable source and guiding principle of all reality)

Instead of perceiving the universe as a continuum and accepting all its various shades and nuances, the dualistic thought process focuses, or 'polarizes,' our attention on the black and white extremes. Polarized thinking convinces us to ignore the continuum and judge only one of the extremes as desirable and worth pursuing. The opposite extreme is then rejected and reviled. That may appear to be both logical and reasonable when we consider opposites such as health/illness, but most of the opposites we construct are not so clear-cut and, for the most part, we create our own sets of opposites. Our own particular set of dualities may not be shared by others or even exist in other parts of the world. To create these extremes, we must constantly compare, categorize and label everything that crosses our path, and to complicate matters, our judgments continually shift.

To illustrate the dilemma, we could consider the opposites of rich and poor. Virtually everyone would agree that they would rather be rich than poor, but consider that it's impossible to accurately define exactly what rich or poor mean. We can only create an arbitrary image in our thoughts of what each condition would look and feel like to us, but this image is fueled by the input of everyone and everything around us, so it's subject to constant fluctuation. Perhaps yesterday being rich meant owning a certain house, but today it means living in a specific up-scale gated community, and who knows what it might mean tomorrow! The perpetual discontent many feel no doubt results from the impossibility of achieving an imaginary, and therefore elusive, goal. If our goal is to reach a state of contentment, dualistic thinking will never allow us attain it. And, the extreme preferences we each create and cling to can't help but make it more difficult for us to understand others or make room for their extreme set of preferences that may be in direct opposition to ours.

When the majority of a society rejects one extreme and chases the other, problems increase exponentially. At times it appears as if all of humanity is chasing the pure white box in the value scale, rejecting the black box and ignoring all the values in between. We witness this happening on a regular basis as fads suddenly sweep across the globe. Suddenly nearly everyone feels they cannot live without a thing that they would have ignored a day earlier. In most cases only a minority will get the desired object, which inevitably results in a belief in scarcity. On the other hand, if something becomes available to everyone who wants it, it's no longer considered special and everyone just as quickly loses interest. Chasing what we deem valuable cannot help but discourage cooperation and intensify competition. As the 20th century spiritual philosopher Jiddu Krishnamurti (1895-1986) explained, "As long as I think in dualistic terms, as long as I am caught in this dualistic process, there must be conflict."

Author/philosopher Jostein Gaarder (1952-) accurately pointed out the inevitable results of our dualistic thought system, "Life is one huge lottery, where only the winning tickets are visible." Like a lottery; duality requires countless contributors to produce the scarce 'jackpot' that only a few can win. Correspondingly, each of life's 'winners' also leaves behind a vast number of life's 'losers.' Consequently, we're taught that we must spend our lives chasing the elusive winning ticket that will guarantee our 'specialness.' But winning is not only elusive, it's ephemeral and transient. Specialness is not only as difficult to define as it is to capture, it can disappear as quickly as a puff of smoke leaving us to chase after the next popular extreme. Is it any wonder that so many experience an underlying feeling of dissatisfaction and frustration? The majority who are considered 'not special,' are not only left wondering why they are unable to win, but also find themselves at the mercy of those who believe they have won. The same holds true for separation gnosis.

As you've discovered, the hallmark of separation gnosis is a 'secret' that's carefully guarded by those few who are considered worthy/special. It includes steps, formulas, methods, rites and rituals that create a division between those who guard the secret and those who want it. Predictably, this system must create 'spiritual winners and losers.' Separation gnosis is based on these tenets:

» The material universe we perceive through our senses is our reality.

» Everything in the universe exists in separation, including God.

» We live in a dualistic universe where extreme opposites like good/evil exist.

» Some extremes are valuable and desirable, others are not.

» The 'valuable' extreme that's desired by the majority is scarce and can only be obtained by a few.

» Obtaining valuable extremes makes us special and confers power.

» Knowing God is a particularly valuable extreme experienced only by an especially favored few. They are trusted with secret/sacred information and thus their worthiness is conferred by God.

» The vast majority must obtain 'sacred information' that's been passed on from one person to another. They must approach God through a 'worthy' mediator and their worthiness must be earned.

III. Oneness Gnosis

To understand oneness gnosis, we must return to the earliest definition of gnosis found in the *Upanishads*: knowing the Divine through direct, personal experience. Since we've been writing about gnosis, we've found that even many sincere spiritual seekers find the concept of personally experiencing the Divine quite shocking and reject it out of hand. This is not at all surprising since most religions see the world from a dualistic perspective and condition their followers to believe that experiencing the Divine is a 'scarce' privilege granted to rare individuals. Although organized religions may not guard their secrets as closely as the mystery religions did, most do teach that only a chosen few are 'called' by God and are able to understand sacred secrets. Quite frankly, the vast majority of religions are in the business of acting as mediators between God and man, and most of them have also made a practice of cruelly censuring anyone who doesn't think they require these 'services.' As philosopher/mystic Carl Jung (1875-1961) observed, "One of the main functions of formalized religion is to *protect people against a direct experience of God.*" [italics ours] Because oneness gnosis eliminates both the concept of 'sacred secrets' and the need for anyone to mediate a relationship with the Divine, organized religion has often considered this form of gnosis to be blasphemy, has persecuted and destroyed those who have practiced it and have hidden the testimony of thousands who have personally experienced the Divine.

Nonetheless, philosopher/mystic Alan Watts (1915-1973) pointed out, "To 'know' Reality you cannot stand outside it and define it; you must enter into it, be it, and feel it." If we're going to have surgery or get on an airplane, we want to know that the surgeon or pilot has had plenty of firsthand experience, and yet, most of us readily accept secondhand spiritual information from people who have never experienced the Divine themselves. We only accept such a pathetic situation because our senses show us a material world of separation and specialness, *and we believe it.* Although the words of the sage Sri Nisargadatta Maharaj (1897-1981) served as the basis for the book *I Am That*, he declared, "Words betray their hollowness. The Real cannot be described, it must be experienced." Simply put, separation gnosis asks you to believe in a God that's based on someone else's experience (or their imagination) and has then passed along through hundreds or thousands of hands that have also never experienced.

Oneness gnosis tells you to 'know' the Divine through your own direct experience. The Indian sage Sri Anandamayi Ma (1896-1982) told her listeners, "God is the one great Reality. To know and experience Him is the whole purpose of human existence. So do not hesitate to strive to achieve this great goal." Another 'experiencer,' the sage Paramahansa Yogananda (1893-1952) explained, "Belief and experience are quite different. A belief comes from what you have heard or read and accepted as fact, but experience is something you have actually perceived. The convictions of those

who have experienced God cannot be shaken."
Separation gnosis offers a belief system based on
the words of others, oneness gnosis offers the surety
of personal experience.

IV. The Science of Gnosis

Still, you may feel that oneness gnosis is 'pie in the
sky' while separation gnosis appears to be logically
based on scientific understanding of the visible,
material universe. Oneness gnosis probably sounds
impossible, or even ridiculous, when we examine it
based on what the senses tell us, but it all fits when
we study the invisible portion of the universe. To
do that, we'll enter the world of quantum physics.
Science may appear to be an odd approach to
understanding a spiritual subject, but as the popular
astronomer Carl Sagan (1934-1996) pointed out, "The
notion that science and spirituality are somehow
mutually exclusive does a disservice to both." And
as physicist Albert Einstein (1879-1955) so precisely
put it, "Science without religion is lame. Religion
without science is blind." After all, how can any
belief system stand on a foundation that's at odds
with the universe itself? Regardless of how tightly
Christianity once clung to the idea that the earth
was the center of the cosmos, their belief could not
stand in the face of scientific proof that earth played
only a minor role within one of the hundreds of
billions of galaxies that exist. We're currently faced
with the same issue; we can cling to beliefs that
cannot withstand the test of what is real, or we can
adjust our views accordingly.

(Even if you are completely uninterested in science please
stick with us, we'll make it as painless as possible, and you'll
find that a brief journey into the quantum world is essential
to understanding oneness gnosis. If, however, you find

that you'd like to know more about the quantum/spiritual connection, may we suggest that you also read our book *The Beginning of Fearlessness: Quantum Prodigal Son*)

Few of us have ever doubted that the material universe is our reality, but as Sagan also observed, "For me, it is far better to grasp the Universe as it really is than to persist in delusion, however satisfying and reassuring" In that spirit, let's begin by questioning our understanding of 'reality.' Physics is the branch of science that studies energy, matter and their interactions. Classical or 'Newtonian' physics (based on the discoveries of Sir Isaac Newton) studies phenomena such as velocity, momentum and gravity that govern how the visible portion of the universe appears to operate. Because Newton's laws had proved to be stable and reliable in the visible portion of the universe since the 17th century, physicists in the 20th century who began to study the portion of the universe invisible to the naked eye, assumed they would they would govern there as well.

As we mentioned earlier, in Newton's day scientists began to visualize the universe as a mechanism or clockwork that was constructed from smaller and smaller separate parts. They believed that for the most part, 'universal mechanisms' were inanimate and once set in motion, the assemblage of parts would continue to operate on its own. Since this supposition appeared obvious, few, if any, questioned the accepted 'fact' that the universe was an objective, independent reality that continued to operate whether or not anyone observed it or interacted with it. This view of the universe continues to take precedence even now. And you might be thinking, "Well of course the universe exists whether I'm observing it or not!

Just because I'm asleep it doesn't mean the stars or my house disappears!" Nonetheless, quantum discoveries demonstrate that our seemingly solid 'material reality' is not something that's 'out there' regardless of whether it's observed or not. Rather, it's actually a phenomenon that requires interaction with a conscious observer to 'materialize!' And even more shocking, that materialization does not take place 'out there' somewhere, but happens *within* consciousness!

However, this discovery is not exclusive to quantum researchers. The ancient, unknown author of the *Muktananda Upanishad* recognized "You are the entire universe. You are in all, and all is in you. Sun, moon, and stars revolve within you." In the 3rd century, the pagan sage Plotinus stated, "We do not pass through the material world; the material world passes through our eternal consciousness." Paramahansa Yogananda also explained, "You are only dreaming that you have a body of flesh. Your real self is light and consciousness," And Ramana Maharshi (1879-1950) observed, "Consciousness…is like a screen on which all this is cast as pictures and move as in a cinema show." Although these words may have sounded crazy to the majority since they were first spoken, science has finally caught up to gnosis. Yes, through the direct experience of the Divine these sages 'saw' universal Reality long before their 'knowing' was confirmed by science. As we continue, you'll understand why everything you thought was 'out there' is actually 'in here,' existing within consciousness. Yes, this means that consciousness is the foundation of the universe, not matter.

Newtonian/Classical physicists assumed that atoms (from the Greek *atomos*, meaning indivisible) were the smallest of the material building blocks, but that was another notion that proved to be incorrect. In 1838 when Michael Faraday (1791-1867) discovered cathode rays, a subatomic (quantum) universe began to emerge. Quantum comes from the Latin word *quanta*, which describes the small increments or parcels of energy, such as electrons or photons, found at the subatomic level. Like Newtonian physics, quantum physics still studies energy, matter and their interactions, but at the invisible, subatomic level. However, as physicists turned their attention to the quantum portion of the universe, they were completely unprepared for the shocking truths that realm revealed. Instead of the smaller and smaller separate building blocks they expected, scientists discovered a sea of interconnected energy where no form or separation existed. Max Born (1882-1970), a physicist and mathematician who was instrumental in the development of quantum physics, said, "We have sought for firm ground and found none. The deeper we penetrate, the more restless becomes the universe; all is rushing about and vibrating in a wild dance."

Nobel Prize winning physicist Werner Heisenberg (1901-1976) stated, "There is a fundamental error in separating the parts from the whole...Unity and complementarity constitute reality." Inventor, engineer and physicist Nicola Tesla (1856-1943) explained, "If you wish to understand the universe, think of energy, frequency and vibration...These ties [between us] cannot be seen but we can feel them—each of us is only part of a whole." Theoretical physicist, father of quantum theory and Nobel prize winner Max Planck (1858-1947) said,

"As a man who has devoted his whole life to the most clear headed science, to the study of matter, I can tell you as a result of my research about atoms this much: There is no matter as such...All matter originates and exists only by virtue of a force which brings the particles of an atom to vibration."

Yes, at the material level we do have the appearance of separate beings and separate objects, but if you were granted special vision and could see the universe at its elemental level, you would find that *everything is one thing*. You would see the perpetual, unrelenting movement of energy, but no separate forms. Finding a separate form would be tantamount to distinguishing between two specific drops of water while they remain in the ocean. This seething field is our universe, and you are one with it. But this was just the beginning of the surprises in store for quantum physicists.

In the face of these amazing discoveries Einstein declared, "There is no place in this new kind of physics both for the field and matter; for the field is the only reality...Our separation from each other is an optical illusion of consciousness." But what exactly did he mean? Our universal 'energy sea' could no longer be described as a mechanism made up of separate parts, but had to be understood as one interrelated, cohesive whole that's more correctly described as a field of quantum 'potential, probability or possibility.' Einstein's statement was literally 'earth shattering' because it infers that everything exists in a state of energy potential *until* consciousness interacts with it. Everything in existence has two natures, particle or wave. As researcher Robert Lanza (1956-) describes it, "...a physical particle or bit of light [photon] only exists in a blurry state of possibility until its wave function collapses." In other words, as long as energy is in the wave state, it *is* infinite potential; it is not material, but it has the possibility of 'being' anything material when the wave function collapses. There is no other way to speak of waves except in terms of probability any more than we can say with certainty which way a pair of dice will land. But how does the wave 'collapse,' and what happens when it does? As noted earlier, consciousness is the key. Nobel physicist John Wheeler (1911 –2008) noted, "No phenomenon is a real phenomenon until it is an *observed* phenomenon." Yes, as the sages knew, consciousness must observe or choose before the wave can collapse and material objects appear.

Newtonian physics had conditioned scientists to assume energy and most matter was inanimate. This view enabled them to think of themselves as objective researchers who stood apart from the data they collected and measured during their experiments. Imagine their shock when they realized that the 'subjects' of their quantum experiments began interacting with them! No matter how determined researchers were to remain detached, their involvement was unavoidable. Why? Quantum particles are conscious; they exist in a state of potential and have no set or stable state until they interact with another consciousness. Since researchers couldn't isolate their own consciousness, their intentions influenced the outcome of their experiments. This was such a startling phenomenon; Niels Bohr, physicist and Nobel laureate, (1885-1962) laughingly said, "A physicist is just an atom's way of looking at itself."

Research has proven again and again that the interaction that takes place between researcher and quantum subject is only possible because *all* energy, and the matter that appears from it, is conscious. Peter Russell (1947-), in his book *From Science to God: A Physicist's Journey into the Mystery of Consciousness* states, "Consciousness is omnipresent...Consciousness is the source and creator of everything we know...Consciousness is... the only absolute, unquestionable truth." Scientists, known as material realists, who continue to insist that only matter exists and that consciousness is just another form of evolved matter, have found their assumptions to be impossible to prove. Whether they like it or not, and many scientists still don't, a growing number of physicists acknowledge that everything in existence makes up one living, conscious and intelligent universal whole. Freeman J. Dyson, a theoretical physicist and mathematician (1923-) explained, "Mind, as manifested by the capacity to make choices, is to some extent inherent in every electron." In other words, the level or type of awareness may differ, but consciousness permeates *everything* in existence. Dyson continued, "[That] atoms...humans...God may have minds that differ in degree but not in kind...is consistent with scientific evidence."

Yes, Dyson did associate a 'God mind' with the consciousness of all beings. His book, *Infinite in All Directions,* describes consciousness much like 'glue' that permeates the quantum and the material, holding everything together within a mind of infinite intelligence:

> *The universe shows evidence of the operations of mind on three levels. The first level is the level*

of elementary physical processes in quantum mechanics. Matter in quantum mechanics is... constantly making choices between alternative possibilities according to probabilistic laws... The second level at which we detect the operations of mind is the level of direct human experience...it is reasonable to believe in the existence of a third level of mind, a mental component of the universe. If we believe in this mental component and call it God, then we can say that we are small pieces of God's mental apparatus.

Werner Heisenberg went a step further when he said, "The first gulp from the glass of natural sciences will turn you into an atheist, but at the bottom of the glass God is waiting for you."

If all this were not enough to turn their understanding of the universe upside down, scientists were also confronted with evidence that the material universe is not our reality. Instead of consciousness being another form of matter that evolved from matter, physicists have realized the opposite is true; all matter is projected from consciousness! As Max Planck stated, "I regard consciousness as fundamental. I regard matter as derivative from consciousness." Quantum physicist Amit Goswami concurs, adding, "You can make sense of this world only if you base the world on consciousness. Consciousness is the ground of all being, and quantum physics makes this as clear as daylight." The unknown sage who penned the *Ribhu Gita*, which many believe may be 7000 years old, gained the same information through gnosis. He/she explained:

The entire world is all Consciousness alone… All matter, time and knowledge are made of Consciousness…The knower and the known are all Consciousness. All causes and effects and also all forms and entities which have no form are all Consciousness…All the permanent and impermanent objects are all Consciousness alone. There is nothing more eternal than Consciousness and nothing is more real…The only existence and the only reality is Consciousness.

Since the late eighteen hundreds, science has begun to catch up with gnosis and is now realizing the material world we assumed was our reality is more akin to a vivid 3D virtual reality. What appears to be solid is actually made up of 99.9999999999999 percent so-called 'empty' space that's actually an interconnected field of quantum information and energy. It is the consciousness and energy potential in this universal field that causes some energy potential (wave) to collapse and appear as mass (particle). Plainly stated, this means consciousness *is* our reality, not the material illusion that consciousness projects. Yes, all energy is permeated by consciousness since this is the information glue that holds everything together and allows for creation, but the consciousness that creates exists at a far greater level of awareness than the consciousness that permeates the creation. This is why the sages who experienced this reality called the material world *maya* or illusion. Earlier we said consciousness collapses the wave function allowing the material object to appear; however, that appearance takes place *within* consciousness rather than outside it. In Reality, you are the puppet master (consciousness), not the puppet (the material body). Here's what a few more noted scientists have said about Reality:

> *Matter is not made of matter* — Hans-Peter Durr, nuclear and quantum physicist (1929-)

> *Everything we call real is made of things that cannot be regarded as real* — Niels Bohr

> *We do not belong to this material world...We are not in it; we are outside. We are only spectators... Our perceiving self is nowhere to be found within the world-picture, because it itself is the world-picture* — Erwin Schrodinger, Nobel Prize winning physicist (1887-1961)

> *Matter is mostly ghostly empty space... In removing our illusions we remove the substance, for indeed...substance is one of our greatest illusions* — Sir Arthur Eddington, astrophysicist (1882-1944)

Physicist David Bohm (1917-1992) clarified the connection between quantum and material phenomenon by comparing the material portion of the universe to a hologram. Although a 3D holographic image appears to be very real, it's actually an illusion projected from holographic film. Bear in mind that holographic film is nothing like photographic or movie film. If you took a picture of a horse with photographic film, you would have a 'negative' image of the horse on the exposed film and a 'positive' 2D image of the horse after the film was processed. If you cut the 'negative' in half and destroyed one of the pieces before the film was processed, you could never have a processed photo that contained more than what was on that half piece of negative. No surprise there, but holographic film works in a very different way because the information needed to project a hologram is spread throughout the film. Instead of showing a negative image, the surface of exposed holographic film looks like the ripples on a pond during a light rain, creating a series of intersecting circles called an 'interference pattern.' Because the information needed for the hologram is spread everywhere on the film, you could cut it into many pieces and still project the entire hologram from any of the pieces. Bohm explained that the quantum (real) portion of the universe is much like the holographic film in that all existing 'information' is spread throughout it.

Remember earlier we used the word 'local' to describe objects that reside at a specific 'address' in the material world; for example, the tree in your front yard has always remained in the same specific location, a location where nothing else can take up residency. However, on the quantum level, there are no 'localities,' 'addresses' or fixed positions where energy potential 'lives.' Because it is, at best, only probable where quantum wave potentials may be, they are considered non-local.

Continuing with Bohm's illustration, the hologram represents the material universe and the holographic film stands for the energy sea of quantum potentiality and consciousness that interacts with it. What our senses perceive is no more real than a sophisticated hologram; in fact, the body, senses and brain that seemingly perceive the material illusion are all holograms as well. They have a level of reality because they are energy potential that consciousness has interacted with causing the energy wave to collapse into a particle that appears to be solid. Nonetheless, they are not The

Reality or true foundation that projects everything in existence. Bohm called the quantum level of the universe the 'implicate order,' from the Latin *implicates*, which means to entwine or enfold. This makes sense because all the information needed to project the material world, consciousness and energy potential, are enfolded throughout it. Like the holographic film, the implicate order may not appear real to a brain that is limited to sense perception, but it *is* our Reality. Bohm called the material portion of the universe the 'explicate order' from the Latin *explicatus*, which means to unfold, because it is the unfolding or projecting of the information held within the implicate order. However, Bohm also pointed out that no matter how different the implicate and explicate orders appear to be, they remain one indivisible whole, what Bohm referred to as a constantly changing 'holomovement.'

Quantum physics has pulled the proverbial rug from under our assumption that we are these bodies and personalities. Although research does not back up the claim, much of medical science continues to point to the brain as the seat of consciousness. But as Robert Lanza, the author of *Biocentrism* points out, "Nothing in modern physics explains how a group of molecules in your brain create consciousness...Nothing in science can explain how consciousness arose from matter." Refusal to look past the material creates an unsolvable paradox: since the brain *is* matter, something that quantum physics demonstrates is produced by consciousness; consciousness has to exist *outside* the brain to bring matter into being. Although we usually take it for granted that our thoughts originate in the brain, Researcher/author Dr. Valerie

Hunt (1916-2014) explained, "The mind's not in the brain. The mind is more a field reality, a quantum reality." Neuroscientist/author Candace Pert (1946-2013) agreed that the brain and mind are not the same when she said, "The mind, the consciousness, consisting of information, exists first, prior to the physical realm, which is secondary, merely an out-picturing of consciousness."

Of course the brain is an exceptionally sophisticated computer-like organ that does not deserve to be discredited. It regulates much of the body's activity, and it also acts as a receiving unit for consciousness that exists outside it. It serves as an extremely sophisticated 'translator' for the senses that allows us to experience far more than the waves and particles that actually make up our universe. Nikola Tesla recognized the parts that both brain and consciousness play when he said, "My brain is only a receiver. In the universe there is a core from which we obtain knowledge, strength, inspiration. I have not yet penetrated into the secrets of this core, but I know that it exists." Neuroscientists have also discovered other intelligent 'receiving units' in the body such as the heart, the gut and the pineal gland. The heart contains at least forty thousand neurons, which rivals the subcortical centers of the brain. Although we've been taught the brain is the body's command center, when the brain sends information to the heart, the heart doesn't automatically submit. But amazingly, when the heart sends a message to the brain, the brain obeys. (You'll be hearing more about the part the heart plays in gnosis later in the book.) Researchers have also discovered that the lining of the intestines are dense with nerve receptors that may play an important part in our intuitive 'gut feelings.' Physicist Amit Goswami points out that the pineal gland, located near the center of the brain, contains "all the structures needed in order to constitute an eye, and even has vitreous fluid as a regular eye does." It also contains a substance similar to the piezoelectric crystals found within the inner ear that pick up sound vibrations. Goswami explains, "This little gland has the ability to pick up audio frequencies and even literal photons of light...It appears to be a little satellite receiver."

Considering what we've just learned, it makes perfect sense that the word 'person' is derived from the ancient Greek word *persona* and Etruscan *phersu* that both meant 'mask.' Those who have experienced the Divine saw past this mask of personhood long before science discovered our quantum reality. Because they 'knew' the Divine through direct experience, they were aware of what was real and unreal. They recognized the body for the virtual reality avatar it actually is. Note that in the following quotations, the capitalized 'Self' stands for your true quantum Reality. The lowercase 'self' symbolizes the limited human we've convinced ourselves we are:

> There are two selves, the apparent self and real Self. Of these it is the real Self...who must be felt as truly existing ... He who sees multiplicity but not the one indivisible Self must wander on from death to death...Those who know they are neither body nor mind but the immemorial Self...find the source of all joy and live in joy abiding... The Self is not known through the study of the scriptures, nor though subtlety of the intellect... Can there be anything not known to That Who is the One in All? Know the One, know all — Katha Upanishad (1200-600 BCE)

To the illumined soul, the Self is all...It cannot be given boundaries. It is ineffable and beyond thought. It is indefinable. It is known only by becoming it... The end...is to know the Self...to realize your identity—Isha Upanishad (1200-600 BCE)

Look as not to direct your intellect to externals. For [Source] does not lie in one place and not in another, but it is present everywhere...At the innermost depths there is one Consciousness, unchanging and the same...Our present life...is a mere shadow and mimicry of the true life... True waking is not of the body, but from the body. Anything else is just a passage from sleep to sleep...Those who identify the body with real being are like dreamers who mistake figments of their sleeping vision for reality—Plotinus, philosopher/mystic (204-270)

You are pure consciousness, the witness of all experiences. Your real nature is joy...You are...the pure unchanging consciousness, which pervades everything...Give up identification with this mass of flesh as well as with what thinks it a mass. Both are intellectual imaginations... Like the waves in the ocean, the worlds arise, live and dissolve in the Supreme Self, the substance and cause of everything...The sage has a body, but does not identify with it. He/she appears to be an individual, yet is present in all things, everywhere...The Self is eternally present. It is revealed by transcendental experience, which is not dependent on place, time or rituals... The waking state is only a prolonged dream. The phenomenal universe exists in the mind...

The Self is One, absolute, indivisible. It is pure consciousness...The Self is pure consciousness... You are the Self, the infinite Being—Shankara, mystic (788-820)

Noted physician and consciousness researcher Pim van Lommel (1943-) explains, "There is no biological basis for our endless and non-local consciousness, which has its root in non-local space...Waking consciousness is experienced via the body but endless consciousness does not reside in the brain." The discovery that we *are* an indivisible part of infinite, eternal, non-local consciousness also puts in question another popular religious belief: the soul. Because sense perception has fooled us into thinking of ourselves as separate bodies, most people that believe in an afterlife also assume they have a separate soul or spirit that resides in a separate heavenly realm with a separate God. However, the Sufi mystic Rumi (Jalâl ad-Dîn Muhammad Rûmî 1207-1273) pointed out quite a different way of understanding the soul when he said, "Consciousness is the soul."

So far we've determined that the material universe is not our reality. Matter is an illusion, a vivid 3D virtual reality projected from consciousness, which is our Reality. We are not the bodies and personalities we've thought we were, but the quantum consciousness that projects them. We've learned that the brain, and probably the heart, gut and pineal gland, all serve as receivers that connect us to the quantum and translate it into the material. There is one more point that holds extraordinary significance for the spiritual seeker. It's also the fact that connects quantum physics to gnosis and explains why we've used the label oneness gnosis:

there is only ONE consciousness! The false premise that our thinking takes place within a separate brain has caused us to assume that we also have private thoughts, but that's yet another misperception that cannot stand up in the face of quantum physics. The unknown sages whose words are included in *The Tibetan Book of the Great Liberation* long ago explained, "It is only because of deluded ideas, which you are free to accept or reject, that you wander in the world. Your mind in its true state…is not realizable as a separate thing, but as the unity of all things."

In his book, *My View of the World*, physicist Erwin Schrodinger wrote, "The multiplicity is only apparent…In all the world, there is no kind of framework within which we can find consciousness in the plural; this is simply something we construct because of the temporal plurality of individuals, but it is a false construction." Remember that our quantum reality is not one of forms, but exists as a sea-like field permeated by consciousness. We may have accepted the idea that we are quantum consciousness, but it may be more difficult to embrace the fact that our consciousness is not separate and private. However uncomfortable that may make us feel initially, it is our truth. As the ancient sage Plotinus put it, "At the innermost depths there is one Consciousness, unchanging and the same. We do not pass through the material world; the material world passes through our eternal consciousness…The awakened being…sees everything filled with Consciousness."

Many physicists who are mining the quantum world for technological advances find consciousness to be an irksome fact they would rather ignore or deny, sometimes vehemently. Regardless of the anger of some, a growing cadre of physicists is now willing to publicly declare that this unified consciousness and the Mind of God are one and the same. Peter Russell explains, "The faculty of consciousness...is a primary quality of the cosmos, an intimate aspect of all existence...The light of consciousness shining in me is the same light that shines in you — and every sentient being." And Max Planck stated, "We must assume...the existence of a conscious and intelligent Mind. This Mind is the matrix of all matter."

No matter how much some may want it to, the quantum universe cannot support the concept of a God that claims, "...my thoughts are not your thoughts, neither are your ways my ways...For as the heavens are higher than the earth, so are my ways higher than your ways and my thoughts than your thoughts." As Rumi put it, "Form comes into existence from the Formless... Fullness resides in the One, the Essence. Everything's empty with the emptiness of itself, and full with the fullness of god. Which means, the One is at the core of all things." Instead of a separate 'outside' god, quantum physics invites us to return to the ancient *Amritabindu Upanishad* for a concept of the Divine that corresponds with our quantum paradigm:

> *It is the mind that frees us or enslaves us. Driven by the senses we become bound...When the mind is detached from the senses one reaches the summit of consciousness...Brahman [The Supreme] is indivisible and pure; realize Brahman and go beyond all change. Brahman is immanent and transcendent. Realizing him, sages attain freedom and declare there are no separate minds.*

> *They have but realized what they always are.*
> *The Self is One…There is only One Self in all*
> *creatures. We see not the Self, concealed by maya*
> *(illusion); when the veil falls, we see we are the*
> *Self. As butter lies hidden within milk, the Self*
> *is hidden in the hearts of all. "I have realized the*
> *Self," declares the sage, "who is present in all*
> *beings."*

As Alan Watts put it, "There is the central Self, you could call It God, you could call It anything you like. And It's all of us." When we understand that our consciousness and Divine consciousness are the same thing, gnosis makes plain and simple sense. When we're willing, we each have the capacity to bypass the brain's chatter and access our own quantum or 'higher' consciousness. The only difficulty is the willingness. To create a world of separation that would appear to be our reality, we chose to hide from our connection with Divine consciousness. It's as if we own a glorious sun-lit mansion, but have chosen to lock ourselves in a tiny, windowless room in the cellar and forget the mansion exists. But this creates one of life's major paradoxes: how we escape from the cellar when we've convinced ourselves the cellar is the only thing that exists? Gnosis opens the door and once more allows the light of Divine Mind to flood our consciousness.

But when we speak of universal energy and consciousness, some philosophies envision a universal ground or matrix that functions only as an impersonal, disinterested source that sustains life. They see consciousness as a computer-like operating system for the universe, but they cannot imagine that this ground would have any personal qualities or take an interest in the creation that has somehow bubbled forth from it. However, simple observation, as well as scientific research, has made it obvious that the consciousness that flows through everything, from human brain to infinitesimally small subatomic photon, is interactive.

Other philosophies claim that the One Mind, being intelligent and self-aware, wanted to 'know' itself through the virtual reality of the material world. To do this, it supposedly projected the material portion of the universe as a stage filled with living actors that could be manipulated to play out its out interests and desires. If that theory were correct, you are little more than a 'meat puppet' doomed to play out whatever scenario is desired. We would also be forced to conclude that the being that was responsible for the drama being played out on earth is little more than an insane cosmic sadomasochist that thrives on war, sexual perversion, addiction, greed, power, violence, hatred and misery. It's extremely difficult to get one's mind around the idea that the source of the world's beauty would also be the source of its suffering.

Although many religions reject the concept of God as an impersonal ground, they end up going in the opposite direction, visualizing God as pure personality. They picture a very human, often juvenile character, who displays a full range of unrestricted emotion, from love to hate, mercy to vengeance. They imagine God to be fully involved in every aspect of human life from the use of our genitals to the outcome of sporting events. In this scenario, humans were created to be obedient worshipers while God acts as the scorekeeper, tallying up good and bad behavior and handingout blessings and curses. This theory supposes the Divine is a weakling who demands our adoration and wreaks havoc whenever thwarted.

Happily, we are not stuck with any of these unsatisfying scenarios. The quantum paradigm suggests that Divine Presence is both a matrix and a personal creator. While the limitless energy and potential of Source serves as a life giving and sustaining ground, consciousness has chosen to bring unbounded intelligence and creativity into existence. Although it would be a mistake to think of Ultimate Reality's transcendent qualities in human terms, there is a third aspect of the Divine that carries special meaning for each of us.

We're all familiar with creation myths that feature gods existing as separate forms, but a few fall closer to the mark and describe the Original Being as pure thought. This Divine Being *is* consciousness and is eventually moved by the desire to experience as well as know. But rather than create humans that could be used like pawns, Source gave the give of consciousness, free will and creativity to other beings. These beings could have been created merely to experience *through*, but that experience would be empty compared to *interacting with* them. Let's look at the beautifully written *Nasadiya Sukta* (also known as the *Hymn of Creation*), one of the most ancient portions of the Hindu *Rig-Veda*. These particular verses may be the first ever written that address what took place before the Big Bang. And along with the *Upanishads*, it may also be the first to discuss 'monism,' the view that the universe is One and everything exists as part of that One.

The following are a few of the remarkable lines taken from *Nasadiya Sukta*:

> *At first was neither Being nor Nonbeing...there was no death...The One breathed without breath by its own impulse; other than that there was nothing at all...Then that which was hidden by Void, that One, emerging, stirring, through power of Ardor, came to be. Desire entered the One...It was the earliest seed, the product of thought...In the beginning Love arose, which was the primal germ cell of mind.*

Keep in mind that the Void mentioned here is not the 'nothingness' or 'emptiness' most Westerners think of when they hear the word. Among ancient and Eastern sages, the interpretation would more correctly be understood as space, but not necessarily space that is empty. Certainly this space is 'void' of duality since it is nothing but the Divine. But in this case, the void 'holds' the quantum sea of infinite energy potential that can become anything consciousness can possibly imagine. As humans, we each understand that we have potential, although we may think of it as something tangible, none of us has ever been able to hold that potential in our hand, put anything into it, or trade it for anything. It's a paradox that we know it exists somewhere because it can become something, yet as soon as it becomes something, it's no longer potential! The same is true of the energy potential of the void. If it's easier, you could imagine the void as a bowl filled with all the ingredients that could be used to make a cake. Because the ingredients haven't been stirred, poured into a pan or baked yet, the cake cannot be said to exist. As every cook knows, the ingredients used to make a cake could just as easily be used to make bread or cookies if the proportions used are adjusted slightly; therefore, the outcome is only a 'potential.' Just because the unmixed ingredients in the bowl are currently 'not cake,' doesn't mean the bowl is empty. Potential is everything and nothing all at the same time, void yet full.

The *Nasadiya Sukta* not only informs us that the Divine contains everything in existence, but also the potential for everything that could ever exist and the consciousness that can put it all into play. Alan Watts observed, "We do not easily grasp the point that the void is creative, and that being comes from non-being as sound from silence and light from space." Because quantum physics has demonstrated that when consciousness acts on energy potential, creation takes place, we might assume that the first creative thought that issued forth from the void brought the material universe into being. Again, our assumptions would be incorrect since the *Nasadiya Sukta* tells us something astonishingly different. In the One Mind a *desire* arose. That desire, the "primal germ cell of mind," was love. Above all else, the Divine *chose to BE love.*

The first century gnostic writer Valentinus (100-160 CE) also described love as the very being of the Divine, and the prime motivation behind creation when he said, "since the Father was creative, it seemed good to him to create and produce what was most beautiful and most perfect to himself. For he was all love and love is not love if there is nothing to be loved." Rather than the Divine creating first and then feeling love for the creation, love came first and the creation of conscious beings who could give and receive love was the logical result. Just as Valentinus pointed out, "…love is not love if there is nothing to be loved." But Ultimate Reality's desire to love could never be satisfied by robotic clones that lack free will. That would be rather like the love a small child has for a stuffed toy—any interaction that takes place is strictly within the child's imagination.

Obviously, love can only be appreciated, exchanged and expressed between beings that can think and choose for themselves. Yes, we are consciousness that has always existed within the One Mind of Source, but that does not preclude a sense of unique individuality. But instead of experiencing the dualistic illusion of separate lives that are in constant competition and striving for specialness, our Reality more closely resembles the facets of a diamond or the cells of the body that find their meaning within relationship. Each of us is unique, each enjoying the gift of conscious thought, yet we all remain equal and connected in love with the One Mind of God. Ancient Hindu sages used an illustration known as "Indra's Net" to explain this phenomenon. Indra, a Vedic deity, was said to have hung a net that connected all of infinity. Within each space in the net, there was hung a jewel that glittered like the stars. If you could inspect one of the jewels, you would quickly discover that all the others were reflected in its surface. While each jewel is unique, they all reflect the magnificence of the whole.

Yes, we realize that our innate oneness and the separation we project in the material universe are diametrically opposed. Gnosis offers us the reason for that dichotomy and its solution. In fact, it was the aim of gnosis to answer the very questions you may be asking yourself right now. Later in the book we'll examine in depth what the sages have to say about the separation we project, but for now, let's return to the reasons why gnosis cannot fail.

Erwin Schrodinger was not only a Nobel Prize winning physicist, but he was also a student of the *Upanishads*. As such, he had a unique opportunity to study the mechanics of gnosis. He explained that 'unity of consciousness' means *the personal self and the omnipresent, all-comprehending Eternal Self are one and the same*! Although it has taken quantum physics to demonstrate the scientific validity of this statement, the same understanding, reached through gnosis, is far from new. Thousands of years ago, the *Chandogya Upanishad* stated, "In the beginning was only Being; One without second. Out of himself He brought forth the cosmos and entered into everything in it. There is nothing that does not come from Him. Of everything He is the inmost Self. He is the truth; the Self supreme. You are that...you are that." And the *Katha Upanishad* adds, "Can there be anything not known to That Who is the One in All? Know the One, know all." Theoretical physicist J. Robert Oppenheimer (1904-1967) affirmed the accuracy of these statements when he said, "What we shall find in Modern Physics is an exemplification, an encouragement and a refinement of old Hindu Wisdom." And of course, sages from every era and location on the globe have experienced the truth of these statements as well. Our oneness, our shared consciousness, is the reason they insist each of us can experience the Divine Mind personally and directly. Yes, later in the book we will discuss how you can experience gnosis.

Although the wisdom contained in the perennial philosophy (the 'knowing' that results from oneness gnosis) encompasses far more, its foundation can be boiled down to these basic concepts:

» There is a Divine life-giving and life-sustaining conscious ground that permeates the universe and holds All That Is within its Oneness. In Reality, separation cannot exist; you are one with the Divine.

» The Divine *is* Love. Since you are one with the Divine, your reality is love.

» The material universe of separation and conflict you think you live in is a temporary projection of consciousness; it is *not* your reality. Quantum consciousness is your reality.

» Everyone has the ability to experience the Divine, directly and personally. There are no secrets, rites or rituals involved. The Divine wants to be known and can be known.

V. Essential Questions

Are we the body or are we the consciousness that projects the body? Quantum physics has answered the question, but what really matters is whether or not we are ready to accept these discoveries and/or the testimony of the sages. How we answer that question will determine how we experience gnosis. The little, false self that believes it's a body requires separation, specialness, mystery and complexity. On the other hand, the *Ribhu Gita* (*Shivarahasya Purana*), thought to be 7,000 years old, defines our Reality this way, "The Self is of the nature that pervades all the world…that transcends the world. The Self is of the nature of all....the nature beyond all...The Self is of the nature of Existence-Consciousness-Bliss. There is nothing apart from the peerless Self. All, ever, is of the nature of Self." When we realize our Reality is that of the Self, we understand that nothing, outside our own willingness, can impede our direct communication with the One Mind of All That Is.

Since we cannot exist outside the One Mind, why have we chosen to reject our awareness of this essential oneness? Why do we choose to cut ourselves off from the One Mind and the 'love exchange' with the Divine that is the reason for our existence? How can we make another choice and open the channel of communication once more? These are only a few of the questions that are addressed and answered by writers who have experienced oneness gnosis. That being said, it's up to each of us to discern for ourselves whether the words we're reading are opening a door to truth or closing it.

> *Belief and experience are quite different. A belief comes from what you have heard or read and accepted as fact, but experience is something you have actually perceived. The convictions of those who have experienced God cannot be shaken —* Paramahansa Yogananda

Part One: Which Gnosis is Which?

Please Note: If you wish to read the gnostic texts we'll be discussing in their entirety, our sources are *The Nag Hammadi Scriptures* edited by Marvin Meyer, International Edition (NHS) and *The Other Bible* edited by Willis Barnstone (TOB) unless otherwise stated. Although there is a great deal of controversy brewing over the person of Jesus and the question of whether or not he existed, our writing assumes that someone lived who shared the concepts that inspired both Christian gnostic and orthodox writing. For the sake of simplicity and clarity, we will refer to that person as Jesus.

Part Two:

The Nag Hammadi Texts:
Gnostic or Not?

Jesus Christ knew he was God. So wake up, and find out eventually who you really are. In our culture, of course, they'll say you're crazy and you're blasphemous, and they'll either put you in jail or in a nut house (which is pretty much the same thing). However if you wake up in India and tell your friends and relations, 'My goodness, I've just discovered that I'm God,' they'll laugh and say, 'Oh, congratulations, at last you found out!!!—Alan Watts

In this section we'll examine texts that scholars have labeled 'gnostic,' most of which are found in the Nag Hammadi collection and a few that are not. As we read, you'll see that the criteria used by scholars to classify gnostic texts does not differentiate between oneness gnosis and separation gnosis; concepts which they do not recognize or understand. Scholars feel they are qualified to analyze and categorize these writings because they have acquired information that has led to academic degrees and what the world views as expertise in a specific subject. It's not our intent to denigrate their intellectual accomplishments; we have spent many years in the university system ourselves and are grateful for the insights and abilities we gained there. However, if any of these scholars have ever experienced separation gnosis personally, let alone oneness gnosis, we are not aware of them. Since researchers base their views on a set of scholarly criteria rather than experiencing gnosis themselves, it's impossible for them to 'know' what the experience discloses or be able to understand the ramifications of how that knowing inevitably and dramatically alters one's perspective. For that reason, scholarly examination of gnosis is best restricted to the context of the work, not the content.

Art historian George Kubler, in his book *The Shape of Time: Remarks on the History of Things*, explained that there are a minute proportion of things in history that can be considered original entities, something without antecedent. As time passes, these prime objects are replicated, but always with a variation that reflects the historical period within which they have been revived. Each time gnosis is experienced, it is without antecedent, it is the original. Unfortunately the replications of this 'prime experience' are the product of those who have not experienced themselves. Eventually, as the replications continue, the words end up bearing little or no resemblance to the original experience and the replication becomes an entity that stands on its own. The direct, personal experience of gnosis could be understood as spirituality while the replication, concocted by someone who has not experienced gnosis, becomes religion.

In his book *The Perennial Philosophy*, author Aldous Huxley (1894-1963) described two classes of scripture recognized in India, and the texts we're about to examine also fit this pattern. Huxley describes the first type of text as the "*Shruti*...which are their own authority, since they are the product of immediate insight into Ultimate Reality." After experiencing gnosis himself, the 9th century Indian sage Shankara noted, "The nature of the one Reality must be known by one's own clear spiritual perception; it cannot be known through a pandit (learned man)...The *Shruti* depends upon direct perception." Simply put, these are the texts that are the direct result of gnosis. Either the sage, as in the case of Shankara, has written down his message himself, or in the case of the Sufi sage Rumi, a scribe wrote down his words from direct dictation. Huxley went on to explain the second type of text this way, "*Smriti*...are based on the *Shruti* and from them derive such authority as they have." Although *Smriti* texts are based on a sage's own writings or spoken teachings, they must be considered 'second-hand' based on the fact that the person who passed them on did not have a direct experience themselves. Since they did not 'know' in the same way as the sage, their writings or teachings will inevitably be altered, interpreted or mistranslated. It's as if a person who has never been on a plane or spoken with a pilot believes they can write an accurate novel with a seasoned pilot as the protagonist.

As you'll soon see, it's also fairly common for 'second-hand' writers to see *Shruti* text as the perfect platform to add their own particular agenda. At times, these alterations have been carried to the point where the replication has little to no real connection with the source material. For these reasons, you'll find that many so-called 'sacred' texts have devolved into a mixture of both *Shruti* and *Smriti*. This is why we've 'armed' you with the tools that will aid you in determining the difference between 'separation gnosis' and 'oneness gnosis.' The former is, at best, *Smriti*; the latter is *Shruti*. We have the choice of hearing the voice of experience or the voice that speculates and philosophizes but does not experience. Again, do you want the surgeon who has performed hundreds of procedures or a person who has only observed or read about the operation? This book will explore both *Smriti* and *Shruti*; and as always, the choice is up to you.

I. How Scholars View the Nag Hammadi

Since the Nag Hammadi library is a treasure trove for Biblical scholars, it's helpful to understand the criteria they use to classify texts as gnostic. At a bare minimum, most scholars agree that gnostic writings include these concepts:

»   The material universe was created by a deluded creature, not the blameless "One," who is the source of all life.

»   The material universe was a mistake that is

irrevocably flawed, at best a pitiful simulacrum of divine realms.

» Humans exist in ignorance, not sin. Within humanity there is a fallen spark of divine substance that allows for the possibility of salvation.

» Salvation is the result of 'awakening' to the true state of things.

As you'll discover, there are as many variations on these themes as there are writers. But the above criteria are very loose, and can often fit either separation or oneness gnosis; as we go through the texts, you'll discover why. Before we begin examining the writings, we'll spend a few moments on some important concepts that can heighten our appreciation.

II. Thought and Language

When we want to understand something new, we're immediately confronted with several barriers that we may not be aware of. Since you're probably discovering information in this book that's new to you, you've already faced the first challenge: the brain's desire to maintain the status quo. Your brain filters out a massive amount of the information that crosses your path simply because it doesn't fit into your current set of beliefs. It's also quick to prepare arguments against any 'different' ideas that interest you. The brain protects itself by reinforcing the wiring that supports our repeated thoughts. Then it goes a step further by instructing the body to create chemicals that reinforce that thinking by giving us a 'hit' in the form of an emotion, each time we repeat the thought. Even if the thought is not serving us, we become 'hardwired' to it and addicted to its corresponding chemical/emotion. Unfortunately, between the brain's filtering system, its argumentative nature and the hardwiring and chemicals the body manufactures to reinforce the brain's familiar patterns of thinking, most people find it easier, and far more comfortable, to let the brain have its way rather than change their thoughts or habits.

The second issue we face is the brain's finite limitation. As we discussed earlier, the brain is a fabulous computer, but when we let it do our thinking, it is unaware of infinite, Divine Consciousness. When we're learning 'about' something, we're using the finite thought system of the brain, which is adept at collecting, categorizing and figuring out how to put information to practical use. In his book *Thought as System*, physicist David Bohm explained the issue we all face, "You may say 'I see a problem here, so I will bring my thoughts to bear on this problem.' But 'my' thought is part of the system. It has the same fault as the fault I'm trying to look at, or a similar fault. Thought is constantly creating problems that way and then trying to solve them. But as it tries to solve them it makes it worse because it doesn't notice that it's creating them, and the more it thinks, the more problems it creates." In our quest to know God, we've made the same mistake; it's impossible to understand something infinite, eternal and beyond the limits of space and time while relying on a finite, mortal instrument bound by space and time. *The infinite can only be found beyond the finite.*

The brain's servant and our third barrier, is our finite, dualistic language system. As Alan Watts pointed out, "Experience is altogether something different from words. The order of the world is very different from the order we create with the rules of our syntax and grammar. To use…words to try to explain life is really as clumsy an operation as trying to drink water with a fork." The brain assumes that because it thinks using an ordered and logical language, it can use that same language to squeeze the infinite into a logical and ordered finite package it can contain and control. The communication that takes place during gnosis arrives without language as we know it. For this reason, it is of utmost importance to remember that it's impossible for words to precisely describe the indescribable. As hard as a sage may try to accurately put the Divine experience into words, they can only convey a partial impression of what they experienced, never the experience itself. The ancient Buddhist *Lankavatara Sutra* testifies, "These teachings are not the Truth itself, which can only be self-realized within one's own deepest consciousness."

The Taoist sage, Lao-tzu (4th – 6th century?), is probably best known for saying, "The subtle truth of the universe is unsayable and unthinkable. Therefore the highest teachings are wordless…The Tao that can be spoken of is not the Tao." This 'wordless teaching' is the communication experienced during gnosis. Although a language system codified to the measurable cannot accurately describe the immeasurable, Lao-tzu did try to distill the basics of his understanding in the *Tao Te Ching*. Thich Nhat Hanh, a Zen Buddhist monk (1926-) explained, "Words cannot describe reality. Only direct experience enables us to see the true face of reality." And yet, he has made over 100 attempts to capture what is unsayable in the books he's written. Few of the many poems penned by the Sufi mystic and poet Rabia (Râbiah al-Basrî, 717–801) have survived, but one of them includes these words, "When I entered God, my vision became like His, it flooded out over existence. I knew no limits…Speech is born out of longing, true description from the real taste. The one who tastes, knows; the one who explains, lies."

In *The Gospel of Thomas* Jesus said, "I shall give you what no eye has seen, what no ear has heard, what no hand has touched, what has not arisen in the human heart." The senses long for what they can hear, taste, smell, see or touch and the brain desires what it can imagine, but its imaginings are limited by its finite language. Since, as Jesus pointed out, gnosis offers us an experience the senses cannot decipher and the brain cannot measure, how could language effectively express the Divine experience? How could one possibly create linguistic order and logic out of an experience that goes beyond both? Rumi captured the impossibility when he said, "Trying to speak about the Ultimate Reality is like sending a kiss through a messenger." Regardless, he was one of the most prolific authors among the Sufi sage/poets.

Although it appears to be a fool's errand to speak of the Divine, while each of these sages knew it was impossible for them to 'transfer' their gnosis to anyone else, they continued to proclaim their message for two excellent reasons. They all shared a burning desire to let others know the divine experience is not only possible, but far grander than anything the brain can envision. And secondly, they knew that if we're willing, each of us can 'feel' the *essence* of truth contained in the words and be inspired to seek the direct experience ourselves. The Sufi mystic Hazrat Inayat Khan (1882-1927) wrote,

"As water flows as one stream but falls in drops divided by time and space, so are the revelations of the one stream of truth." To access that stream we must bypass the intellectualizing of the brain and gain entrance through the foremost conduit of consciousness, the heart:

> *On this path let the heart be your guide... Everyone sees the unseen in proportion to the clarity of the heart...Turn to the heart and go forward, travelers of the night; there's where you'll find...streams of Living Waters...There is a rope of light between your heart and [Source] that nothing can weaken or break, and it is always in His hands* — Rumi

> *Mind creates the abyss, the heart crosses it* — Nisargadatta

> *The heart outstrips the clumsy senses, and sees...an undistorted world* — Evelyn Underhill (Christian mystic, 1875-1941)

> *Your vision will become clear only when you look into your own heart* — Carl Jung

> *The heart brings us authentic tidings of invisible things* — James Hillman (psychologist 1926-2011)

> *Don't listen with your ears but with your heart...don't listen with your mind but with your spirit* — Chuang-tzu

> *Work of the eyes is done, now go and do heart-work* — Rainer Maria Rilke (mystic poet (1875-1926)

III. About Ancient Writing

Art history students quickly learn that context is as important to understanding a work of art as content. Unless they learn something about the artist, the times the artist lived in and the ideas that influenced them, it's very easy to make incorrect assumptions about the work. When we read a novel, that sort of information may not be necessary, but when we read nonfiction, especially works written in a different time and locale, it's extremely helpful to understand the context in which it was written. Although some staunchly maintain that the direct words of God exist in written form, we can't move forward if we remain stuck in that belief. It may be comforting and appear to make life easier if we believe God dictated a no-fail directive that remains as pure today as the day it was given, but research has demonstrated again and again that is simply not the case.

Every word that has ever been written has been penned by a human hand and filtered through a human brain. No matter how impartial a writer or copyist might like to believe they are, they cannot help but see things through the lens of their own range of experience, limited sense perceptions, personal opinions, attachments and aversions. And yes, we include ourselves in this observation. When we accept the fact that every written work in existence, no matter how 'spiritual' it sounds, has been influenced by human hands and minds, then we are free to accept truth when it resonates as such, no matter what the source, and reject what is left even though it may have been labeled 'holy' or 'sacred' by so-called experts. Keep in mind that works resulting from a Divine experience cannot escape this fact either. As the ancient Hindu text *Srimad Bhagavatam* advised, "Like the bee gathering honey from different flowers, the wise man accepts the essence of different scriptures"

To understand ancient writings, we must also take into consideration factors that we rarely run into when reading modern texts. Various writing systems began to be developed around 3500 BCE, but up until the last 200 years, education of the masses generally consisted of hands on training in the trades and military. Literacy was largely restricted to wealthy or noble families and those who had to be equipped to serve them. And of course, printed material was not widely accessible for some time after Gutenberg invented his version of the printing press in the mid-1400s. Since the inability to read and write rarely kept the illiterate masses from craving information, the majority relied on oral readings, recitations, and orators who drew crowds in both religious and public venues.

While many who relayed and listened to oral teachings were quite skilled at accurately remembering what they heard, there is no way for us to know how many times a story or teaching went through minor or even major alterations as it was passed along. We would also be mistaken if we assumed that ancient information remained protected by isolation. Along with goods that were traded over long distances, information was also valued and 'traded.' As information moved across the known world, it was generally translated into several languages and influenced by countless diverse cultures long before it was written down. Honest errors were undoubtedly made, but information was also purposely altered to more closely fit differing modes of cultural understanding or to coincide with personal agendas. This will become particularly evident when we discuss the disparity between Jesus' apocalyptic and gnostic followers later in the chapter.

All the factors that produced changes in oral teachings also held true when these teachings were finally written down and recopied by hand. No matter that a teaching was considered holy, few, if any, manuscripts remained intact after passing through many hands, languages and cultures. For example, although many take it for granted that the *New Testament* gospels are historically accurate eye witness accounts written by Jesus' closest followers, we must understand that it was extremely unlikely that any of those followers could read or write. A mere 3-10% of the population of Jesus' day was literate, and certainly not those who were from the lower classes Jesus associated with. Instead, his words were passed on orally until they were finally written down 15-77 years after his death by educated people trained in Greek rhetoric, a persuasive style that Jesus' Aramaic speaking disciples would not have been exposed to. Obviously, these writers had not heard Jesus speak and probably had never met anyone who had actually known Jesus. By the time these accounts were written down enough time had passed for countless conflicting ideas about Jesus to blossom and take root.

Many have clung to the idea that God has protected their preferred holy book and kept it pure. However, the rough handling of gospels (both biblical and gnostic) becomes more comprehensible when we understand what the word 'gospel' meant when the manuscripts were originally written. Although we currently assume the word signifies an inspired, accurate account, the Greek word for gospel, *euaggelion*, originally meant a style of writing we would refer to as 'self-help.' Like modern self-help books, these writings were aimed at personal transformation. More accurately, they were mainly written as 'conversion propaganda' meant to convince readers to adopt the author's views or belief system. (Of course this is ultimately true of every non-fiction book, including ours, which is why there is no substitute for experiencing the Divine yourself.) We must also take into account the fact that hundreds, or more likely thousands, of these gospel accounts were circulated, each written from a different perspective. Since none of the accounts were originally penned with the expectation of becoming part of a holy book, they were not considered sacred and were copied, passed around and altered at will. Hopefully very few of us confuse the writings of modern day self-help gurus with a direct message from the Divine, but mainline Christianity has trained millions to do just that by teaching them that the 'self-help' gospels found in the *New Testament* retain unquestionable sacred status.

Even a superficial comparison of the *New Testament* gospels of *Matthew*, *Mark*, *Luke* and *John* demonstrate that the 'Jesus story' was purposely changed to refute objections and make it more appealing. (For a detailed discussion of the changes that took place in the *New Testament* gospel accounts, see *The Beginning of Fearlessness: Quantum Prodigal Son*.) Biblical scholar Robin Lane Fox noted, "The Christian scriptures were a battlefield for textual alteration and rewriting in the first hundred years of their life." By the fourth century when the Catholic Church began organizing early Christian writings into what is now known as the *New Testament*, thousands of copies had been made from original manuscripts, but none of the originals had survived. These copies disagreed with each other, and they all contained mistakes. These errors "number in the hundreds of thousands" and as *New Testament* scholar Bart Ehrman (1955-) points out, "there are more differences in our manuscripts than there are words in the *New Testament*." Many of these errors and rewrites altered the meaning of words, verses, chapters, and even entire books. Scholars feel that in many cases the actual meaning will never be known. Since these texts, zealously guarded by an organization that viewed them as sacred God-given directives for salvation could not be protected, we can safely assume that unprotected gnostic teachings, both oral and written, underwent even rougher treatment.

During periods of heightened spiritual interest, both ancient and modern, (which usually coincide with times of escalated unrest and fear) seekers eagerly exchange ideas. They draw from a milieu of contemporary thought, refuting it, elaborating on it and adapting it to fit their views. But they also turn to the past and build new concepts from the bricks and boards of older teachings. While established religious institutions aggressively guard against such change, merging, modifying and reinventing has been a more common practice among those seeking the Divine outside the walls constructed by religion. This will quickly become apparent throughout the texts we're about to consider. Although we'll continue to recognize basic concepts that characterize gnostic texts and signposts that differentiate separation gnosis from oneness gnosis, you'll soon realize that the nature of gnosis dictates that *no uniform gnostic belief system or text exists.* Rather than being considered sacred, dictatorial or legalistic, gnostic writings were meant to be thought provoking and interactive. Especially in the earlier texts, the reader was not expected to accept them as irrefutable, but to use them as a means of searching their own heart or as a jumping off place for their own contemplation or experience.

Oneness gnosis, by its very definition, does not lend itself to belief in a unique God inspired religious text or a literal interpretation of any sage's teachings since 'knowing' can come *only* through a direct, personal experience of the Divine. In the case of separation gnosis, you'll discover that some of the earliest texts do contain concepts associated with oneness gnosis but as time went by, they moved closer and closer toward institutionalization, and began to focus on secrets, mysteries, rituals, obedience and the belief that only a few were worthy of salvation. Still, when compared to religious standardization and the compliance demanded by the church, at least some freedom of individual understanding and expression continued to appear. Yes, those who practiced separation gnosis guarded their 'secrets,' but worthy initiates were still encouraged to 'experience' the secrets that were shared with them individually. Confusing as this sounds, the relative freedom separation gnosis offered was certainly an escape from the oppressive spiritual suffocation of the nearly all-powerful early church.

On the other hand, throughout history and in every locale, texts based on the direct experience of oneness gnosis consistently include the same basic concepts. Even so, it would be a mistake to assume there was any forced conformity or collusion on the part of writers. Since sages were separated by time and location and rarely knew each other, or even knew of each other, we can only conclude that their consistent message is the result of the same changeless truths they all experienced. Despite the fact that these truths never change, they can be expressed in as many different ways as there are experiencers. Rumi explained why we see the same concepts expressed in very personal ways:

> *Make everything in you an ear, each atom of your being, and you will hear at every moment what the source is whispering to you, just to you and for you, without any need for my words or anyone else's. You are – we all are – the beloved of the Beloved, and in every moment, in every event of your life, the Beloved is whispering to you exactly what you need to hear and know.*

Simply put, the Divine crafts each experience to best fit the understanding of the experiencer, making gnosis uniquely personal. In turn, each sage's writings reflect their individuality. For example, when explaining that we must see past the illusion of the material body, the mystic poet Hakim Sanai (1080-1131/1141 ?) said, "Break free from the chains you have forged about yourself. You will be free when you are free of clay." While references to chains and clay may not be meaningful to us, Sanai and his readers would have associated chains with slavery, which was common in his day. Since they regularly used clay jars, they would have readily grasped that the value of the jar lies not in the clay itself, but what the clay contains and hides. Using these common word pictures, he helped his listeners understand that attachment to the body kept them in the material world. Hafiz (Hâfez-e Shîrâzî 1325-1390), a Persian Sufi master and mystic poet with a penchant for humor, expressed the same idea this way, "Why pretend your expansive existence, your Imperial Nature, have all been squeezed into a tiny red hot skillet?" Nisargadatta Maharaj, who was aware of modern scientific discoveries spoke with that in mind when he said, "The ultimate value of the body is that it serves to discover the cosmic body, which is the universe in its entirety." Regardless of time, location or language, the same truth shines through the words of each sage that expresses it.

IV. Signs, Symbols and Myths

The symbols, myths and parables that play an important part in ancient texts often appear laughable or childish to the logical mind that leans toward literal interpretation that confuses signs and symbols. What is the difference? A sign clearly tells us what something is or what we should do, while a symbol points to something beyond the literal. For example, the word 'God' can be used as either a sign or a symbol. If you were discussing the *Bible* with a group of Christians and used the word God, it would carry with it an agreed upon description of a male, fatherly spirit being that resides in heaven with a host of angels. In that case, the word would be a sign. On the other hand, a New Age writer may use the word as a symbol of the indescribable "That Which Is," expecting the reader to mentally 'fill in the blank' with whatever image was most comfortable to them. Signs and symbols can also be confused when they collide with a reader's personal perceptions, attachments and aversions. For example, when Jesus told his followers that he came "not to bring peace but a sword," many of his listeners, especially those who were looking for a leader to fight against their Roman oppressors, interpreted his words as a call for physical weapons and warfare. Those who understood that Jesus taught using symbolic language and parables came to an entirely different conclusion. For them, the saying meant that Jesus' words would not be a soothing solace, but would cut through their comfortable illusions like a sharp instrument.

Unless we understand the twofold nature of symbolic language, it can add to the confusion. As we've learned, some use symbols to hide information from the 'unworthy' while others employ it to make information more easily understood by a wider audience. If the meaning of a symbol is revealed only to those who are considered worthy, as is the case in separation gnosis, the wording will appear nonsensical to outsiders no matter how hard they work at puzzling it out. And, since the meanings behind much of the arcane symbolism used in separation gnosis have been lost, it's often nearly impossible for the modern reader to understand anything past the most basic ideas, and even then they cannot be certain their interpretation is correct.

In contrast, symbolic language, parables and myths can also be used to create mental pictures, metaphors and analogies that are common to the human experience, simplifying a complex subject. No doubt this is why Jesus regularly used parables as teaching tools when he spoke with the crowds. Like love and laughter, symbols and stories are something that people of all languages, nationalities and time periods share and understand. If we don't brush these stories off as childlike or primitive, we find that they use something we do understand to open our minds to something on a higher plane of thought that we don't yet understand. As Joseph Campbell noted, "Mythologies and the symbols they contain...embody collective and universal themes. The symbol...is thus a doorway that leads the open mind into a higher more integrative space."

The texts we'll be considering contain elaborate mythologies, signs and symbols that are either arcane or inaccessible. Although we'll point out many of the differences, your own experience is the surest means of 'knowing' which they are and more importantly, which gnosis they're associated with.

Understanding Gnosis

Part Three:
Examining the Nag Hammadi Library

Leaving aside speculations, we can say categorically that the Bible...has given us a highly censored and distorted version of ancient religious literature—Willis Barnstone, editor, *The Other Bible*

As we begin to examine The Nag Hammadi Library, please keep in mind that although this collection consists primarily of texts scholars have associated with Christianity, gnosis is not a phenomenon limited to Christianity. In our opinion, the term Christian more aptly describes those associated with organized religion than those who have been labeled 'gnostic Christians.' Why? Institutionalized Christianity professes Jesus as a god, a savior whose spilled blood atones for the sins they claim humans both inherit and commit. They teach that Jesus planned to start a new religion and appointed a successor. However, many early writings describe Jesus as fully human, a beloved friend and teacher who shared "sayings of everlasting life." Their Jesus did not take on the role of messiah or savior and did not die to atone for sin. In fact, many of Jesus' followers didn't even believe in the Christian concept of sin!

In the Nag Hammadi text, *The Dialogue of the Savior*, Jesus' disciples asked him to reveal the source of his teaching. Recognizing that he differed from his companions only in their current depth of understanding he answered, "Light the lamp within you…Knock on yourself as upon a door and walk upon yourself as on a straight road." Here we meet a human who had become aware of truth through gnosis. Like other sages, he understood his experience could not be institutionalized. In *The Gospel of Thomas*, Jesus said, "I am not your master… He who seeks will find and he who knocks will be let in." If there is one key theme that persistently recurs in writing associated with oneness gnosis, it would have to be that truth resides within each of us. How so? Because, whether we choose to deny it or recognize it, we always have been, and always will be, one with the Divine. Lack of recognition (ignorance) is the only error recognized in oneness gnosis and many texts associated with separation gnosis. Here are a few examples from the Nag Hammadi Library:

The Gospel of Philip: Ignorance is the mother of all evil. Ignorance is a slave, knowledge is freedom.

The Gospel of Truth: Ignorance of the Father brought about anguish and terror; and the anguish grew solid like a fog, so that no one was able to see…This is the way everyone has acted, as though asleep at the time when they were ignorant…It is within Unity that each one will attain himself; within knowledge he will purify himself from multiplicity into unity…The end, you see, is the recognition of him who is hidden, that is, the Father, from whom the beginning came forth and to whom will return all who have come from him.

The Gospel of Thomas: If you bring forth what is within you, what you bring forth will save you…the kingdom is inside you and it is outside you. When you know yourselves, then you will be known, and you will understand that you are children of the living Father. But if you do not know yourselves, then you dwell in poverty.

As we turn to the Nag Hammadi texts, let's take a moment to clear up the meaning of the word Gnosticism. Since we've learned that gnosis and gnostic are regularly associated with either separation or oneness gnosis, it may seem logical that Gnosticism could also be applied to these two contradictory concepts. However, when we add the suffix 'ism' to a word, it then describes a distinctive doctrine, philosophy, theory, system or practice that groups of people adhere to such as Catholicism, Judaism or Buddhism. As for the many organizations that claim to practice Gnosticism, you would be correct in assuming they fit the separation model since they each hold to their own set of specific doctrines, rituals and practices that are passed on to others. Of course the same cannot be said for oneness gnosis since it's impossible for a direct, personal experience of the Divine to be second-hand. Unfortunately, language is often inexact at best, so we will run into texts that use the word Gnosticism in connection with oneness gnosis. In that case, we suggest that you think of it as a dynamic spiritual approach rather than something that can be organized, joined, believed or ritualized.

Again, context is extremely important to our understanding of these texts. We cannot emphasize enough that Jesus' earliest followers held an extensive variety of disparate beliefs, every bit at odds with one another as the forty thousand or so Christian denominations and sects that exist today. This was as true for those who claimed they were 'gnostic' as it was for those moving toward an institutionalized church. These differences also explain why the writings are often a mish-mash of ideas, many containing wild contradictions within the same text. (To be fair, wild contradiction is no stranger to the *Bible* either.) But by 200 CE this diversity was all but swallowed up by the institutionalized Roman church. Backed by Emperor Constantine's military might, the church not only decimated its spiritual enemies, it succeeded in destroying almost all their writings and nearly every shred of proof they had ever existed. Willis Barnstone, editor of *The Other Bible*, pointed out that this campaign of literary genocide resulted in a *New Testament* that presents, "…a highly censored and distorted version of ancient religious literature." But scholars began to realize there had been other forms of early Christianity when they found orthodox writings that refuted their opposers' beliefs. Sadly, these writings offered only the church's view and shed little light on the dissenter's actual beliefs.

Finally, one of the banned writings surfaced in Egypt in 1769. Scholars were elated to discover the manuscript claimed to be a record of Jesus' conversations with his disciples. A tiny but tantalizing trickle of manuscripts appeared through the years until an epic find was accidently made near the village of Nag Hammadi, Egypt in 1945. An earthenware jar was discovered buried in the sand that contained fifty-two texts bound into thirteen books. These writings had been translated from ancient manuscripts approximately 1,500 years ago and had probably originally resided in the library of a near-by monastery. The books were most likely buried by monks who realized the church would destroy them. There is no way to know why each of these texts was chosen for preservation. The only accurate comment that can be made about them is that they are an eclectic combination of works that demonstrate an extremely wide range of early thought. Some of these books were attributed to Jesus' earliest followers and a few of the manuscripts they were copied from (*The Gospel of Thomas* in particular) may well have predated the *New Testament* gospels. These books presented a remarkably different view of Jesus' earliest followers, one that corresponded to the "heresies" the church had denounced. Since it's impossible to prove the *New Testament* gospels are any more authentic than the writings found at

Nag Hammadi, these texts are equally deserving of our interest.

Although the oneness gnosis of the perennial philosophy was first described in the *Upanishads* as early as the 6th century BCE, many biblical scholars claim that gnosis originated when early Christians adapted ideas from a Jewish movement influenced by earlier Egyptian, Greek and Hermetic philosophies. Regardless of the veracity of that assumption, what scholars label 'Christian Gnosticism' refers to loosely organized groups or individuals who understood Jesus' message to mean that salvation was attained independently as each one awoke to their true Divine nature. Since they saw no need for a savior, church or clergy to mediate their awakening from spiritual sleep, they instantly became enemies of those who were determined to structure and police Jesus' message.

Unlike orthodox Christianity where significant changes took place only from the top down, gnostic fluidity allowed for major changes to take place from the bottom up. This meant that any speaker or writer had the power to influence others with their views. Their words were used as lures to entice new initiates, as teaching texts or, in the case of separation gnosis, as a means of argumentation or a way to air complaints about other teachers or groups. *The Testimony of Truth* didn't stop at speaking out against orthodox Christianity, but also railed against the views held by another gnostic group the writer had just left. In *The Interpretation of Knowledge*, the author claimed the equality the gnostic community had been known for was giving way to the levels of status and petty jealousies that were more common in institutionalized religion.

And some writings, *The Dialogue of the Savior*, for example, demonstrate a 'cross-fertilization' that resulted in gnostic-orthodox hybrid texts and anticipated the eventual establishment of organized Gnosticism. The word 'rowdy' isn't commonly used in spiritual discussions, but we'd be misled if we thought of these turbulent, mud-slinging times as peaceful.

Of the fifty-two texts, bound into thirteen books, that were discovered at Nag Hammadi, six were duplicates, five were previously known and ten were in fragments. This left scholars and seekers with thirty-one texts dating from the second to fourth centuries AD that were previously unknown. All the manuscripts were originally written in Greek and translated into Coptic, an Egyptian language spoken as late as the 17th century. We'll also be discussing several texts from sources other than the 1945 find at Nag Hammadi that are usually included as part of the Nag Hammadi Library. Listed in order of their discovery:

The Askew Codex, discovered in 1773, was purchased from the heirs of Dr. Anthony Askew by the British Museum in 1785. Made up of 365 pages known as *Pistis Sophia* (aka *Faith Wisdom* or *Faith in Wisdom*), the work claims Jesus remained on earth to teach his disciples for eleven years after his death and resurrection.

The Bruce Codex (also called the *Codex Brucianus*) was purchased in Upper Egypt by James Bruce in 1769. The codex contained two unnamed 'gnostic mystery texts' that appear to have been written to facilitate ritual initiations.

The Berlin Codex, also known as *The Akhmim Codex* due to its discovery in Akhmim, Egypt in 1896. *The Berlin Codex* includes *The Gospel of Mary, Apocryphon of John* (aka *Secret Book of John*), *The Sophia of Jesus Christ* (aka *Wisdom of Jesus Christ*), and *The Acts of Peter* which were first published in 1955.

The *Codex Tchacos* has an intriguing history unfortunately far too involved to relate here. It contains *The Gospel of Judas,* a text that was rejected as heresy by the early Roman Church and then lost for 1700 years. The codex resurfaced in Egypt in the 1970s and also includes *The Letter of Peter to Philip, The First Apocalypse of James* and a fragment of *The Book of Allogenes* (aka *The Book of the Stranger,* not the same as *Allogenes* found at Nag Hammadi.)

(Note: A codex, codices plural, is simply a manuscript containing scriptures, classic literature or ancient annals.)

As we've stated earlier, the point of this book is not to offer yet another scholarly rehash of gnostic texts, but to *examine them from the sage's point of view.* We'll be searching out the tidbits of information that identify separation and/or oneness gnosis and examine the context that influenced the writers' choices. Scholars generally divide the Nag Hammadi texts into four schools of thought that share similar concepts, which we'll examine later. But each writer also chose a particular, and usually well-known, writing style that would best serve their message. Since we can learn much from the differences in these styles and the reasons authors chose them, we'll begin our examination by comparing texts that were produced in similar writing styles.

I. Dialogues and Revelations

Revelations given by Jesus and dialogues that supposedly took place between Jesus and his disciples after his resurrection appear to have been very popular formats since many of them were preserved at Nag Hammadi. Keep in mind that although the titles attribute these texts to Jesus' siblings, apostles and disciples, they were *not* the authors. Many texts were written anonymously and titled later using the names of prominent early Christians to champion the 'special' disciple, add credibility and confer an air of sacredness to the work. This practice was similar to the endorsements by famous authors that writers use today, except the early writers appropriated the names without anyone's permission. Since the works were written long after the reported revelations or dialogues could have taken place, it's impossible to know if they include any factual happenings or are the product fertile imaginations bent on creating an attractive means of advancing their favorite gnostic concepts. Regardless, there are some gems waiting for us in these texts.

In most of these texts, one of the disciples was considered 'special' or gifted with greater understanding than the others and was rewarded with 'secret sayings' that were denied to the group. Although some of these dialogues include sayings that support oneness gnosis, the fact that they highlight specialness and secrets demonstrate that they also stray into separation gnosis. These texts also inform us that the bestowal of secret teachings not only caused jealousy and wrangling between the disciples, but reflected and encouraged the arguments that were proliferating among seekers of that time:

1. *The Book of Thomas*

(aka *The Book of Thomas the Contender*. This is *not* the same book as *The Gospel of Thomas*)

Thomas is an especially important figure in gnostic literature. Some believe the name Thomas was commonly appropriated because Judas Thomas was supposedly the brother of Jesus. And, since the name Thomas also meant twin, some early writers believed Thomas was Jesus' literal twin. Mark, the earliest of the *New Testament* gospels, mentions Jesus' siblings, but this bit of biography was soon dropped by the church since it couldn't co-exist with the belief that Mary was free of original sin and remained 'ever virgin.' However, if you consider the use of the name as a symbol rather than a sign, it takes on a completely different meaning. Although *The Book of Thomas* opens with these words, "The secret words/hidden sayings that the Savior spoke to Judas Thomas," Jesus also says, "…while you are still in the world, listen to me and I shall reveal to you what you have thought about in your heart. Since it is said that you are my twin and true friend, examine yourself and understand who you are, how you exist and how you came to be. Since *you are to be called* my brother, it is not fitting for you to be ignorant of yourself." [Italics ours] Instead of speaking to a sibling, this verse was directed toward a potential spiritual brother. In this case, brotherhood was contingent on the awakening of the person Jesus was addressing.

In *The Book of Thomas*, the listener/reader is also charged with letting go of the ignorance that blinded them from understanding their true spiritual reality. Of course the direct route to this 'knowing' is gnosis. Once we have experienced for ourselves what Jesus had experienced, we become his spiritual twin. When we understand the name Thomas as a symbol rather than a sign, we realize that Jesus was offering an invitation to each and every one of us to share his level of awareness and spiritual oneness.

2. The Secret Book of John

(aka *The Apocryphon of John.* Apocryphon means secret writing.)

(Note: Scholars feel that *The Secret Book of John* is part of a larger school of gnostic thought labeled 'Sethian.' Later in the chapter we'll examine the differences between the major schools of gnostic thought.)

We've learned that both oneness and separation gnosis recognize ignorance of the true Self as the only human error, but what happens if we do not wake from ignorance before the body dies? *The Secret Book of John* tells us the soul will be "thrust into flesh again," repeating the life/death cycle until it acquires understanding. Clearly, the writer was referring to what many of us think of as reincarnation. Since resurrection is associated with Christianity, not reincarnation, we might assume that the author of *The Secret Book of John* had learned something of Eastern philosophies, but this may not be the case. Surprisingly, the Jews believed that important prophets returned by reincarnating, and in fact, many Jews suspected that John the Baptist and/or Jesus was actually the prophet

Elijah returned. Christianity now professes only one human lifetime that results in either an eternal blessing or curse as stated in the *New Testament* book of *Hebrews*, "...man is destined to die once, and after that to face judgment." (Hebrews 9:27) However, the first century Jewish historian, Flavius Josephus offered another perspective. He wrote that the legalistic Jewish sect known as the Pharisees believed that the souls of 'bad men' received punishment after death while the souls of 'good men' were "removed into other bodies" and given the "power to revive and live again." Since Jesus often interacted with the Pharisees, it's reasonable to assume that he and his followers were familiar with these views as well. Although the Pharisees considered reincarnation to be a reward rather than a punishment, gnostics wished to transcend the cycle of birth and death in the flesh.

Although the concept of reincarnation is commonly found in gnostic writings, the entire Christian faith hinges on the resurrection of Jesus. Unlike reincarnation, which supports the view that life may take on different forms while remaining eternal, resurrection requires the possibility of mortality and immortality, plus a separate god who chooses which you will experience. But as we've learned, quantum research informs us that there is no life other than that which is One and eternal. We can join the religionists and wonder whether resurrection is of the body or of the spirit, or what is required to attain it, or we can forget the theological arguments and accept the fact that the Self cannot be held hostage to either the promise of bliss, the threat of torment or eternal annihilation.

From a quantum standpoint, we would understand reincarnation in a slightly different way than the author of *The Secret Book of John* explained it. Remember that Rumi stated, "Consciousness is the soul." Since it would be impossible for our infinite, non-local consciousness to be 'thrust into flesh,' it makes sense that consciousness uses a body much as a video game player is represented by an avatar. When you play a video game, you are never inside the game or the avatar; you manipulate the action from outside the game. Just as an avid gamer often begins to identify with their gaming persona, consciousness can become as attached to the human avatar it projects. And as passionate gamers often find, the game can begin to feel more real to them than their daily life. Although consciousness may have projected hundreds, or even thousands, of human avatars, it forgets its true identity and the many lifetimes it has previously projected and instead identifies with the latest body and personality it's using. Of course this makes each lifetime feel like the only one and the death of each avatar quite painful.

Consciousness, being eternal and infinite, can play whatever game interests it. It is certainly not limited to gaming in this world since it can pretend to inhabit whatever plane it can imagine. Theoretical physicists are currently investigating anomalies of the microwave background that may suggest that our universe is influenced by other planes of existence, perhaps parallel universes or multi-verses. Anecdotal evidence abounds concerning 'otherworldly' experiences that also contain separation and a dualistic thought system. Since the aim of our experiment in separation is specialness, it makes sense that we would want to play over and over again until we reach our goal. In an attempt to increase our odds of winningthe game of specialness, we may well be playing on many different planes just as gamers may be involved in several different games.

The little self does everything within its power to keep us from understanding this truth: *specialness is such an unquantifiable and ephemeral quality, there's really no way to secure it.* But considering how popular the lottery is even though we all know the odds against our winning are impossibly high, we must still feel that we have a chance or we wouldn't keep playing. The same blind hope must also drive us to project one lifetime after another. However, when we finally realize the futility and no longer wish to play at separation and specialness our dualistic games end and consciousness returns to oneness. This does not mean surrendering our unique Self (although that Self is not any of the personalities that have been associated with a body), only that we once again create in oneness and harmony for the good of all instead of competing and hoarding.

One lifetime, ending in reward or punishment meted out by a God that exists separately from his/her creations, is one of the main concepts of dualistic/separation thinking. On the surface, this appears to be correct because this is what we think we're seeing. However, gnosis has not only consistently revealed the oneness of All That Is, but also the impossibility of death. Yes, material illusions pass before us, and within those illusions bodies come and go, but we are not those bodies. Science confirms that the universe is a closed energetic system where energy can change forms, but it cannot escape the system. Of course a tree dying and its energy transforming into fertile soil that supports other plants is not the type of immortality most of us want. In his book *Biocentrism*, researcher Robert Lanza states, "If I am only my body, then I must die. If I am my consciousness, the sense of experience and sensations, then I cannot die for the simple reason that consciousness may be *expressed* in manifold fashion sequentially, but it is ultimately unconfined." In other words, the energy that consciousness interacts with and projects can change into countless forms, but consciousness, the prime mover and foundation of All That Is remains unchanged.

The Indian sage, Shankara, explained our innate immortality this way:

> *The mind of the experiencer creates all the objects which he experiences while in the waking or the dreaming state…You are pure consciousness, the witness of all experiences. Your real nature is joy…The Self is pure consciousness…You are the Self, the infinite Being…the pure unchanging consciousness, which pervades everything. Your nature is bliss, your glory without stain.*

Oneness gnosis and quantum physics agree that we project bodies, we are not bodies. Just as we can play one DVD movie after another and identify with the hero in each, we can project one lifetime after another, completely convinced we're living it. There are probably thousands of ideas floating around about what the soul actually is, but Rumi's explanation that the soul is consciousness, fits the quantum model perfectly.

3. "The One"

Early in *The Secret Book of John* we also discover a passage where the resurrected Jesus describes "The One" or "Spirit of Unity" this way:

> *The Spirit is a Unity, over which no one rules. It is the God of Truth, the Father of the All, the Holy spirit, the invisible one, the one who is over the All, the one who exists in his imperishability, the one who exists in pure light into which no sight can look.*

Now let's compare this translation, which came from *TOB*, with the translation found in *NHS*:

> *The One is the Invisible Spirit. We should not think of it as a god or like a god. For it is greater than a god, because it has nothing over it and no lord above it. It does not exist within anything inferior to it, since everything exists within it, for it established itself. It is eternal, since it does not need anything. For it is absolutely complete. It has never lacked anything in order to be completed by it. Rather, it is always absolutely complete in light.*

No doubt you've already recognized a basic foundation concept of oneness gnosis and the perennial philosophy that's supported by quantum physics: There is a life-giving and life-sustaining ground that contains and supports the universe. Within this Reality, it's impossible for separation to exist except as illusion. Like *The Secret Book of John*, many gnostic texts contain a description of "The One," the Divine Source that's revealed by direct experience. But as you'll see over and over again, a text may contain a basic concept or two that resulted from oneness gnosis but then disintegrates into dualistic thinking.

Many who came into contact with a sage resonated with some of their wisdom and were willing to repeat it, but instead of experiencing the Divine themselves they manipulated or altered those truths to fit more comfortably with their own dualistic thought pattern. Since they weren't grounded in the truth of gnosis, these tales often grew fantastically intricate, as if each writer was trying to outdo the last. Like many gnostic texts, *The Secret Book of John* contains just such a tale. Many have found it intriguing for the simple reason that's it's virtually opposite of the story told in the *Bible*. The warp thread of this story became very popular among gnostic writers, but they each wove their own variations into the weft of the foundation cloth. Since it would be impossible to cover every variation, and would add little to our discussion, we'll present a condensed version that covers the basic concepts related in these stories:

Instead of "The One" creating the universe and declaring his creation 'good,' these stories claim that the material universe is the result of a cosmic disaster. While the *Bible* teaches that evil came into the world through human sin, this version declares that the entire material universe was innately evil from its inception. Although the Bible claims there is only one God, *The Secret Book of John* takes on the attributes of separation gnosis when it describes a pantheon of gods that begin to flow from The One described in the two earlier quotes. Instead of being direct creations that The One chose to bring into existence, we're told that they could be thought of more accurately as light that had no choice but to emanate from a star or water that poured from melting mountaintop snow to become streams, rivers and oceans. *The Secret Book of John* explains it this way, "The Father is the one who beholds himself in the light surrounding him, which is the spring of living water and provides all realms. He reflects on his image everywhere…and becomes enamored of his luminous water…His thoughts became a reality…and she who appeared in his presence in shining light came forth." Because of this passive emanation, The One is never considered responsible for the chaos that results. In all, 182 pairs of gods, called Aions, were said to have come into being, each pair flowing from the pair that came before it. Somehow, one more being came into existence, but the 365th god, known as Sophia or Wisdom, had no partner.

Seeing that all the other pairs that had preceded her had created another pair, she longed for a partner and the same creative experience. Some versions of the story claim Sophia did have a partner, and in some texts this partner is Jesus, but she ignored him because she wanted to create on her own. *The Secret Book of John* tells us, "Sophia wanted to bring forth something like herself, without her partner and without his consideration… and because of the power within her, her thought was not an idle thought. Something came out of her that was imperfect and different in appearance from her… it was misshapen." Ultimately, she managed to produce an "abomination," a defective child called Yaldabaoth, Sabaoth, Ialdabaoth or the Demiurge. (Yaldabaoth is Aramaic for 'child of chaos.')

Disgusted by what she had given birth to, Sophia rejected her flawed creation and left it on a lower plane in isolation and ignorance. The author of

John added, "When Sophia saw what her desire had produced...she cast it away from her, outside that realm so that none of the immortals would see it." Sophia eventually repented, was forgiven and allowed to remain in a position higher than her abominable son, but she remained close enough to him that he was able to steal some of her power. At some point, this flawed and deluded being decided it was The One. Using the small spark of divine power he had stolen from his mother, Yaldabaoth created angels called Archons, which were counterfeit versions of the divine Aions. *The Secret Book of John* says, "He mated with the mindlessness in him and produced authorities for himself."

But Yaldabaoth didn't stop there; he also used cosmic forces to create the material universe. Gnostic texts claimed that Yaldabaoth and the creator god of the Old Testament, Yahweh/Jehovah, are one and the same. As a result of Sophia's error, her creation, and in turn, her child's creations, were fatally flawed and beyond redemption. But this is not how Yaldabaoth saw things. *John* states, "When [Yaldabaoth] saw creation surrounding him, and the throng of angels around him, that had come forth from him, he said to them, 'I am a jealous god and there is no other god beside me." As you probably recognize, this statement mimics the beginning words of the Ten Commandments found in the *Bible* at Genesis 20: 3 and 5, "You shall have no other gods before me... for I the Lord your God am a jealous God."

The Secret Book of John also tells us that it was Yaldabaoth who created the first human, Adam. Each of the 365 flawed Archons Yaldabaoth created also contributed a bit to the human creation that was "after the image of God and with a likeness to ourselves." Nonetheless, Yaldabaoth was unable to imbue this creation with life. Some stories say that the Archons helped out by stealing life-giving heavenly light that brought Adam to life. *John* speaks of a spirit known as "the Mother and Father of All," who tells Yaldabaoth to "Breathe some of your spirit into the face of Adam and the body will arise." But the author explains that it was not really Yaldabaoth that gave life to Adam because, "The spirit was the power of his mother, but he did not realize this because he lives in ignorance."

John tells us the Archons placed Adam in a paradise setting, but "their beauty is perverse… Their pleasure is a trap…their tree a sacrilege…their fruit is deadly poison, and their promise is of death." Some stories also claim the Archons raped Eve, which resulted in the birth of Cain and his semi-divine offspring. Nonetheless, gnostic texts generally agree that the "tree of knowledge of good and bad" symbolized enlightenment, and the serpent that enticed Adam to eat the fruit was not evil, but was the Christ trying to awaken him.

The creation account in the *Bible* book of *Genesis* says that God gave the breath of life to Adam and through that breath, he became a living soul. But it goes on to explain that by disobeying God's command not to touch the fruit of the tree of knowledge of good and bad, Adam and Eve condemned all humans to a life of sin, suffering and inevitable death. The *Bible* holds out a hope for all humans: anyone's sin can be forgiven *if* they put faith in the spilled blood of Jesus. Again, the gnostic *Secret Book of John* tell a very different story, one that divides humans into three distinct and unequal groups:

» *Hylics* or *Sarkics*, known as the 'wooden' ones: These creations of Yaldabaoth are irredeemable. Like animals, they live for pleasure and when they die, they're gone forever. Some writings say that the Hylics are the condemned progeny of the angelic Archons and human women. This idea corresponds with the *Bible's* Nephilim, the sons of human women and fallen angels that the *Bible* says were destroyed in Noah's flood.

» *Psychics*, the 'soulish' or 'natural' ones: These are the descendants of Cain. They are said to have a soul, but not a 'Divine Spark.' It's possible for these 'natural ones' to be saved, but this can happen only through great effort and/or special circumstances.

» *Pneumatics*, the 'spiritual' ones: The Pneumatics are the only humans that carry the 'Divine spark' of The One, but they don't realize it. Their only duty is to remember that they are among this very special group. This is not easy, because the Archons are busy trying to distract them. Until they remember, they continue to reincarnate as a body. When they do remember, they return to the spirit realm, take their place among the Aions, and enjoy a special afterlife dwelling in the presence of The One.

Texts that share the basic belief system that we've just outlined explain that Jesus' death was not a sacrifice arranged by God to atone for sins but the evil work of the Archons. They teach that Jesus was a divine emissary sent by The One to awaken the Pneumatics from their sleep and his words were meant for them alone. There were several theories explaining why Jesus came to earth and what he was doing here, but many gnostic followers agreed that the spirit of the divine Christ entered a human body known as Jesus when he was baptized. While preaching, the Christ spirit used this body like a puppet, and many gnostics agreed that the Christ spirit left the 'Jesus body' when the Archons caused humans to crucify it. They claimed that the human Jesus was speaking to the Christ spirit when he cried out, "Why have you forsaken/left me?" before dying.

After the Christ spirit left the body of Jesus, and before it ascended to The One, many Gnostics believed this spirit took control of other bodies and used them to spend time (up to eleven years) with the Pneumatics he had identified during his preaching work. It was said that this spirit shared with these special ones (pneumatics) the 'secret information' they would need to wake up to their true identity and return to the realm of The One. They, in turn, infiltrated organized religion seeking to identify others who carried the very special Divine spark. After they had identified candidates for salvation, they would act like the mystery schools, drawing their initiates further and further into their ring of secret knowledge. Of course this became one of the main reasons why the early Christian church was so rabid in its destruction of this group of early opposers.

It was believed that once all those with the divine spark had returned to The One, the creations of Yaldabaoth would collapse into nothingness and the suffering endured on the earth would finally come to an end. This was all well and good for the Pneumatics and the few Psychics who were saved, but it left nothing but meaningless misery for the rest of Yaldabaoth's abominable creation. But the wholesale destruction of the world and its inhabitants meant nothing to most gnostics; to them, both the body and the earth were thought of as disgusting prisons where those with the divine spark was enslaved by natural and human laws. Their goal was a place of glory and the route back consisted of 'waking up' and realizing they didn't belong in a body on the earth. This seemed far too simple for orthodox Christians who had added many rules of behavior, sacraments and creeds to their requisite belief in Jesus' sacrifice. It became a regular ploy of orthodox Christians to accuse gnostics of grossly immoral behavior, which included sex orgies, to lure new initiates. But in fact, they were usually very strict and harshly denied and punished the' evil body' to keep it line for fear that they would succumb to the desires of the flesh and fall asleep once again.

In contrast to the flight of imagination focusing on separation and specialness in *The Secret Book of John*, *The Gospel of Truth* speaks of The One this way, "… the Father's Word goes out in the All as the fruition of his heart and expression of his will. It supports all and chooses all." The gnostic *Treatise on the Resurrection* tells us that it was our own desires that caused us to project a material avatar so we could experiment with the separation and specialness not available in oneness. The text goes on to explain that it's our realization that separation and the pursuit of specialness is doomed to fail combined with our desire to return to oneness, that finally ends our experiment:

> *For where there is envy and strife there is deficiency but where there is unity there is completeness.*

Since deficiency came about because the Father was not known, from the moment when the Father is known, deficiency will cease to be. From then on the world of appearance will no longer be evident, but rather it will disappear in the harmony of unity. Now the works of all lie scattered. In time unity will make the heavenly places complete, and in unity all individually will come to themselves. By means of knowledge they will purify themselves from multiplicity into unity, devouring matter within themselves like fire, darkness by light, death by light.

Envy and strife require a dualistic system to exist, which is deficient compared to unity. One might think this would be self-evident, yet the majority continue to champion the separation and pursuit of specialness that inevitably leads to misery in the material world. As the text promises, gnosis (in this case translated as knowledge) will open our heart to what is, and we will realize our oneness. Although the text appears on the surface to say that matter will be destroyed, it is actually the *misperception that matter is our Reality* that will be exposed and devoured.

4. *The Revelation of Peter*

Earlier we mentioned that in several gnostic texts one of Jesus' disciples is singled out for special treatment. This inequality not only identifies separation gnosis, but highlights the fact that there were countless factions vying against one another for 'spiritual supremacy.' To understand the context of *The Revelation of Peter* and *The Gospel of Mary* that follows, we must take a look at early Christian/ gnostic history. Very early on, Jesus' followers met casually in public places or in each other's homes. Since there was little organization and few rituals (none standardized), their meetings generally consisted of open discussions facilitated by men or women who had no priestly function. No doubt the proliferation of new, and oftentimes conflicting, ideas about Jesus' revolutionary message gave early seekers much to consider.

Contrary to popular belief, Christianity did not explode on the world scene as an organized belief system with a large, following. Instead, interest in these new ideas grew very slowly for the first two centuries after Jesus' death and developed rapidly only as the Roman Empire began to decline. Why? Fearful pagans began to embrace the 'Jesus story' en masse when they thought the gods that were supposed to have made Rome invincible had failed them. In turn, Roman rulers began to blame the odd new religion for their problems and began persecuting those who took up the name of Christ. At first these early followers caved under the pressure and Christianity nearly collapsed, but after a decade of abuse, martyrdom became a badge of salvation and Christianity grew once more.

During these early growth years, Christianity retained is diversity and bitter disagreements between opposing factions began to escalate. It became common for each group to declare their allegiance to a certain apostle or disciple and put them forth as Jesus' favorite. Although both gnostic and orthodox writings make it clear that Jesus disdained the hypocrisy, greed and burdensome requirements of organized religion, his followers did not necessarily get the point. One group based in Rome claimed Jesus had started a church, named Peter as his successor and gave him exclusive responsibility for the "keys of the kingdom." (Matthew 16: 18, 19) Although this claim was by no means accepted by all early Christians, the 'Peter group' began to gain power. The leaders of this group were legalistic literalists who wanted to both institutionalize and control Jesus' message as they understood it. In this case, literalists are not the same as fundamentalists who take every word literally. Instead, it refers to those who believe there is one unique text inspired by God that represents the *only* belief system that leads to salvation.

As the Peter group grew, leaders began constructing a unified system of belief and rituals that would separate them from other Christians. They called their organization a church or 'body of believers,' and named themselves orthodox (straight-thinking) and Catholic (universal) to signify the worldwide scope of their agenda. Equality also gave way to class distinctions as a clergy class made up of deacons, priests and bishops presided over a laity class. As a side note, the word clergy signified an "office of dignity given to a person of learning" or "professional" while laity meant "unlearned" or "amateur." These meanings made sense at the time because hand copied manuscripts and the education necessary to read them were privileges open to only a tiny minority.

As the chasm between clergy and laity widened, church leaders began to feel the congregation could not be trusted to understand Jesus' teachings or know right from wrong. In an effort to protect the congregation from itself, they deemed it necessary to control both the content and quantity of spiritual food given to the people. Heterodoxy (literally 'different opinions') was no longer tolerated and any teaching that disagreed with the group's dogma was considered heretical, a 'crime' punishable by excommunication. In our day, this may not seem like much of a penalty, but at the time it made a pariah of the 'offender' who usually lost not only their family and place in the community, and also their livelihood — in many cases a virtual death sentence. Once the Catholic Church had fully aligned itself with Emperor Constantine, it also gained the military backing it needed to literally destroy its 'enemies.' By the time Theodosius became emperor (379-392 AD), the little 'Peter group' had grown into the state religion of the Roman Empire and it wielded the power needed to crush Jews, pagans and gnostic Christians out of existence.

Jesus' gnostic followers were not immune to the controversies that were brewing when the 'Peter group' began to form, so you'll discover that some gnostic texts, including *The Revelation of Peter*, also champion Peter as a friend of gnosis, while others ignore him or go out of their way to make him appear to be a bombastic moron incapable of understanding Jesus' teachings (for example, *The Gospel of Mary*, *The Gospel of Thomas* and *Pistis Sophia*). But in *The Revelation of Peter*, Jesus tells Peter, "…you are to become perfect in keeping with your name, along with me, the one who has chosen you, for through you I have begun a work for the remnant whom I called to knowledge." (Note: Peter means rock and the 'remnant' referred to is a small group of Pneumatics with the Divine spark.)

The Revelation of Peter demonstrates the enmity that existed between opposing groups as the text identifies Peter's gnostic supporters as "the little ones" and "true believers" while using the word heretic to describe the Peter supporters aligned with the institutionalized church. Unlike sages who have experienced oneness gnosis and proclaim that all have the ability and opportunity to experience the Divine, *The Revelation of Peter* declares, "Not every soul is of the truth of immortality...some souls are destined for eternal destruction."

5. *The Gospel of Mary*

Although *The Upanishads* records the teachings of both male and female sages and oneness gnosis recognizes gender equality, the society where Jesus' teachings were first heard was patriarchal to the point that women were considered to be little more than unclean chattel. In *The Gospel of Thomas* Peter reflects this view when he says, "Mary should leave us, for females are not worthy of life." Keeping these facts in mind, we come to an amazing document that's credited to a female writer, claims this woman is Jesus' favorite and depicts Peter as a misogynist buffoon! Although *The Gospel of Mary* is the only gnostic manuscript attributed to a woman that still exists, we cannot take that to mean it was the only one. When we consider that hundreds, if not thousands, of writings were destroyed, it stands to reason that a group that was 'gender blind' would have produced texts by several women. And, since few who were named as authors had actually written the text, some of the texts attributed to men could just as easily have been written by women.

Texts found in the *New Testament* demonstrate that during a time when harsh anti-feminine attitudes were common, Jesus treated women respectfully, had women friends, spoke to women publicly and included them among the followers who traveled with him. Unless we understand the context, we might not realize just how rebellious and shocking this behavior must have been! In the *New Testament* the apostle Paul followed Jesus' example and declared, "There is neither Jew nor Greek, neither slave nor free; there is not male and female, for all of you are one in Jesus Christ." (Galatians 3: 27-28) And in the 16th chapter of Romans, Paul greeted many women as co-workers, including Phoebe, who he addressed as a deacon of the church. Some groups chose to follow Jesus' and Paul's examples of equal treatment for all while others clung to their misogynist attitudes and continued to relegate women to servitude and silence. To reinforce their own prejudice, intolerant copyists made deletions and additions to several manuscripts and changed names of prominent early Christians from female to male. Sadly, to this day, very few women within institutionalized Christianity have been accorded the spiritual equality that was a hallmark among many of Jesus' earliest followers.

The Gospel of Mary is also unique because it not only highlights the early arguments over the equality of women in the Christian community, but it also claims Mary as Jesus' favorite disciple. After the book presents a short post-resurrection dialogue between Jesus and a group of close followers, the fearful male disciples turn to Mary for comfort. Surprisingly, Peter acknowledges, "Sister, we know that the Savior loved you more than all other women" and then asks if she would share any secret teachings Jesus may have given her. After she complies, Peter rudely inquires, "Did Jesus then speak with a woman in private without our knowing about it? Are we to turn around and listen to her? Did he choose her over us?" Obviously Peter's initial question was meant to be a trap rather than a sincere inquiry. A weeping Mary asks Peter if he is accusing her of lying or making up the teachings she shared. Levi reprimands Peter by saying, "Peter, you have always been a wrathful person. Now I see you contending against the woman like the adversaries. For if the Savior made her worthy, who are you then for your part to reject her?" Although Peter eventually capitulates and decides to work with the group, this account undoubtedly made a strong argument against misogyny and the claim that Peter was chosen to succeed Jesus or build a church.

To some, *The Gospel of Philip* implies an intimate relationship between Jesus and Mary when it states, "The companion of the Savior is Mary of Magdala. The Savior loved her more than all the disciples, and he kissed her often on the mouth." This text may be confirmation of the gnostic view that Jesus was a human teacher, and as such, had sexual interests and intimate relationships. However, it's also important to note that when the disciples asked why Jesus loved Mary more than all of them, Jesus' answer explains that his attraction to Mary went far beyond the body. Jesus said, "If a blind person and one who can see are both in darkness, they are the same. When the light comes, one who can see will see the light, and the blind person will stay in darkness." Obviously Mary was spiritually awake and aware while the others remained blind. His answer may also infer that Mary had experienced the Divine as well; creating a bond of understanding between them that would not register with anyone who thought they could attain awareness simply by listening to Jesus' teachings. This theme is played out to the maximum in *The Gospel of Mary*.

Even more significant than the book's arguments against Peter and for gender equality, it leads us to a key point of oneness gnosis: *our true nature has nothing to do with the body*. Here the body is likened to a garment which disguises the true Self. In fact, the manuscript opens with the question, "Will matter then be utterly destroyed or not?" Jesus' answer echoes quantum discoveries when he says, "Every nature, every modeled form, every creature exists in and with each other. They will dissolve again into their own proper root. For the nature of matter is dissolved into what belongs to its nature." Simply put, everything is, always has been, and always will be the Divine despite illusionary appearances of separation. In *The Gospel of Thomas*, the disciples similarly ask, "Tell us how our end will be." Again Jesus refers to our eternal Oneness with Source when he answers, "Have you discovered the beginning then, so that you are seeking the end? For where the beginning is the end will be. Blessed is one who stands at the beginning: that one will know the end and will not taste death." Experiencing the Divine removes the material 'veil' and exposes the illusion of separation. Then we see that we cannot be other than what we have always been, making the 'end' the same as the 'beginning.'

Later in *The Gospel of Thomas*, Jesus tells his disciples they will enter the kingdom, "When you make the two into one, and when you make the inner like the outer …the upper like the lower and when you make male and female into a single one." In other words, until we're willing to let go of dualistic/

separation thinking and attachment to the body, we'll be unable to experience our true oneness with All That Is. As in *The Gospel of Mary*, Jesus likens the body to a garment when he tells his disciples to be like little children that unashamedly remove their clothing and trample it underfoot. Simply put, this metaphor urges Jesus' followers to identify with the Self, not the body, gender or the personality that we associate with it.

(Note: As you'll discover during our discussion, some gnostic texts demonstrate utter disgust for the human condition and condemn all acts of the flesh. However, oneness gnosis recognizes the fact that everything is the Divine, including the material portion of the universe. While recognizing the need to wake up from the illusion that convinces us we *are* material beings, these writings do not condemn the material portion of the universe, ask us to renounce it or expect us to become celibate aesthetics.)

The Gospel of Mary and *The Gospel of Thomas* also share two more significant hallmarks of the perennial philosophy: no sin and no rules. Those who first listened to Jesus' words were Jews, also known as the "people of the book." Why? Moses was said to have received the Ten Commandments directly from God, but this was only a small portion of the voluminous set of written laws the Jews considered sacred and tried to scrupulously follow. Although the law was impossible to keep and constantly reminded them of their shortcomings, they were still expected to obey it perfectly. Based on the belief that they had inherited Adam's sin, this was a daunting, and probably extremely discouraging task. However, they also believed it was possible to atone for their sins by participating in rituals and by making the proper blood sacrifices. Those whose wealth or position made it easier for them to carry this heavy burden began to look down on those who could not, and an unspoken caste system began to form, separating the supposedly 'clean' from the 'unclean.'

Imagine the outrage on the part of those who enjoyed pointing out the failings of others when Jesus challenged their views by saying, "What sin have I committed or how have I been undone?" In this quote from *The Gospel of Thomas*, Jesus wasn't claiming exemption from sin because he was "the only begotten son of God," since this idea did not begin to surface until long after his death. Instead, he was making the point that sin was not inherited, nor did one have to keep strict laws in order to atone for it. In fact, he was saying the notion of sin was a misperception manufactured by confused minds. Through gnosis, Jesus understood he was not a body and more importantly, that his true Self was without sin. He understood that our experiment in separation and specialness was exactly that, a legitimate experiment that the Divine had allowed. This becomes clear in *The Gospel of Mary* where Peter asked Jesus, "What is the sin of the world?" Jesus replied, "There is no such thing as a sin" and explained, "This is why you get sick and die; because you love what deceives you. Anyone who thinks should consider these matters." We continue to project the cycle of birth and death, and the misery that accompanies them, only as long as we continue to desire the game of separation and specialness more than the oneness and equality of Reality.

in *The Gospel of Mary,* as Jesus was about to leave his disciples, he warned them that creating rules and laws would keep them locked in duality. He said, "Do not lay down any rule...nor promulgate law like the lawgiver or else you might be dominated by it." These words also find clarification in *The Gospel of Thomas* when his disciples asked, "Do you want us to fast? How should we pray? Should we give to charity? What diet should we observe?" Of course these questions would have seemed perfectly logical to a group of people who had spent a lifetime observing laws that covered even the most intimate aspects of their lives. Instead of giving them a new set of rules, Jesus simply replied, "Do not lie, and do not do what you hate." Introspection tells us whether we're doing either, not rules, laws or someone else's judgment. Later in the text he added, "If you fast, you will bring sin upon youselves, and if you pray, you will be condemned, and if you give to charity, you will harm your spirits." Why? Repainting an old barn does not change the fact that the barn is ready to collapse, nor can the creation of another set of man-made rules bring about liberation. In effect, *they* would be creating the concept of sin through their own belief in rules. As Jesus said, "I am not your teacher. Because you have drunk, you have become intoxicated from the bubbling spring that I have tended." Freedom can never come from rules, but it can come by drinking from the fountain of gnosis just as Jesus had.

6. *The Secret Book of James*

Although scholars agree that this text is a carefully crafted fiction, it contains several bits of information that portray the difficulties experienced by Jesus' followers as they attempted to sort out and understand his life and teachings. The work is written in the form of a letter from the apostle James to an unknown recipient who was judged 'worthy' of the secrets it contained. The text opens by stating, "You have asked me to send you a secret book revealed to me and Peter by the master...so I have written it...and have sent it to you, and to you alone...do your best to be careful not to communicate to many people this book that the Savior did not want to communicate even to all of us, his twelve disciples." Obviously, separation and specialness quickly became a priority among many who claimed to follow Jesus and the mystery school structure already appears to be in place.

The dialogue in this text supposedly begins 550 days after Jesus' resurrection. The disciples are sitting together trying to remember Jesus' teachings and write them down. Either the author didn't know that the disciples were unable to read or write and probably didn't even have access to expensive writing materials, or he/she chose to ignore the fact. Nonetheless, this text highlights the fact that many of Jesus' followers became enthralled with his words rather than his example. They were focused on becoming believers in, and followers of, his words rather than being experiencers. This scene is especially odd, since the resurrected Jesus is still supposed to be with them and could have repeated and clarified the teachings for them. Considering their behavior, it makes sense that the text highlights several examples of Jesus' frustration with his closest follower's inability to 'get it.' At one point Jesus says, "First I spoke with you in parables, and you did not understand. Now I am speaking with you openly, and you do not grasp it." This is a theme that's prominent in the *Bible* gospels as well as gnostic texts. In this oft repeated testimony, we find that the disciples were more interested in competing with one another for their own specialness and the elevated roles they wanted to claim in God's kingdom, such as sitting at Jesus' right hand.

In *The Secret Book of James,* Jesus chooses James and Peter to receive secret information. After taking them aside he tells them, "The other disciples also have written my sayings in their books as if they have understood, but be careful. They have done their work without really understanding. They have listened like foolish peoples, and they have not understood." The author set up this scene for three reasons; first, to establish the 'mystery school' version of separation gnosis. Here Jesus, as the high priest and keeper of secrets, decides who is worthy of receiving them and who is not. Secondly, although we're given the initial impression that both James and Peter are worthy, the reader quickly sees that Peter was unable to understand what Jesus was saying. Since the Peter group claimed Jesus had commissioned Peter to build a church, his inability to grasp the deep meaning of secret knowledge not only demonstrated his unworthiness, but also symbolized the unworthiness of the church he represented. And most important, James is pictured as the one who will succeed Jesus as the one who holds and disseminates secret teachings.

In *The Second Revelation of James*, James is again the chosen vehicle for secret teachings as Jesus explained, "...it would be fitting that others would come to knowledge *through* you." [Italics ours] Whether these texts discredit Peter and honor James is not nearly as important as the fact that gnosis was no longer considered a 'do it yourself' experience, but rather a secret that had to be passed from one 'worthy' person to the next.

The Secret Book of James also contains an odd amalgamation of oneness gnosis, separation gnosis and orthodox teachings. In some verses Jesus is considered fully human and his words reflect oneness gnosis. For example, Jesus said, "Be eager to be saved without being urged. Rather, be fervent on your own and, if possible, outdo even me, for this is how the Father will love you." Jesus also chastises James and Peter saying "Do you still dare to sleep when from the beginning you should have been awake so that heaven's kingdom might receive you?" Here 'waking up' from ignorance is the key, not putting faith in a savior or being privy to secrets. To do this, Jesus tells them to, "…know yourselves," and "Understand what the great light is." Jesus also said, "The Father does not need me. A father does not need a son, but it is the son who needs the father." This is quite a contrast to orthodox thought that eventually claimed that Jesus *is* God. Nonetheless, the author also goes on to claim that Jesus is the savior of mankind when Jesus makes the declaration, "None will be saved unless they believe in my cross."

Why would the writer embrace teachings central to the institutionalized religion that was busy crushing gnostic thought? We must remember the tumultuous times and realize that with the vast array of belief systems to choose from the writer may have been unsure of his or her own beliefs, or they may have thought it would be safe to hedge their bets by keeping a foot in both camps. Although it's impossible to have it both ways, many early Christians who had lost the true meaning of gnosis were ready to try.

7. *The Revelation of Paul*

Although this text is another example of separation gnosis, it contains several interesting side points. As usual, an especially privileged person, in this case the apostle Paul, is treated to 'sacred secrets' by means of an allegorical ascent to heaven. In this mystery school style text, Paul's journey symbolized the steps that would lead an initiate through the rituals and mysteries that eventually culminated in a divine revelation. Sadly, instead of being a joyful ascent, his journey is fraught with danger which includes a dualistic hell where Paul helps several angels judge seekers and beat them with a whip. Reincarnation is once again seen as a punishment when a sinful soul is cast into another body to suffer through another miserable lifetime on earth. Paul ultimately reaches the tenth level of heaven where he meets his fellow apostles, but not before he has visions of vengeful angels, is made to correctly answer a series of questions and 'give a sign' before he can ascend upward. Texts like *The Revelation of Paul* veer far from our model of gnosis as the direct, personal experience of the Divine. Returning to Rumi, we find a far different portrayal of our return to oneness:

> *The second you stepped into this world of existence a ladder was placed before you to help you escape. When you pass beyond this human form…plunge into the vast ocean of consciousness. Let the drop of water that is you become a hundred mighty seas. But do not think that the drop alone becomes the ocean. The ocean, too, becomes the drop.*

Rumi's gnosis clearly showed him that All is One, and All is consciousness. There is nothing to fear in this return since, in Reality, we can never separate ourselves from what we truly are. We can take particular comfort in the fact that an escape route from illusion has always been in place. Since Source does not decide for us, our 'escape ladder' had to be part of a Divine plan that we each willingly agreed to *before* we entered our experiment in duality, separation and specialness. Although the little self has done its best to encourage us to lose ourselves in illusion, the escape route is always available to us. In *The Crest-Jewel of Discrimination*, the sage Shankara explains how easily we can choose to end our experiment in separation and specialness. In this text, Atman is the true Self that has become mired in illusion and Brahman is our Source:

> *The Atman is pure consciousness...It is the eternal reality, omnipresent, all pervading...It is the real I...Know the Atman, transcend all sorrows...Be illuminated by this knowledge, and you have nothing to fear. If you wish to find liberation, there is no other way of breaking the bonds of rebirth...You must realize absolutely that the Atman is Brahman...He who has become liberated in this life gains liberation in death and is eternally united with Brahman, the Absolute Reality. Such a seer will never be reborn.*

Unlike the picture painted by many gnostic texts, oneness gnosis tells us that although our experiment in separation and specialness is a mistake, we are not. There are no steps, no purification, no assessment of our worthiness required. But what can we do to overcome this mistake? Since the mistake was based on choice, choice is the way out. We chose duality, separation and specialness; we can just as easily choose oneness and equality. The

Divine *is* love, and we chose not to be. However, we can also make the choice to let go of everything that is not love, and BE love once again. But as Einstein pointed out, we "...can't solve a problem with the same thinking that created it." Therefore, a different choice can't be made until our thinking changes. However, surface changes cannot take us where we want to go; instead of whacking at the branches, we'll need to tear out the roots of our misperceptions.

In his book *The Perennial Philosophy*, Aldous Huxley listed three fundamental qualities common to those who have successfully made a different choice and sought the Divine experience. Notice that none of these basic characteristics requires anything other than a particular mindset and the willingness to have our misperceptions corrected. These qualities are free and available to all, no matter what our circumstances might be and they involve no organizations, mediators, gurus, secrets or rituals. Every successful spiritual master Huxley studied spoke about these three qualities being essential to their spiritual maturity. (Note: we're using both the words sage and master to designate those who have personally experienced the Divine.) Huxley used the terms "pure in heart" and "poor in spirit" to describe two of these basic conditions. Although the terms appear cryptic, they're actually quite straightforward.

A "pure heart" does not mean that we need to 'clean up our act' before we can experience the Divine. Living up to man-made rules (religious or secular) may keep us out of trouble with society, but it carries no weight with the Divine. In this case, a pure heart symbolizes our core motives and our willingness to have our misperceptions corrected so they don't veil what the Divine wants to show us. This actually means that *agnosia*, a state of unknowing/emptiness, comes before gnosis can take place. Simply put, your deep desire must be for the chalkboard to be wiped clean and written on anew. Pseudo-Dionysius the Areopagite (5th or 6th century), author of *Theologia Mystica* explained it this way:

> *And at times he who is set free of things seen and of things seeing, enters into the truly mystical darkness of unknowing, wherefrom he puts out all intellectual knowledge, and cleaves to that which is quite beyond touch and sight — the entire essence of Him who is beyond all. Thus through the voiding of all knowledge, he is joined with the better part of himself not with any creature, nor with himself, not with another, but with him who is inwardly unknowable; and knowing nothing, he knows beyond the mind.*

Simply put, we let go of the preconceived notions, attachments and aversions that make up this body's personality, knowing that it is little more than a construct of society and not our Reality. This may sound like a great deal of work, perhaps akin to the torturous ascension of Paul through ten heavens, but that does not have to be the case if we're willing. If we cling to our ideas they cling to us, if we fight against them, they become stronger. If we willingly allow them to, they fade away. Since we've created layer upon layer of illusion this usually doesn't happen overnight, but even though it may take some time for each veil to disappear, it doesn't have to be painful. Happily it's the willingness, not the effort, that matters. Heartfelt willingness has no motivation other than the sheer joy and freedom inherent in the Divine experience. Jesus displayed the attitude of a pure heart when he recognized that, "Man cannot live on bread alone, but by every word that proceeds from the mouth of God." (Matthew 4:4) Clearly, gnosis was as much sustenance to him as food was to the body. And as you probably have already figured out, no one else can create or mediate your willingness for you.

During the well-known Sermon on the Mount, Jesus also said, "Blessed are the poor in spirit, for theirs is the kingdom of heaven." (Matthew 5:3) Was he talking about an ascetic who renounces all material comforts and desires? It's easy to confuse literal poverty with a poor spirit; however, living in poverty can be as much of a spiritual detriment and distraction as wealth. In this case, "poor in spirit" symbolizes the understanding that imperturbable peace, love and joy cannot come from outside us. This doesn't mean that we find no happiness in physical life or material comforts, but rather that we no longer see things or other people as an end in themselves. We know the world can give us pleasure, but it also brings us pain; it can make us rich, but it cannot enrich us. We can be called "poor in spirit" when we see through the impossibility of ownership or the illusion that there is anything separate from us that we could own. This also applies to the 'ownership' of information, that is, clinging to a particular belief system.

In some cultures, these concepts are expressed as "empty hands." When we hang on to this world or try to corroborate our preexisting beliefs, our hands are already full. When we cling to preconceived notions, the brain works overtime trying to prove that our views are correct. Instead of letting in new ideas, it filters out anything that contests their validity. Obviously, full hands cannot hold anything new. Empty hands are just that, empty and ready to receive. The seeker has willingly let go of preconceived notions, attachments and aversions and is willing to accept *whatever* the Divine shows them. The 8th century *Ashtavakra Gita*, penned by an anonymous sage, puts it this way, "My child, you may read or discuss scripture as much as you like, but until you forget everything, you will never live in your heart." In Zen, this 'clean slate' is also known as "beginner's mind," since the beginner's mind is open and ready to receive, while the expert's mind is full and ready to argue.

The third item that Huxley discovered is the subject of this book, gnosis. Masters have never been satisfied learning 'about' the Divine but have expected to 'know' the Divine directly. The 2nd century Arab gnostic, Monoimus, insisted that we each, "Look for God by taking yourself as the starting point. Learn who it is within you…you will find Him in yourself." Shankara wrote, "Study of the scriptures is fruitless as long as Ultimate Reality has not been experienced. And when Ultimate Reality has been experienced, it is useless to read the scriptures" Shankara also shared, "A clear vision of the Reality may be obtained only through our own eyes, when they have been opened by spiritual insight—never through the eyes of some other seer." In *XinXin Ming*, attributed to the Third Chinese Zen Patriarch Jianzhi Sengcan (d. 606), we find gnosis explained this way, "The Great Way is not difficult for those who have no preferences. Let go of longing and aversion, and it reveals itself."

(Note: other texts contained in the Nag Hammadi library that use the format of dialogue or revelation include *Dialogue of the Savior*, *The First Revelation of James*, *The Second Revelation of James*, *The Letter of Peter to Philip* and *The Revelation of Adam*.)

II. Sayings Gospels and Wisdom Sayings

1. *The Gospel of Thomas*

Although *The Gospel of Thomas* is a very well-known part of the Nag Hammadi library, it is one text in the collection that many scholars refuse to think of as gnostic. Ironically, this is because it lacks the separation, specialness, ritual and secrecy evident in texts they do consider gnostic. Of course it would be unfair to expect scholars to understand the difference between separation and oneness gnosis since scholarly pursuits are limited to learning 'about' and categorizing. Unfortunately, where gnosis is concerned, direct, personal experience is the only legitimate teacher. Marvin Meyer, scholar and editor of *The Nag Hammadi Scriptures*, explains that *The Gospel of Thomas* is more often classified as a 'sayings gospel' or collection of 'wisdom sayings.' Nonetheless, we personally regard this text as the best example of oneness gnosis in the collection for one very simple, yet significant, reason; it overflows with concepts that are hallmarks of the Divine experience.

The Gospel of Thomas is presented as a dialogue between Jesus and his followers, yet it is more essentially a collection of rapid-fire sayings and short parables. These verses offer virtually no geography, history or biography that would draw attention to the person of Jesus or identify him as anything other than completely human. Since sages want the Divine experience to stand on its own rather than focus on them personally, collections of sayings that result from gnosis are often presented in this 'wisdom sayings' format. Although the book opens with the words, "These are the hidden sayings that the living Jesus spoke," they also add, "And Jesus said, 'Whoever discovers the interpretation of these sayings will not taste death.'" In other words, *these are 'secrets' only in the sense that they are hidden from those who refuse the direct experience, never by Source.* Instead of passing on secret information through initiation or ritual, each person who listens to these words will be expected to make their own experiential 'discovery,' just as Jesus did.

Many scholars believe *The Gospel of Thomas* may predate the *New Testament* gospels, and therefore, would present a more accurate view of Jesus and his teachings. This text is similar in style to a compilation of sayings known as *The Sayings Gospel of Q* or *Quelle* (German for Source) *Q* is not part of the Nag Hammadi library, nor do any manuscripts survive that could absolutely prove its existence. Although most Christians are unaware of *Q*, it's well known among *New Testament* scholars. Based on evidence found within the *New Testament* gospels, it's assumed that an earlier text in the 'wisdom sayings' style must have been passed around among Jesus' early followers before the *New Testament* gospels were written. Countless similarities found in *Matthew* and *Luke* make it obvious that both authors used the gospel of *Mark*, as one of their primary references, but scholars also detected an additional 4,500 words shared by *Matthew* and *Luke* that were not found in *Mark*. These portions of text agreed so closely in word choice, order and inflection, scholars had little choice but to conclude that they were copied word-for-word from a second common source that predated all four of the *New Testament* gospels. Since 1838, scholars have meticulously reconstructed a facsimile of this missing source document.

Like *The Gospel of Thomas* and other very early manuscripts, *Q* consists solely of Jesus' sayings. This suggests that Jesus' earliest followers were far more interested in his teachings than they were in him personally. This would hardly have been the case if they believed he was something other than wholly human. Both texts feature references to rural life and agriculture that urban audiences may not have understand, and in both Jesus urges his followers to personally come to an understanding of the wisdom he's sharing. Jesus is presented as a teacher in *The Gospel of Thomas* and the latest in a long line of Jewish prophets in *Q*, but he is *not* identified as a messiah nor does he die for anyone's sins in either book. However, in *Q*, Jesus does speak of the "One to Come" who will eventually resurrect the faithful, including himself. Although similar in many ways, of the two, *The Gospel of Thomas* appears to present the clearest representation of oneness gnosis.

Before we examine *The Gospel of Thomas*, we'll take a moment to look at the context of this work and understand why it differs so radically from most other so-called gnostic texts. We'll also examine the reasons why there are radical and irreconcilable differences between it and the gospel accounts preserved in the *New Testament*.

In our information age, we might think that if video equipment would have been available when Jesus spoke, the factions that quickly arose between his earliest followers would have had no reason to form. But even if video equipment could have provided word-for-word documentation, it would have had little impact on the diverse perceptions of Jesus' listeners. As we've learned, the brain 'protects' us from new ideas that appear frightening and instead filters what we hear through the information the brain has already vetted. The early stories about Jesus don't agree simply because each listener came away with the information their attachments, aversions and opinions allowed them to hear. Although there are wide variations in interpretation within each group, Jesus' listeners generally fell into one of two camps, apocalyptic or gnostic. Neither of these groups was static and both underwent numerous transitions over time, but for the moment, let's concentrate on the beginnings of each.

2. Apocalyptic View

Long before Jesus' day, Jewish thinkers wrangled with a seemingly unsolvable question. Although they felt certain they were God's 'chosen' people, they couldn't comprehend why their nation experienced so much suffering. Their prophets claimed the suffering was just punishment for falling short of the law code given to Moses. Few argued with that logic, but they couldn't understand why they continued to suffer even when the law was carefully followed. This question finally led to a decidedly dualistic 'apocalyptic' perspective that's illustrated in the *Old Testament* book of *Job*. The story opens with Satan, an angelic creature, openly challenging God. Satan has noticed the righteous man Job, and the riches God has blessed him with. Satan claims that humans do not worship God because they love Him, but for the material rewards alone. To answer the accusation, God not only hands the earth over to Satan but gives him permission to test human loyalty using every form of suffering imaginable. Job, who was considered the most faithful of all humans, becomes Satan's 'test case, and systematically robs him of his family, his wealth, his health and his friends. Eventually God steps in and replaces what Job has lost, but not before pointing out just how ignorant Job was. Ultimately, the point of the story is that humanity is the rope in a cosmic tug of war between good and evil and as a result, humans suffer even when they are good. Institutionalized Christianity absorbed this Jewish rationalization and still maintains that all of humanity remains under attack by Satan and his hoard of powerful demon helpers.

Job's restoration pictured the Jewish belief that that the cosmic war would also eventually come to an end after sufficient testing had taken place. At that point, God would step in to destroy the wicked and make things right for those who remained faithful. The Jews of Jesus' day had many reasons to hope that the day of God's reckoning would take place in their lifetime. Their nation had already endured a lengthy and miserable history of exile and alien rule, but approximately 65 years before Jesus' birth, the Roman Empire took Judea and appointed a Roman ruler over them. This wretched state of affairs stirred massive Jewish unrest that produced well over twenty religious/political factions vying for attention. Among them were apocalyptic groups that expected a messiah.

The English word messiah, the Hebrew *mashiach* and the Greek *khristos* all mean 'anointed.' The word originally referred to Jewish kings, priests and prophets who had oil poured on their head to signify that they were favored by God or chosen for a special task. Because of this history, the Jews expected the messiah to be a military leader like King David, who would physically defeat their enemies and bring peace and material blessings to the faithful of Israel. Their victory would not only herald a restoration of the balance between good and evil on earth, but in heaven as well. But where would this messiah come from? In Jewish scriptures, God had promised there would always be a king from the line of David on their throne, but that promise went unfulfilled. Nonetheless, some reasoned that a descendant from the line of David could be a likely candidate to avenge the Jewish people. During Jesus' lifetime, there was no shortage of apocalyptic preachers and self-professed messiahs who claimed they were the one who would fulfill that role. Other apocalyptic thinkers believed the messiah could not be a man, but would have to be a supernatural "cosmic judge" they called "the Son of Man" or the "One to Come" mentioned in Q. Regardless of whether apocalyptic thinkers believed in a physical or cosmic savior, they all envisioned the messiah as an indestructible force who would establish God's kingdom as a political power on earth.

From *The Gospel of Thomas* we see that Jesus' earliest followers didn't think of Jesus as a possible messiah, and in Q, Jesus himself is looking for the coming of a cosmic warrior. It's rather surprising then that some of Jesus' followers began to imagine that this rural teacher could be the warrior messiah they longed for. In Jesus' day it was common for one person to hold both religious and political power. When a king went astray in his religious duties, powerful prophets sometimes appeared in God's name to chastise them and set things straight. Jesus' message, which was radically different from the teachings and corrupt behavior of the priesthood, may have reminded them of the powerful priests of old. It's also probable that after filtering Jesus' message through their own perceptions; followers heard something very different than what Jesus actually said.

We all might feel sure that if we had been on the scene, we would have processed Jesus' words correctly. But as Dr. Candace Pert's research in the areas of physiology and biophysics reveals, it is not only the brain, but our emotions that also act as a powerful filter for perception. Simply put, the chemical messengers that connect the brain and body regulate what we believe we're experiencing. Dr. Pert wrote, "Our emotions decide what is worth paying attention to." Pert felt that we cannot objectively define what's real and what's not real in light of the chemical charge we receive from our emotions. That being said, we could safely assume that the emotionally charged political/religious scene of Jesus' day strongly influenced the perception of everyone involved.

Imagine the horror when, just as Jesus' apocalyptic followers were expecting to witness their salvation, the Romans easily dispatched their messiah. This inconceivable event left them with two choices. They could look at Jesus' teachings from a different perspective, which his gnostic followers already had. Or, they would be forced to manipulate Jesus' story and teachings to fit their new circumstances. Among the second group was the apostle Paul. Desperate to understand how someone who was executed as a common criminal could possibly be God's chosen warrior messiah, Paul figured out how to give purpose to Jesus' ignominious death. The end of Jesus' earthly story couldn't be changed, but a new beginning could be constructed that would explain the end in a more meaningful way. Paul's teachings provided an explanation that many disheartened followers were seeking; instead of seeing Jesus' death as a defeat, it was reinterpreted as a victory.

Since it was impossible for Paul to imagine that Jesus actually deserved crucifixion or that his death had no meaning, he assumed there had to be a noble purpose behind it. Building on that foundation, Paul recalled that the Jews were required to make animal sacrifices to "atone" for their sins and deduced that Jesus' body and blood must have been a human sacrifice meant to atone for sin in a far grander way. Although the 'Adam and Eve' story condemned all humans as sinners, the atonement sacrifices made at the Jewish temple were not meant to cover the world of non-Jewish gentiles. Paul reasoned that a human sacrifice could fill the bill and wipe away the entire world's inherited sin. Although the earliest 'sayings gospels' did not include crucifixion, sacrifice, atonement or resurrection, all of these became necessary parts of the apocalyptic story.

Paul began likening Jesus' resurrection to a plant that grows out of a seed; in effect, the seed gives up its life so the plant can grow. Paul claimed that Jesus' mortal body had been sown in death and had become an immortal spiritual body when he was resurrected. With this entirely new thought, the Jesus story made a dramatic shift. According to Paul, all of Jesus' followers had to undergo this transformation because, as he said, "flesh and blood cannot have any inheritance in God's reign." (1 Corinthians 15:50) Nonetheless, Paul did not believe all of Jesus' followers would die. In fact, he was certain that Jesus would return in all his spiritual power and glory during Paul's own lifetime. When that happened, all those of faith who were alive at the time would be instantly transformed and rule with Jesus in heaven. When that did not occur, Christians began pushing Jesus' glorious return farther and farther into the future. Although predictions of his eminent return still regularly surface, generation after generation of Jesus' apocalyptic followers still continue to wait.

Both the gnostic gospels and the *New Testament* gospels make it clear that the majority of Jesus' followers completely misunderstood his teachings. Based on this repeated testimony, we should not be at all surprised that:

» Many of Jesus' listeners already had a messianic agenda, one they deeply desired because it was tied to their immediate well-being. As long as a thought remains precious to us, we inevitably filter everything through that thought and the emotions that support it.

» Very few of Jesus' listeners were willing to experience gnosis as Jesus had. No matter how sincere their desire, until they had a Divine experience they could do no more than interpret his words based on their own limited understanding.

» Although it's impossible to accurately put a Divine experience into words, Jesus' teachings and behavior were still such a radical departure from the values accepted within the culture, very few had the willingness to comprehend them.

3. Gnostic View

Many scholars, including some that are well versed in the gnostic gospels as well as the *New Testament*, insist that Jesus was an apocalyptic preacher. If *Q* were our only reference, that may appear to be true. If we had only *The Gospel of Thomas* to refer to, the answer would be a resounding NO. Without further ado, let's allow *The Gospel of Thomas* to speak for itself. As we've already mentioned, the text opens by making it clear that 'salvation' comes through personal understanding and cannot be mediated by a 'savior.' Here are a few examples from the text:

Whoever discovers the interpretation of these sayings will not taste death.

Jesus says, "Let one who seeks not stop seeking until one finds. When one finds, one will be astonished, and having been astonished, one will reign, and having reigned, one will rest. (Greek version)

And God's kingdom is inside you and outside you. Whoever knows oneself will find this. And when you know yourselves, you will understand that you are children of the living Father. (Greek version)

Jesus said, "Have you discovered the beginning, then, so that you are seeking the end? For where the beginning is the end will be. Blessed is one who stands at the beginning: that one will know the end and will not taste death.

Jesus said to them, "When you make the two into one, and when you make the inner like the outer and the outer like the inner...then you will enter the kingdom.

If you do not fast from the world, you will not find the kingdom...be passersby.

If you bring forth what is within you, what you have will save you.

Jesus said, "Seek and you will find. In the past however, I did not tell you the things about which you asked me then. Now I am willing to tell them, but you are not seeking them....One who seeks will find; for one who knocks it will be opened."

Doesn't Jesus say, "Whoever has found oneself, of that person the world is not worthy?"

As you'll notice, each of these statements puts the burden of salvation on the listener/reader. In just these few lines, Jesus used the word 'whoever' twice, one/oneself twelve times and you/yourself twenty times. In fact, not only does Jesus *not* claim to be a mediator or savior in *Thomas*, he clearly states, "I am not your teacher." In *The Apocryphon of James*, Jesus encouraged his followers to "...become better than I," reflecting the desire of every sincere teacher. However, he does admit to offering the priceless gift of gnosis, calling it a "bubbling spring," but as we can see in Jesus' statement, the gift has value *only* when it is accepted and experienced *for oneself*: "Jesus said, '...Because you have drunk, you have become intoxicated from the bubbling spring that I have tended.'" Rumi used similar symbolism when he said, "Be thirsty for the ultimate water. Then be ready for what will come pouring from the spring." Sages can point the way but they all know it's impossible for them to save anyone else since each of us must be our own savior. As Jesus said, "How miserable is the body that depends on a body, and how miserable is the soul that depends on these two." No other body/person can give you salvation or carry you on their understanding. Depend on the Self within and you can't go wrong.

Let's continue to discover the numerous hallmarks of oneness gnosis contained in *The Gospel of Thomas*:

1. Faith, obedience, rites, rituals or intellectual learning are not the way:

   "Jesus said, 'Whoever discovers the interpretation of these sayings will not taste death...Let one who seeks not stop seeking until one finds.'"

Notice the word 'discovers' is used not 'figures out' or 'receives the secret.' Since truth cannot exist in the material realm, to 'know' or understand it, we must go past the material and connect with the One Mind where truth actually exists. Again, we see the word discover used to symbolize gnosis when 20th century sage Eknath Easwaran, says, "The seers discovered a core of consciousness beyond time and change...they discovered Unity." Since our Reality is consciousness, the discovery is possible for each of us. Jesus recognized the uselessness of 'intellectual spirituality' when he said, "One who knows everything but lacks in oneself lacks everything." Nisargadatta also clarified who the 'oneself' is with these words, "When I say

'I am'...I mean the totality of being, the ocean of consciousness, the entire universe of all that is and knows." Why would anything outside us be needed to know the Divine when we already *are* the Divine?

2. 'God's Kingdom' is everywhere:

> *"Jesus said, 'If your leaders say to you, "Look, the kingdom is in heaven," then the birds of heaven will precede you. If they say to you, "It is in the sea," then the fish will precede you. Rather, the kingdom is inside you and it is outside you'...the Father's kingdom is spread out upon the earth, and people do not see it."*

The words of physicist Erwin Schrodinger sound very similar:

> *You are a part, a piece, of an eternal, infinite being, an aspect or modification of it... This life of yours which you are living is not merely a piece of this entire existence, but in a certain sense the whole...This, as we know, is what the Brahmins express in that sacred, mystic formula which is yet really so simple and so clear; tat tvam asi, You are That... The mystical experience of the union with God regularly leads to this view, unless strong prejudices stand in the way. Multiplicity is only apparent, in truth, there is only one mind.*

Unless we're attached to the notion that God's Kingdom must be a literal government, the symbolic language Jesus used is clear. The Kingdom is the very being of the Divine, which encompasses everything in existence. It is not something we need to look for, hope for or expect a savior to restore since it is, always has been, and always will be, What Is.

3. The body we project is a little, false self, a tiny misguided portion of the true quantum Self we must claim:

    "Jesus said, 'When you know yourselves, then you will be known, and you will understand that you are children of the living Father. But if you do not know yourselves, then you dwell in poverty, and you are poverty"

No matter what riches we might believe we possess in this world, we're in poverty as long as we believe our material projections are real. Jesus also explained what was necessary for him to realize who he actually was when he said, "Blessed is one who stands at the beginning: that one will know the end and will not taste death." Our beginning is pure quantum consciousness and gnosis allows us to tap into that state, and see the truth of our beginning.

Also remember that Jesus used garments to symbolize the flesh when he said, "when you strip without being ashamed and you take your clothes and put them under your feet like little children and trample them, then [you] will see the child of the living one and you will not be afraid." We can understand that the body is merely a costume that disguises our true nature, but the trick is in letting go of our attachment to that concealing garment and value it no more than something we'd easily trample underfoot. Nisargadatta repeated Jesus' counsel when he said:

    Save all your energies and time for breaking the wall your mind had built around you...Don't burden yourself with names. Just be. Any name or shape you give yourself obscures your real nature…Meet your own Self. Be with your own Self, listen to it, obey it, cherish it, keep it in mind ceaselessly. You need no other guide. When all the false self-identifications are thrown away, what remains is all-embracing love.

4. Rituals, rules, laws, secrets, practices and organizations are obstacles on the spiritual path:

As for secrets, Jesus promised, "Know what is in front of your face, and what is hidden from you will be disclosed to you. For there is nothing hidden that will not be revealed." Clinging to the law code they were used to, his disciples continued to believe they could find Divine favor by obeying rules. When they asked, "Do you want us to fast? How should we pray? Should we give to charity? What diet should we observe?" Jesus answered, "Do not lie, and do not do what you hate…If you fast, you will bring sin upon yourselves, and if you pray, you will be condemned, and if you give to charity, you will harm your spirit." Once again, everything comes back to the individual and what is going on within. Ironically, rules, rituals, secrets and practices are traps we manufacture to catch and condemn ourselves. Even when we use them to prove our own righteousness, they condemn us to remaining in the rut of this world's thinking. The little self loves this since its greatest fear is that you'll actually begin to see through the illusion that "is in front of your face, and what is hidden from you will be disclosed to you."

5. Everything is One:

We've learned what quantum physics has to say about the oneness of everything in existence but nearly two thousand years earlier, Jesus saw this truth in action when he personally experienced gnosis. In *The Gospel of Thomas*, he makes it clear that our desire for separation and specialness, compounded by our dualistic thought system, is the only issue standing between us and Reality. Again, he explains that reversing our thinking dissolves the problem, "When you make the two into one, and when you make the inner like the outer and the outer like the inner and the upper like the lower, and when you make male and female into a single one, so that the male will not be male nor the female be female...then you will enter the kingdom." We're repeating this portion of the text because, although it's an extremely simple thought, it's absolutely key for the seeker to understand. We've learned that this world divides one into two, and clings to extremes, but Jesus said, "I am the one who comes from what is whole...For this reason I say, if one is whole, one will be filled with light, but if one is divided, one will be filled with darkness." Here Jesus was asking *each person* who heard his words to look at the world of separation we've created and decide whether or not it was working. Choice turned one into two, only choice can turn two back to one. In the shorter Greek version of *The Gospel of Thomas*, Jesus points out that the separation we project also causes us to think in terms of separation from the Divine, "Where there are three, they are without God, and where there is only one, I say I am with that one." By thinking of the Divine as separate, we separate ourselves from Source. It is only in oneness that the Divine is revealed to us.

It would be a simple thing for a person who had not experienced gnosis to misinterpret the quote we're about to examine:

> *Jesus said, "I am the light that is over all things. I am all; from me all has come forth, and to me all has reached. Split a piece of wood; I am there. Lift up the stone and you will find me there."*

As shocking as these words might sound at first, from the perspective of non-local consciousness, each and every one of us can correctly make the same statement. Similarly, Rumi said, "I am the life of life. I am that cat, this stone…I have thrown duality away like an old dishrag, I see and know all times and worlds, As one, one, always one." Unfortunately, those who had not experienced the Divine could easily take these words to mean that Jesus was claiming to be the God they worshipped. Since they believed God was an unapproachable spirit being who was separate and higher than creation, they judged the statement to be unadulterated blasphemy. The *New Testament* gospels of *Luke* and *John* both tell us that the Jewish Sanhedrin (high court) wanted Jesus killed because he had the audacity to claim that he was the Son of God. Since they had no authority to put anyone to death, they were forced to turn Jesus over to the Romans. The Romans didn't much care about Jesus' spiritual claims, but they were willing to comply because they feared the Jews might rally around someone they believed might be a politically potent messiah, a "King of the Jews." (Luke 22:70-23: 39 and John 19: 1-7)

Jesus was not the only sage who paid the ultimate price for testifying to oneness with the Divine. In 922, the Sufi master Mansur al-Hallaj was put to death for saying *Anâ l-Haqq* meaning "I am The Truth," which also translates "I am God." al-Hallaj repeatedly uttered these words while "in the presence of God," i.e. during gnosis. Like Jesus, al-Hallaj had angered religious leaders who labeled him a heretic because he openly shared the concepts of mysticism/gnosis with the masses. He taught that one must go beyond religious rites and deep into the heart to discover the Divine. For al-Hallaj the Divine was the "Beloved Friend," a relationship he knew was the birthright of each and every one of us. Forgetting body and personality, he claimed "[My] only Self is God." To attain that relationship, he taught, "Love means to stand next to the Beloved, renouncing oneself entirely and transforming oneself in accordance to Him." For al-Hallaj, "renouncing oneself" was simple because it was only the projected virtual self that was renounced, allowing the true Self to once again stand with the Beloved. Because al-Hallaj spoke continually of union with the Divine, his captors chose to enforce separation and duality on him by cutting him into pieces. Eye witnesses reported that until the moment of death, he smiled and repeated "I am the Truth." Although religious leaders see the claim of oneness with the Divine as either blasphemy or a privilege held out for only a very special few, Rumi took the opposite stance saying:

> *This is what is signified by the words Anâ l-Haqq, "I am God." People imagine that it is a presumptuous claim, whereas it is really a presumptuous claim to say Ana 'l-'abd, "I am the slave of God"; and Anâ l-Haqq, "I am God" is an expression of great humility. The man who says Ana 'l-'abd, "I am the servant of God" affirms two existences, his own and God's, but he that*

says Anâ l-Haqq, "I am God" has made himself non-existent and has given himself up and says "I am God", that is, "I am naught, He is all; there is no being but God's." This is the extreme of humility. (Translated by Victor Mansfield)

6. In this world, we are asleep to Self unless we choose to wake up:

The Gospel of Truth uses sleep and dreams to symbolize our material projections:

> *Ignorance of the Father brought about anguish and terror; and the anguish grew solid like a fog, so that no one was able to see…there were many illusions at work…and there were empty fictions, as if they were sunk in sleep and found themselves in disturbing dreams…When those who are going through all these things wake up, they will see nothing, they who were in the midst of these disturbances, for they are nothing. Such is the way of those who have cast ignorance aside as sleep, leaving it behind like a dream in the night.*

In *The Gospel of Thomas*, Jesus uses the stupor of drunkenness to symbolize our forgetfulness:

> *I found them all drunk, and I did not find any of them thirsty. My soul ached for the children of humanity, because they are blind in their hearts and do not see, for they came into the world empty, and they also seek to depart from the world empty. But now they are drunk. When they shake off their wine, then they will repent.*

And *Creation of the World and the Alien Man,* a text that's not a part of the Nag Hammadi library but is attributed to the Mandaeans, the only gnostic sect that survived into the 20th century, used both symbols when it said, "Life is a dualistic scheme…a sleep, a drunkenness, an oblivion…our ignorance is a form of unconsciousness." For many gnostics, Adam's sleep in the Garden of Eden symbolized the dream state we continue to experience as long as we desire the separation of virtual reality rather than oneness.

7.   Duality exists only in illusion:

Remember that our polarized, dualistic thought system ignores the continuum and either rejects or clings to, extreme opposites, clinging to one and rejecting the other. Religion has done such a thorough job of convincing us that 'evil' exists as a powerful outside force personified by entities such as Satan and his demon cohorts, that few even question the idea that the world is locked in a perpetual struggle between good and evil. And sadly, countless numbers have lived in fear of these non-existent entities, believing they could easily be overpowered and used by them. From a quantum perspective, the entire scenario is both ridiculous and impossible. As we've learned, everything exists in a harmonious relationship; there can be no 'cancer' eating away at the oneness of All That Is. If there were, the Divine would have had to create evil and then 'infect' Self with its poison. This is something no sane being would even consider doing; nonetheless we do see evil in the world. How can we understand this seeming paradox?

First of all, we need to keep in mind that the material portion of the universe is an illusion. You are not here, and although what you believe you see and feel convinces you it is real, both quantum physics, and the sages, assure us it is not. Secondly, although many believe that karma, fate, destiny or determinism rules their life, we do live in a universe of free will and choice. How do we know that? Our quantum model demonstrates that everything comes into being because consciousness is interacting with energy; simply put, nothing happens until consciousness makes a choice. However, our freedom is relative in one sense: it is impossible for us to make a choice that will actually harm or destroy Ultimate Reality (which of course, includes our true Self). Nonetheless, we can make any choice we wish up to that point, including the choice to project a world of separation and dualistic thought where we can pretend to hate and harm one another. We can project the belief in evil entities so effectively, (or fairies, abominable snowmen or aliens for that matter) we're certain we're seeing them or suffering from their machinations. We can even go so far as to deny or curse the Source that sustains us, and yet the Divine loves all, plays no favorites and lovingly waits for our inevitable return.

In *The Gospel of Thomas* Jesus testifies to the fact that we are the ones who choose everything we project in the material world, not God or an evil entity: " A good person brings forth good from the storehouse; a bad person brings forth evil things from the corrupt storehouse in the heart and says evil things. For from the abundance of the heart this person brings forth evil things." Both Jesus and Buddha were said to have been tempted by evil entities who offered them great power before they began teaching publicly. But the *New Testament* gospel of *Mark* agrees with *The Gospel of Thomas* when Jesus states, "What comes out of a man is what defiles a man. For from within, out of the heart of man, come evil thoughts." (Mark 7: 20-23) Boethius, a 6th century Roman philosopher recognized the truth beyond appearances when he pointed out, "Evil is thought to abound on earth. But if you could see the plan of Providence, you would not think there was evil anywhere." And Plotinus, a 3rd century Greek philosopher made it clear that duality was a thought system, not our Reality, when he said, "The soul must remove from itself good and evil and everything else that it may receive the One alone, as the One is alone." (Note: In some cases, the title 'philosopher' actually refers to a 'sage.')

8.   The universe *is* Light:

The following illustration is found in both the *New Testament* gospel *Matthew* (5:14-16) and *The Gospel of Thomas* where Jesus says:

> *Whoever has ears should hear. There is light within a person of light, and it shines on the whole world...For no one lights a lamp and puts it under a basket, nor does one put it in a hidden place. Rather, one puts it on a stand so that all who come and go will see its light...If one is whole, one will be filled with light, but if one is divided, one will be filled with darkness.*

Most Christian churches use this short parable to teach their followers not to hide their faith and/or to make use of their talents in Christian service. However, when seen from a quantum perspective, it takes on far greater significance. The creation account found in the *Bible* book of *Genesis* chapters 1 and 2 is scrambled and repetitive, but if we look closely we'll see something interesting. Genesis

1:3 states, "And God said, 'Let there be light,' and there was light.'" When seen from a quantum perspective, this statement clearly identifies consciousness collapsing energy potential into form. We might assume this verse referred to the creation of the light produced by the sun, moon and stars; however this light is mentioned before their creation. An ancient Jewish manuscript called the *Haggadah* verifies this when it states, "The light created at the very beginning is not the same light emitted by the sun, the moon and the stars, which appeared on the fourth day." In his book, *The God Theory*, astrophysicist Bernard Haisch asserts that quantum light was "…the first manifestation of creation." As we've learned, the zero-point field is a sea of quantum light energy. Research conducted by Haisch and physicist Alfonso Rueda, "suggests that the solid, stable world of matter is sustained at every instant by this underlying sea of quantum light." Rueda proposes that matter does not innately possess mass. Instead, the quantum light of the zero-point field exerts an illusion of mass.

Science has also discovered that tiny particles of light called biophotons are emitted by *all life*. Although gnostic writers felt "The One" personified perfect love and goodness, they also understood Source to be a universal ground, which *The Secret Gospel of John* identifies as "immeasurable light." The early gnostic writing, *Creation of the World and the Alien Man* agrees saying, "There is no boundary for the light and it was not known when it came into being. Nothing was when light was not, nothing was when radiance was not. Nothing was when the Mighty Life was not, there never was a boundary for the light." In *The Gospel of Thomas*, Jesus tells his followers they have come from God's kingdom, and therefore, they can return to it. He instructs them that if anyone asks them where they're from, they should answer, "We have come from the light, from the place where the light came into being by itself, and established itself'…If they say to you, 'Is it you?' say 'We are its children.'" Now, when we look back to Jesus' 'bushel basket' illustration, we can see that he was not talking about something as simplistic as letting our faith or our talents shine for others to see. Instead, he was going to the heart of the matter by pointing out that all of us who project the material realm and see ourselves as a body are 'under the bushel basket.' Until we reclaim 'the light,' of our true identity, we remain in hiding.

9. We must choose between the little, false self and the true Self:

One of Jesus' parables found In *The Gospel of Thomas,* illustrates this point: A man prepares a feast and sends his servant out to invite his friends to share it with him. The servant finds each of the friends too occupied with worldly interests and problems to accept the invitation. When the servant returns alone, the man instructs him to go out into the street and bring back anyone who would like to share in the feast. Of course the man preparing the feast symbolizes Ultimate Reality, the servant stands for the sage who offers spiritual invitations, and the feast pictures truth. Each one of us, whether we're aware of it or not, have a standing invitation to this feast.

The dramatic point of the story, if we're willing to take it to heart, is that we choose between this world and our true nature countless times each day, albeit often totally unwittingly. This parable also has a second meaning. The 'friends' who are invited first represent the religionists who loudly proclaim their friendship with God. As we can see, the friendship they boast of is merely a sham to cover their intense involvement in the world. Those out on the street who choose to respond to the invitation picture those with the 'pure heart, 'poor spirit,' and 'empty hands' we spoke of earlier. They gladly attend the feast because they want truth instead of the pseudo-spiritual food dished out by the world. In *The Gospel of Thomas* Jesus also said:

A person cannot mount two horses or bend two bows. And a servant cannot serve two masters, or that servant will honor the one and offend the other. No person drinks aged wine and immediately desires to drink new wine. New wine is not poured into aged wineskins, or they might break, and aged wine is not poured into a new wineskin, or it might spoil. An old patch is not sewn onto a new garment, for there would be a tear.

Over and over, in both the gnostic and *New Testament* gospels, Jesus emphasizes the fact that a choice must be made. Although many try to keep a foot in two opposing camps, it's impossible to be both the little, false self and the true Self. In the Greek version of *The Gospel of Thomas* Jesus draws a line when he says, "If you do not fast from the world, you will not find God's kingdom."

4. The Teachings of Silvanus

The Teachings of Silvanus is another collection of 'wisdom sayings,' and like *The Gospel of Thomas*, it is not considered gnostic by most scholars. Although we've called this text a 'collection,' it could more aptly be considered a 'conglomeration.' Actually, it's an excellent example of a text that has been altered, added to and abused from the early 1st century through the late 4th century. Scholars also believe it includes a mish-mash of wisdom sayings from Egyptian, Jewish and Greek sources. As you'll see, the early verses contain many of the same clues to oneness gnosis as *The Gospel of Thomas*. After that, additions made by orthodox tinkerers openly contradict the earlier sayings.

Although the second half of the text insists that Jesus is the only savior, the first half states, "…before everything else, know yourself." And how do we do that? Again we hear the words, "Bring in your guide and your teacher. The mind is the guide…Live in accordance with the mind…Get strength for yourself because the mind is strong… Illuminate your mind with heavenly light, so that you may turn toward the light." As in other gnostic works, when *The Teachings of Silvanus* uses the word 'mind' it is referring to consciousness rather than the brain. The text also connects this mind to the One Mind saying, "May God dwell in your camp…and may the Divine Mind protect the walls…Do not flee from the Divine and the teaching within you." One of the more interesting subsections in the text asks the question "Is the Mind in a Place?" Of course quantum physics has made us aware of the non-local nature of consciousness, but *The Teachings of Silvanus* offers the same information hundreds of years earlier when it answers, "…in terms of the thought process, the mind is not in a place. For how can it be in a place when it contemplates every place?"

In stark contrast to the orthodox belief that God is a separate entity that dwells in a separate heavenly realm, these verses from *The Teachings of Silvanus* clarify the non-local nature of the Divine and support the truths that become evident during the direct experience of oneness gnosis:

> *Do not think in yourself that God is in a place. If you localize the Lord of all in a place, then you could say that the place is more exalted than the one who dwells in it. For what contains is superior to what is contained. For there is no place that can be called incorporeal. It is not right for us to say that God is corporeal…Consider these things about God: He is in every place; on the other hand, he is in no place. In terms of power, he is in every place, but in terms of divinity, he is in no place…In terms of his power, he fills every place, but in his exalted divinity nothing contains him. Everything is in God, but God is not in anything. What is it to know God? Everything that partakes of the truth is God…For it is necessary to know God in the way he is…Do not confine the God of All to mental images.*

The Teachings of Silvanus also reminds us, "When you consider sin, it is not anything real." As *Silvanus* explains, "…thoughts that are not good are evil beasts." This statement agrees with several other gnostic gospels that evil is not an entity or a cosmic force, but the result of our own choices. Simply put, there is no devil tempting us or forcing us to his will. This is an extremely upsetting thought for some, but it's also the key to our liberation. If we are responsible for the thoughts and actions we don't want, then we also have the power and freedom to change them! Again, it's ignorance of our true nature that continues to separate us from the Divine. And the author of *Silvanus* reminds us of our own responsibility when he writes, "He crowns himself with ignorance, and seats himself on a throne of incomprehension...he leads only himself astray, for he is guided by ignorance and he follows the ways of every passionate desire... The poor wretch who goes through all these things will die because he does not have the mind as a helmsman." Ignorance of our true nature is once again symbolized by sleep, drunkenness and forgetfulness when *Silvanus* says, "My child... bring an end to the sleep that weighs heavily upon you. Come away from the forgetfulness that fills you with darkness...O obstinate soul, be sober and shake off your drunkenness, which is the work of ignorance."

Unlike many gnostic texts that blame Yaldabaoth for the human predicament, *The Teachings of Silvanus* puts the responsibility squarely on our own shoulders. *Silvanus* infers that when we chose to coopt the human body and use it for a purpose it was not originally intended, we opened the little self to the influence of the human body's 'animal nature.' Under the subheading, "Know Yourself," the text reads, "But before everything else, know yourself, that is, from what substance you are." It goes on to explain the difference between the Self and the human animal, "The body came into being from the earth with an earthly substance...The created, however, is the mind that came into being according to the image of God," and then *Silvanus* admonishes, "If you mix yourself...you fall from heavenly virtue into earthly inferiority. Live in accordance with the mind. Don't think about the things of the flesh. Get strength for yourself because the mind is strong." The text also asks, "Did you wish to become animal when you came into this kind of nature? Wouldn't you rather take part in the true nature of life?" From the perspective of oneness gnosis, this is not an insult to the body or to its physical desires; it's merely an acknowledgement of the fact that without our interference, the human animal would be exactly what it was supposed to be, and we would be free of this unnatural dual nature.

Biologists and paleontologists have long been confused about radical changes that took place in the human brain. Animal brain mass had always developed proportionately with other organs and physical structures. About 250,000 years ago, mammals reached the height of their brain size and efficiency. Then spontaneously, the human brain experienced a 20% increase in the mass and density of the neocortex, but the body increased by only 16%. This may not seem like much of a difference, but it was an extreme variation in the usual mammalian body-brain ratio. Because the human skull didn't keep pace with brain size, the brain was forced to fold in on itself and took on the appearance of a walnut. This folding increased mental capacity so much, we have still barely tapped the brain's full potential. From a purely evolutionary standpoint, this type of 'overkill' makes absolutely no sense. It is our contention that this sudden brain increase was an accommodation that allowed consciousness to exploit the human animal to the farthest reaches of its capabilities.

Of course the drives, instincts and urges natural to the human animal can be delightful to experience, but they also create a constant push/ pull for domination over consciousness. Non-local consciousness can't successfully exist as form, nor can a human body happily be what it truly is when commandeered by consciousness. At a deep level we all understand there's a clash between our higher leanings and the body's lower drives. Misunderstanding the reason for this dichotomy, most religions attempt to explain the problem away via the concept of sin. They assign humans two conflicting natures, a good portion associated with a soul that's supposedly trapped in the body, and an evil portion associated with the body itself. Most teach that we must suppress the body so the soul can win the struggle. However this mysterious dichotomy interests science as well as religion.

Research has been regularly conducted to explain the paradox of the so-called "moral animal." Evolutionary psychology rationalizes human behavior from a biological standpoint, claiming humans have evolved on an intellectual and moral level, but remain prisoners of biological drives that originated in prehistoric times. This theory asserts that the majority of the decisions we believe we're making are actually steered by prehistoric safety and survival instincts, while the loftier aspects of human behavior are the anomaly. The writer of the ancient *Kena Upanishad* clearly understood that the dichotomy in human behavior was not caused by evolution nor could it be explained by the concept of sin. Rather, the explanation lies in the fact that our true Self is attempting to be something that it's not:

The ignorant think the Self can be known by the intellect, but the illumined knows he is beyond the duality of the knower and the known. The Self is realized in a higher state of consciousness when you have broken through the wrong identification that you are the body, subject to birth and death.

Like everything else in existence, the human body is the stuff and substance of the Divine; however, trying to combine the Reality of quantum consciousness with virtual reality forces both to exist in an unnatural way. Unfortunately, like mixing oil and water, this incompatible combination can be extremely difficult to sustain, resulting in continuous physical, intellectual and moral dilemmas. Many attempt to bend one nature to the will of the other; however, this strategy carries its own frustrations. If we struggle to sublimate the body we may become disgusted by it or feel continual frustration in our failure to conquer it, a common theme in both separation gnosis and Christianity. If we choose to serve the body, we can just as readily become disillusioned by its empty and incessant desires or wracked with guilt when we give in to its more outrageous and hedonistic demands. And so, the third option, shutting out the conflict by deadening ourselves to the issue, often becomes the default mode. Happily, the choice to return to Source completely eliminates the issue.

5. *The Gospel of Philip*

This text has the appearance of a personal notebook used to jot down quotes and concepts that interested its owner. The writer pulled information from so many diverse sources, it's impossible to detect any form of underlying continuity. Nonetheless, the text is interesting for that very reason. Why? The mish-mash of contradictory information serves as a window into the thoughts of an early gnostic seeker who was faced with countless spiritual concepts, just as we are today. Evidently the writer was trying to use the intellect to logic his or her way to the Divine rather than allowing the Divine to show them truth via personal experience. Hopefully some of the words they collected eventually moved them from an intellectual pursuit to gnosis. One of the more interesting gems of oneness gnosis the writer gathered is a comparison of oneness and duality. This portion of the text begins by saying:

> *Light and darkness, life and death, and right and left are siblings of one another and inseparable. For this reason the good are not good, the bad are not bad, life is not life, and death is not death. Each will dissolve into its original nature, but what is superior to the world cannot be dissolved, for it is eternal.*

These verses take us back to the continuum of the gray scale and the yin/yang symbol where everything exists in relationship rather than as a stand-alone opposite or extreme. Next, the text discusses how language reinforces duality:

> *The names of worldly things are utterly deceptive, for they turn the heart from what is real to what is unreal. Whoever hears the word "God" thinks not of what is real but rather of what is unreal… though the words refer to what is real. The words that are heard belong to this world. Do not be deceived. If words belonged to the eternal realm, they would never be pronounced in this world, nor would they designate worldly things. They would refer to what is in the eternal realm.*

Dualistic language is designed for separating, labeling and judging; it defines and describes the unreal but it cannot be used to accurately explain the Real. Lao-Tzu observed, "Today I speak in this fashion, tomorrow in another, but always the Integral Way is beyond words and beyond mind."

This brings to mind Lao-Tzu's most oft quoted words, "The Tao that can be spoken of is not the Tao." Gnosis requires no language since you are immersed within the experience and understand it because you've become one *with* it. As Jesus said, gnosis conveys "what no eye has seen, what no ear has heard, what no hand has touched, what has not arisen in the human heart." Sages testify that 'knowing' comes instantaneously and completely, without words. The always humorous Hafiz put it this way, "If you think that the Truth can be known from words, if you think that the sun and the ocean can pass through that tiny opening called the mouth, O someone should start laughing! Someone should start wildly Laughing Now!" But Rumi clarified how truth can be 'heard' when he said, "Let silence take you to the core of life…Let silence tell you the secrets of the world…Silence is the language of God, all else is a poor translation." The Danish philosopher/sage Soren Kierkegaard (1813-1855) confirmed this saying, "I became silent, and began to listen. I discovered in the silence, the voice of God." Of course a silent voice is an oxymoron, except in gnosis, where the silence speaks volumes.

Like many gnostic texts, *The Gospel of Philip* contains contradictory information about the nature of evil. At one point it truthfully tells us, "Let each of us also dig down after the root of evil within us and pull it out of our hearts from the root. It will be uprooted if we recognize it. But if we are ignorant of it, it takes root in us and produces fruit in our hearts…It is powerful because we do not recognize it." And what is the source of the evil in our hearts? The text agrees with many other gnostic sources when it adds, "Ignorance is the mother of all evil.

Ignorance leads to death." Reminiscent of Jesus' words found in the *Bible* at *John* 8:31 *The Gospel of Philip* reminds us, "If you know the truth, the truth will make you free. Ignorance is a slave, knowledge is freedom. If we know the truth, we shall find the fruit of truth within us. If we join with it, it will bring us fulfillment...Whoever knows the truth is free." Yet in another section of the text, the writer penned the opposite, "There are forces that do favors for people. They do not want people to come to salvation." Spiritual seekers do not want to remain conflicted, but as long as we look outside ourselves, believing we're victims of powerful cosmic entities and forces beyond our control, we're blinded to the fact that everything we see on earth is the outworking of consciousness that we've chosen to limit and misdirect.

The text also repeats an interesting variation on Jesus' 'bushel basket' parable: "No one would hide something valuable and precious in a valuable container, but countless sums are commonly kept in a container worth only a cent. So it is with the soul. It is something precious, and it has come to be in a worthless body." Our quantum discoveries have shown us that consciousness is not 'in' the body, but the text also makes the point that the consciousness that projects the body is not the same nature as the body when it states, "Adam ate of the tree that produces animals, and he became an animal and brought forth animals." As we discussed earlier, we struggle with the conflict between our divine consciousness and the animal nature of the body we have co-opted. But *The Treatise on the Resurrection* explained that each of us was "...originally from above, a seed of the Truth, before this structure of the cosmos had come into being." And the *Tripartite*

Tractate describes our existence within the One Mind saying, "His offspring, the ones who are, are without number and limit and at the same time indivisible... existing eternally in the Father's Thought, and he was like a thought and place for them." These texts infer that a vague recollection of our choices and their resulting outcome remains deeply imbedded within the little self to be remembered when we're ready to wake up. This thought is also expressed in *The Gospel of Philip*:

> *If a pearl is thrown into mud, it will not lose its value, and if it is anointed with balsam, it will not increase its value. It is always precious in its owner's eyes. Likewise, the children of God are precious in the eyes of the Father, whatever their circumstances of life*

This statement is in direct opposition to many gnostic writings that claim only a tiny fraction of humanity is worthy of life. Nonetheless, this verse offers us an assurance via oneness gnosis that we are all playing a 'sanctioned' game, one that we can quit at any time with no penalties. Although this verse also explains exactly what the pearl symbolizes, many gnostic writings are not nearly so transparent. *The Gospel of Philip* hints at the reason why:

> *Truth, which has existed from the beginning, is sown everywhere, and many see it being sown, but few see it being reaped. Truth did not come into the world naked, but in symbols and images. The world cannot receive truth in any other way...The mysteries of truth are made known in symbols and images.*

Why is truth couched in symbol, myth and image? If our return to Oneness is all important, why doesn't the Divine send one perfectly crafted set of instructions for the entire world to follow? It's not to make things more difficult for us since there is nothing more the Divine desires than our return. As Rumi assures us, "…when the love for Source brims over in your heart, know that love for you is also brimming in His…You are — we all are — the beloved of the Beloved" And Hafiz concurred, saying, "Always assume you are on the best of terms with God, for, dear, each of us is like His only heir." However, for any experiment to be valid, it must adhere to strict guidelines. If the criteria for the experiment are ignored, the outcome is null and void. Since our experiment is based on our ability to use free will in whatever way we would like, Divine interference would essentially revoke our free will and invalidate the experiment.

Free will is not free will if God mandates how it must be used. This issue is obvious in the *Bible* book of *Genesis* and has become a sticking point for many former Christians. Free will is inferred in the creation story since God initially appeared to give Adam and Eve the freedom to either obey or disobey the 'rule' forbidding them to partake of the fruit of a certain tree. When they chose to disobey and eat the fruit, they're quickly and severely punished, as are their innocent progeny. From that time forward, it's clear that choices can be made, but many choices will exact an extremely steep price. The system of rewards and punishments set out in the Bible can hardly be compared with the 'victimless' free will the Divine has blessed us with.

In contrast to the pronouncements, demands and rules laid out in most 'holy books,' symbols and images are spread throughout the universe *if we choose to see them*, but they remain invisible to us if we don't. Source has complete confidence that we will return, and the patience to allow each of us to take as long as we need to either wake up or remain asleep until our experiment ends in disaster, which it surely will. Either way, the result will be our joyful return to Oneness. As Rumi explained, Divine justice has nothing to do with blessings or punishments, but is concerned with "...putting each thing in its real place." Since we all belong in oneness, justice will be served when we embrace the whole once again.

As you read the next verse quoted from *The Gospel of Philip*, you'll see the depth of the gift of free will we have received, "Love never says it owns something, though it owns everything. Love does not say, 'This is mine,' but rather, 'All that is mine is yours.'" Keep in mind that The One is often referred to as Love by gnostic writers, we're reminded that we were not created to be obedient robots or slaves, but as free beings whose greatest joy is to engage in a love exchange. Even if we choose not to see the signs and symbols that hide in plain sight all around us, Rumi explained, "There is a rope of light between your heart and Source that nothing can weaken or break, and it is always in His hands." Although that rope can never be broken, it's also so transparent we can forget that it's there. But this rope was not forced upon us; it would not tether us to the Divine if it were not also our own will that it did so.

(A few examples of the 'wisdom sayings' style from other eras and cultures include: Chuang Tzu's *Inner Chapters* (China, 4th century BCE), Hakim Sanai's *The Walled Garden of Truth* (Persia, 12th century), Shankara's *The Crest Jewel of Discrimination* (India, 8th century), Patanjali's *Yoga Aphorisms* (India, 120 BCE), Jianzhi Sengcan's *XinXin Ming* (Japan, 7th century) or the anonymous *Ashtavakra Gita* 500-400 BCE. Some of these texts will be discussed later in the book.)

III. Allegories

Like Jesus' parables and ancient mythologies, allegories (an extended story-like metaphor) are a means of conveying a complex idea in an understandable format that appeals to an audience that may not be familiar with the subject. Although some allegories use symbolism to veil hidden information, *Exegesis on the Soul* and *Authoritative Discourse* were both likely created as a means of promoting gnostic ideas to a wider audience. In both texts, the central character is a soul with a feminine nature. The story begins with her 'fall' from heaven to earth (spirit to body), the trials she endures, her ultimate awakening and return to her original place and finally, her triumphant reunion with her spiritual bridegroom. If you think this sounds strangely like the plot of a romance novel, you would be correct. Madeleine Scopello, who introduces *Exegesis on the Soul* in *The Nag Hammadi Scriptures*, points out that both Hellenistic and Jewish romance 'novels' were well known by the 3rd century. No doubt the two authors thought they could take advantage of this popular genre to spread their gnostic teachings. However, there is one unexpected and very surprising difference between the popular Jewish/Hellenistic novels and the gnostic texts written during the same period.

In a popular romance, the female character scrupulously preserved her purity/virginity at all costs regardless of the trials and tribulations she endured. In the gnostic allegories, the hero remained a 'pure' spirit being, but the once pure maiden is corrupted by taking on an 'impure' human form and becoming a whore! Like Sophia and Eve, it was the woman that fell from grace, however in these works; she also has the strength and courage to 'wake up' and realize she has traded everything for nothing. No matter how odd these texts sound, they would not have been written, circulated and protected unless there was an audience ready to read them and be influenced by them. Both texts promote separation gnosis, but, as we've learned to expect, they also carry remnants of exposure to oneness gnosis that are worth examining.

As we know, the foundation of our quantum reality is consciousness. Since nothing comes into being until consciousness and energy interact, free will (choice) is a necessary component of all quantum creativity. In these allegories, its choice that gets the main character into trouble, but it's also choice that gets her out again. The *Discourse* makes this clear when it points out, "Before anything was, the Father alone existed, before the worlds in the heavens appeared, or the world on earth…Nothing came to be without the Father's will." Note that the word 'will' carries the same meaning as thought or choice, so we would also be correct if we say that 'will' interacts with the quantum field and brings matter into being. Since Source imbued us with will, our will (aka our thoughts and choices) constantly interacts with energy and manifests in the world. But unlike recent popular depictions of the universe as a gigantic vending machine or genie waiting to serve up our every desire, there is a catch. *It's our most deeply rooted will, thoughts and emotions that interact with the quantum field, not our surface desires.*

Our subconscious, conditioned core 'will,' may be so deeply buried we're hardly aware of it. Unfortunately, this hidden will has far more power than our surface thoughts and choices. Why? This part of our consciousness most accurately reflects our conditioned self, who and what we actually see and feel ourselves to be despite the outer appearance we show to those around us. Of course this body and personality and the little self are not who or what we truly are, but as long as we feel certain it is who we are, this is the part of us that interacts with the quantum field. For example, if on the surface you act as if you are extremely capable and successful, but deep inside you feel like a failure, the quantum field will bring you situations where you appear to be capable but keep failing. Affirmations have become extremely popular, but if they are out of sync with our deep-seated fears and desires, they have no weight on a quantum level. (However, affirmations can, over time, aid in retraining the brain and emotions.) Also, we can't forget that the world is not just our personal construct; it's the result of the 'soup' of the countless choices that are being made by every consciousness that's projecting it. Because our will, thoughts and choices effect far more than our little portion of the world, free will should be considered among our greatest treasures, a gift to be used judiciously and guarded carefully.

Both texts clearly illustrate the point that choice can be used to remain in oneness or to project separation. In the beginning of *Exegesis*, we're told the virgin soul "fell down into a body" as if she had nothing to say about it. But when she wishes to return, she has another story. Here we see free will at work when she begs the Father to save her while promising to "...tell you how I left home and fled from my maiden's quarters." At that moment, when she took responsibility by owning up to the part her own free will played in the matter, she opened the way for change. In the *Discourse*, free will is prominently featured in this verse, "Death and life are placed before everyone, and people choose for themselves which of these two they want." Each choice we make that supports our continuing projections of separation keeps us in the illusory life/death cycle of this world. As we 'wake up' we see past this illusion and can make the choice to transcend it. The *Discourse* uses the symbolism of the fallen maiden to illustrate the choice for separation when it explains, "She has abandoned knowledge and has fallen into the life of an animal." Nonetheless, it also tells us that her true mind/consciousness was never actually a part of this illusion since it "remained in a treasure house," a "storehouse which is secure." Just as we've learned from quantum physics, our consciousness 'resides' safely in the non-local quantum world while a tiny, closed off portion of it makes the choices that projects the virtual reality where we continually repeat the birth/death cycle struggling to claim specialness.

In each of these allegories, the maiden experiences the worst possible abuses at the hands of her many lovers. Nonetheless, she continues to deceive herself because she is no longer in direct communication with her Source and her true Self and has forgotten her origins. Similar to other gnostic texts, these two texts describe her as "drunk, forgetful, dreaming and ignorant." Nonetheless, the *Discourse* tells us that the fallen maiden demonstrates her desire to wake up because of her "constant labor in seeking the inscrutable one." As we've seen in other texts, those who seek *will* find. Like a true heroine, the *Discourse* dramatically describes the part our misguided maiden plays in her own salvation:

> *Our soul is sick because she lives in a house of poverty, and matter strikes her eyes in order to blind her…The soul who has tasted these things has come to realize that sweet passions are fleeting…the soul disdains this life, because it lasts only for a time. She learns about the light, and she goes about and strips off this world. Her true garment clothes her within and her bridal gown reveals beauty of mind rather than pride of flesh.*

No matter how magnificent our life in this world appears to be, it's a life of poverty compared to Reality. As we've all witnessed, material comforts and indulgences have the power to blind us. Regardless, the maiden finally realizes that pleasure and pain are minted into a two sided coin; one side cannot be spent without experiencing the other as well. And no matter how much we would hope otherwise, every object and experience is inevitably fleeting. When the maiden finally faces this truth, she strips off the outer garment made up of the body, the personality and little, false self that have hidden the beauty of her true Self. In another part of the *Discourse*, the maiden smears medicine on her own eyes to cure her blindness and chooses "the food of life."

Exegesis explains the soul's awakening in a slightly different way when it says, "The beginning of salvation is repentance." Religion generally uses the word repentance in connection with sin, but for gnostics, the only 'sin' was ignorance. Where religious sin is concerned, many repent but then go on to repeat the sin, perhaps many times. Where our 'ignorance' of the Divine is concerned, the word takes on a completely different meaning. The Hebrew word for repentance is *shuh*, meaning 'to return,' a far more accurate way to understand what was meant. Awakening from ignorance implies a return to our original state. Of course that doesn't mean that the body instantly dies and we become pure consciousness in a flash, but it does mean that we no longer think with the tiny portion of consciousness we blocked off to project this world. Instead, that small portion of consciousness melts back into the whole, and we live from the Self, the One Mind of All That Is. We may continue to project the body for many more years until its natural death, but we have actually already stripped off this garment that disguises us and "given it back" as did the maiden in the story. As Jesus said, we continue *in* this world, but we are no longer *of* this world, using the body and personality, but no longer attached to them. The experiences of this lifetime become a quaint story that we can recall but no longer identify with.

Although *Exegesis* also makes it clear that while we must act as our own savior by choosing to 'wake up,' everything we are, have and enjoy comes to us through grace, "In this way, through rebirth, the soul will be saved. This is not because of practical lessons or technical skills or learned books. Rather it is the grace of the Spirit, it is the gift of the merciful God, for it is from above." Not only does grace allow us to play the game of separation, the 14th century Sufi sage and poet Hafiz proclaimed, "God wants nothing in return for your existence. What madness to ever think you owe Him/Her/It anything...Mercy and Grace are just there; they are attributes of light, they want nothing but to be... this is the time for you to compute the impossibility that there is anything but Grace." Many believe that grace equates to God forgiving us even though we are actually unworthy of that forgiveness. But from a quantum perspective, grace means that we always have been, and always will be, worthy because we are one with the Divine. Grace is a given, an attribute of the Love that Source is. Nonetheless, its preciousness should not be forgotten or taken for granted.

Regardless of its gnostic label, the *Authoritative Discourse* and the *Bible* share many similarities; both tell stories with a dualistic foundation that feature a cosmic struggle between good and evil in which humans become the hapless pawns. We've learned that the *Bible* book of *Job* set up a struggle between God and Satan that tested human loyalty. In the *Authoritative Discourse*, a vainglorious God sets up an even stranger "contest" and vies with Satan for winners. The *Discourse* tells us, "The Father wished to reveal his wealth and his glory, and so he established a great contest in this world. He wanted to make the contestants come up and leave behind what is of the created world." The text makes it clear that while God is luring humans with his heavenly wealth and glory, Satan seduces them with the world's physical pleasures. Since God and Satan are both bent on serving their own insatiable lust for adoration and power at the price of human suffering, the thinking person cannot help but loathe them both. However, these stories generally have a far more subtle, yet potent, effect on everyone that reads them.

Both scenarios offer an explanation of human suffering that shifts the blame away from our own free will choices and places it squarely on the power struggle between good and evil. While many swallow these stories whole and accept the impossibly incongruous idea that God can be love *and* hate, good *and* evil, when we see past duality we cannot. Hafiz reminded us that free will offers us both wisdom and foolishness when he said "You carry all the ingredients to turn your life into a nightmare—Don't mix them! You carry all the ingredients to turn your existence into joy, mix them, mix them!" Although quantum physics demonstrates the oneness of the universe, we are still given the choice of either believing our dream or recognizing it for what it is, blaming God or taking responsibility for our own choices. No matter how much we might want to have it both ways, that's one choice that is impossible.

IV. Schools of Thought

In the epilogue of *The Nag Hammadi Scriptures*, Editor Marvin Meyer notes that among the collection "there are substantial differences of perspective and theological and philosophical point[s] of view." We've examined several styles of presentation; now let's shift our attention to a few of the 'schools of thought' represented in the collection. Although the title of this section infers that these schools were institutionalized like the church, they were not literal schools. Rather, 'school of thought' is a concept used by scholars to conveniently identify and categorize texts that are similar. But once again, although basic ideas can be identified in the texts belonging to each school, the details vary widely.

1. Sethian School

With fourteen texts, the Sethian school claims the largest representation in the Nag Hammadi library. There was no historical group that referred to themselves as Sethian, but as Nag Hammadi scholar John D. Turner points out, "…this convenient term was used by certain of the fathers of the early Christian church who opposed this form of Gnostic thought.

As you may recall, the *Bible* book of *Genesis* tells us that after God drove the disobedient Adam and Eve from the Garden of Eden, Eve gave birth to two sons, Cain and Abel. In an attempt to worship God or offer atonement for their inherited sin, Cain, who was a farmer, made an offering to God of the best of his produce while his brother Abel, a shepherd, sacrificed an animal. As *Genesis* 4: 4-5 tells us, "And the Lord had regard for Abel and his offering, but for Cain and his offering he had no regard. So Cain was very angry, and his countenance fell." This scenario is important because it establishes God as the arbitrator of duality, an entity focused on judging and establishing who/what is special and who/what is not. These verses also imply that specialness is a scarce commodity, one that demands fierce competition to acquire. Since each brother offered the best of what they had, God's arbitrary judgment in favor of a blood sacrifice could not be expected to sit well with Cain. In the heat of jealousy, Cain killed Abel. God quickly retaliates by banishing Cain from his homeland and condemning him to wander endlessly as a fugitive. Eventually Adam and Eve have another son, Seth. According to *Genesis* 4: 25, Eve announces, "God has appointed for me another child instead of Abel for Cain slew him." In the *Genesis* account there is little more said about Seth except to place him within a genealogy and report his death at the age of 912. However, early Jewish gnostics saw things from a completely different perspective that caused them to focus on Seth.

Why did Seth become so important? Jewish gnostics based their views on the words in *Genesis* 5:3, "When Adam had lived a hundred and thirty years; he became the father of a son *in his own likeness, after his image*." [Italics ours] They reasoned that the Divine 'image' or 'spark' within Adam had bypassed both Cain and Abel, but was reborn in Seth. If you'll remember, in the dialogues and revelations section, we discussed the Sethian text, *The Secret Book of John*. In it, we discovered that some gnostics had divided humanity into three categories, but only one group, the 'pneumatics' or 'spiritual ones,' were automatically worthy of heaven. Why? Gnostics claimed the pneumatics were the biological progeny of Seth and therefore carried the Divine spark/seed of Seth within them. The 'Sethian' gnostics took this a step further and declared they alone were the legitimate heirs of Seth. Of course these 'pneumatics' still had to wake up, but like the Jews, the Sethians felt certain they were God's chosen people. However, in their case, they believed they had been chosen by 'The One,' not the *Bible* God, which they believed was a far higher calling. As you'll recall from the information we covered on *The Secret Book of John*, Sethians told a creation story that took place long before the story recorded in *Genesis*. For them, the creator God of the *Bible* was the "child of chaos," Yaldabaoth, and the Garden of Eden, made by Yaldabaoth's flawed angels, the Archons, was a trap rather than a paradise. In their view, the serpent was a savior that offered Adam and Eve freedom from Yaldabaoth's insanity. Eating from the tree symbolized waking up to the upside down condition of this world.

For Sethians, Jesus was the heavenly figure or incarnation of Seth. In Sethian texts, such as *The Second Discourse of the Great Seth,* when Jesus/ Christ speaks it is taken as the words of Seth. (Don't bother looking for *The First Discourse of the Great Seth,* it's mentioned in other texts, but it has not survived.) Since the Sethians believed the *Bible* was a joke, it should come as no surprise that this text resounds with Jesus' laughter as he ridicules one *Bible* character after another. In fact, Jesus also describes the crucifixion as a joke he played on a gullible crowd. The 'joke' began when the heavenly Seth/Jesus hijacked a human body, saying, "I approached a bodily dwelling and evicted the previous occupant, and I went in…I was in it, and I did not look like the previous occupant. He was a worldly person, but I am from above the heavens" However, "The whole multitude of Archons was upset, and all the material stuff of the rulers and the powers born of earth began to tremble at the sight of the figure with a composite image." Since Yaldabaoth and his cohorts could not overpower the Divine Seth, they plotted the death of the body he inhabited. Their plan was doomed at its inception; as easily as Seth co-opted a human body, he was able to exit, leaving the hijacked man to die in his stead. Jesus laughingly states, "The death they think I suffered they suffered in their error and blindness...someone else wore the crown of thorns...I did not die in actuality but only in appearance...And I was on high, poking fun at all the excesses of the rulers and the fruit of their error and conceit. I was laughing at their ignorance." As you've probably observed, this portrayal of Jesus is at irreconcilable odds with the humble, human wisdom teacher we met in Q and *The Gospel of Thomas*.

Scholar John D. Turner explains that Sethians "... divide themselves into two basic groups depending on the way one attains...enlightenment." Texts either describe the seeker ascending to Seth/Christ by attaining higher and higher levels of conscious awareness or by having Seth/Christ descend to the seeker and perform a baptismal rite called the "Five Seals." Although Sethian texts often contain fragments of oneness gnosis (as outlined in the discussion of *The Secret Book of John*) they inevitably fall into the same dualistic patterns so evident in the *Bible.* No doubt these gnostic writers were unable to deny their senses and fully accept the testimony of those who had experienced the oneness of the Divine. In his book, *Biocentrism*, noted research scientist Robert Lanza explains that we misunderstand the universe because we accept the testimony of our senses, which have wrongly convinced us the universe is an independent entity, something that exists 'out there' whether we interact with it or not.

Since the renaissance the universe has been thought of as a lifeless collection of gears and mechanisms that, once set in motion, continues ticking regardless of whatever goes on around it. Because we've been conditioned to believe that the material universe exists independently outside us, it's no stretch to also imagine that independent heavens and hells filled with spirit creatures also exist. Once we've gone that far, it's a simple matter to believe that other beings can influence our lives in both positive and negative ways. Although it may be difficult to let go of this scenario, it could not be further from the truth. We may take it for granted that our sight, hearing, touch, taste and smell give us an accurate picture of what's going on 'out there,' but sense perception actually takes place *within* consciousness. There are no images, sounds, textures, flavors or odors that exist outside of conscious observation. And what does consciousness observe? Everything in existence has a particle nature and a wave nature. As Lanza describes it, everything exists "...in a blurry state of possibility until its wave function collapses at the time of observation." Strange as it sounds, your home, your neighborhood, even the body you assume is you, exist as energy patterns until consciousness interacts with it. As philosopher George Berkeley (1685-1753) proclaimed, "The only things we perceive are our perceptions." Simply put, there is no material universe 'out there' that exists on its own independent of conscious observation.

2. Valentinian School

The Nag Hammadi library contains six books (listed in Appendix I) based on the teachings of Valentinus (100-160 CE). Although the terms gnostic and theologian are rarely used together, in Valentinus' case they can both be accurately applied. As we noted earlier, before the line was irrevocably drawn between orthodox and gnostic Christians, people who favored one view over the other often mingled and freely shared ideas. Valentinus, who was born in Egypt, was a Christian convert who claimed to have received the secret teachings of the apostle Paul through Paul's disciple Theudas. These esoteric secrets were said to have been given directly to Paul by the resurrected Jesus when he appeared to Paul in a vision. And like the other secret teachings we've discussed, they were reserved for the worthy few. Valentinus was such a popular teacher within the early Orthodox Church; he was very nearly elected Pope in 143 CE. When he lost by a few votes, it was said that he left the church in anger and began his own group in Rome. Since he had been so influential and drew many away from the church, he was excommunicated in retaliation.

Considering Valentinus' background, it should come as no surprise that his writings combined orthodox and gnostic teachings, but they were also mixed with Platonic philosophy that he may have picked up in Egypt. In fact, Valentinus may have been one of the first to combine these thought systems and propose the notion of a divine trinity of three persons in one. For gnostics, the trinity was comprised of God the Father, Sophia the Mother, and Logos the Son. In contrast, the so-called 'Holy Trinity' of the Orthodox Church consisted of God the Father, God the Son and God the Holy Ghost. Unlike the gnostic trinity, the Orthodox trinity evolved out of an extremely bitter controversy over the identity of Jesus and was not fully accepted until the 4th century. In an attempt to end the rivalries that were tearing the church apart, the Roman Emperor Theodosius (347-395) made Christianity the state religion and used his power to declare that "all true Christians" must profess belief in the trinity doctrine. A quick look at what happened clearly reveals a wide divergence in early Christian thought.

Some said Jesus was a human who had been adopted by God; this meant that everyone had an equal opportunity to become the son or daughter of God just as Jesus had. Another faction, one more closely aligned with pagan converts, said that God had fathered a divine son, Jesus, who was part-god, part-human. This made perfect sense to pagans who were used to a pantheon of half-human, half-immortal demigods. Others felt certain humans were beyond redemption and could not be saved without the intervention of Jesus, who was separate from God, but equal to God. Yet others argued that God the Father and God the Son were the same being, which meant that God had sacrificed himself on behalf of humanity. And to further muddy the waters, other factions felt certain something they called the Holy Spirit was also a God.

As each group staunchly supported their own view, fighting within the church reached epic proportions. Street riots, lies, threats, dirty tricks, intimidation, kidnappings, beatings and excommunications became common place and several assassinations occurred. Christians were now faced with the virtually unsolvable problem of being monotheists who had to somehow explain the reason they now had more than one god. The new trinity doctrine appeared to be a way to tie up all these loose ends, but it radically changed Christian beliefs. Now, each 'part' of the trinity was considered equally God, all were eternal and all were the same substance, yet all were different. Many church members found this new triune Godhead impossible to understand, but they were told the trinity was "a mystery beyond their comprehension, analysis or conceptualization" that they must accept without question. The Jewish God, the God of the early Christians and this new triune god could no longer be considered the same God, and "The One," who had been revealed through gnosis by Jesus and other early gnostics, was, for all intents and purposes, forgotten.

Although Valentinus' teachings inspired many variations, the 'Valentinian system' was the most wide spread and prominent of the gnostic schools. A high percentage of Valentinian literature was destroyed by the church, but it is thought that Valentinus himself may have been the original author of the salvaged *The Gospel of Truth*. In this text, "The One" is referred to as either the "Depth" or the "Father." Regardless of the fact that Valentinus' ideas may have, in part, inspired the concept of the Christian trinity, *The Gospel of Truth* also appears to shy away from duality and lean toward the idea that everything in existence is contained within the whole. The text tells us the Father created a son because he wanted to be known, and together, Father and son emanated more spiritual beings. Although these beings had individual personalities, they remained one with the All. Oneness fell into duality when Sophia, who failed to understand how oneness worked, was introduced. She split in two and while one part of her remained with the Father, the other confused half began projecting matter. Until Sophia enters the picture, this description matches the quantum paradigm and oneness gnosis, but from that point on, *The Gospel of Truth* more closely resembles Sethian thought than oneness gnosis. Again, a demiurge (a creative sub-deity), this time known as "error" does the actual construction work of the visible world and, unwittingly believes he is God. Humans are separated into three categories:

» The Spiritual ones: This group is made up of Valentinus' followers who are considered innately worthy of returning to the All.

» The Psychical ones: Christians who can receive a form of salvation, but are not considered worthy to return to the All.

» The Material ones: Those who are doomed no matter what they do.

Valentinus' Jesus comes from the spirit world to offer salvation. This takes place via a baptism ritual that was said to heal the split between the higher spiritual self and lower material self, between duality and unity.

3. Hermeticism

As you read earlier, John Moffitt's book *Occultism in Avant-Garde Art* outlined a progressive interest in a trendy, trashy, kitsch variety of occultism that began with the founding of Theosophy in 1875. Moffitt's research led him to conclude that this trend culminated in a pseudo-religious/self-help/mysticism now commonly known as "new age" spirituality. Moffitt described this phenomenon as, "…another twist on the venerable theme of ancient wisdom." This is also true of the ancient wisdom, Hermeticism. Although current revivals of Hermeticism focus on its magical/occult aspects, scholars agree that in its original form, Hermeticism was a spiritual path. In fact, some scholars classify Hermeticism as a gnostic religion, and believe that it was one of two great branches of Gnosticism, with Christian Gnosticism being the second.

Early practitioners claimed that Hermeticism was rooted in *prisca theologia*, a doctrine that asserts there is a single spiritual truth that was given directly to humanity by God in antiquity. This may bring to mind the perennial philosophy, and while these concepts have similarities, they also have two extremely important differences. While both models propose the existence of unchangeable, universal truth, those who accept *prisca theologia* say that truth was given by God once for all time. On the other hand, the perennial philosophy has demonstrated that truth is revealed in gnosis, an experience that's been open to willing seekers throughout time. Both principles do agree that threads of truth exist within all religions. But as you've learned, the perennial philosophy clarifies that many religions were created by followers who could not understand a sage's gnosis. *They preferred to worship the sage's words rather than emulate his experience.* Although these followers may have preserved some seeds of truth, they could not help but contaminate the foundation of truth with their own dualistic perceptions. As a result, the perennial philosophy tells us the *only* way to know truth is to experience the Divine yourself. Since *prisca theologia* was thought to have existed in its pure form only when it was first given, hermetic practitioners claim seekers must reject all but the earliest teachings in order to avoid the corrupting influence of human interference. For this reason, gnostic Hermeticism returned to its earliest Egyptian roots for inspiration.

There are three Hermetic texts included in the Nag Hammadi library, *The Discourse on the Eighth and Ninth, The Prayer of Thanksgiving* and *Excerpt from the Perfect Discourse*. It's impossible to get a comprehensive picture of this thought system from these three slim texts, and like all other writings that are categorized as belonging to a certain school of thought, variations and contradictions exist both between and within the texts. Originally there may have been forty-two foundation books that made up the *Hermetic Corpus*, but most were believed to have been lost when the ancient Library of Alexandria was destroyed. The author credited with writing these books was called Hermes Trismegistus or "thrice great Hermes," a mystic and prophet who was said to have lived around 1200 BCE. Later scholarship has placed the origins of the writings within the 1st to 3rd centuries CE, the heyday of gnostic texts, and attributed them to a group or a series of contributors rather than a single person.

Trismegistus was said to be the successor of the Egyptian god Thoth and the Greek god Hermes. The ancient Egyptians believed Thoth, depicted as a man with the head of an ibis or baboon, was responsible for all science, religion, philosophy and magic. Hermes, a god of transitions, was said to be equally at home in both the divine and mortal realms. He was also known as a 'trickster' who used his talents to benefit humans while outwitting other gods. From the 2nd century BCE through the 3rd century CE, Hermeticism was a wide-spread and influential mystery school type system that combined astrology, alchemy and theurgy (magic) with rituals, prayers, secrets and ceremonies. The goal? Transcend the desires of the body that keep humanity locked in the material realm and return to The Father of All:

This is the good, the aim of those who have gnosis: to become God. The closing of my eyes became the true vision...I became God-inspired, God-Minded, and came with the Truth...Let me not be removed from Gnosis...with your grace, let me bring Light — Hermes Trismegistus

This verse clearly echoes the aim of the perennial philosophy and oneness gnosis. Let's take a closer look at several other similarities:

» The end is found in the beginning. The quest will inevitably take us back to where we started.

» Salvation comes through 'knowing' the true Self. While intellectual pursuits may be helpful, *all seeking must finally come down to direct experience. No one else can do this for us.*

» The material world is not our home. Since we cannot exist fully in the material and spiritual realms simultaneously, we must choose between them. We cannot be 'whole' until we return to our true nature.

» The Divine is referred to as The All, The One, The One Who Is and The Father of All. Source is understood to *be* everything that exists. The hermetic text, *Asclepius*, not part of the Nag Hammadi library, states, "...the nature of God is will. And his will is the good. He is in every place and he looks out over every place."

» Although everything exists within the Divine, Source is not directly involved in the doings of the material world.

» Humanity is Divine, but has allowed itself to

become trapped by the material world and distracted from its true nature.

»   Until we stop projecting the material world, we'll be caught up in a continuing cycle of birth and death.

»   Ignorance of truth is the only 'sin' that exists, and that is more appropriately understood as a mistake that can be corrected.

Nevertheless, there are also several differences. Like separation gnosis, Hermeticism operated within a mystery school type system where carefully guarded secrets were passed from one 'worthy' seeker to another. To return to Source, initiates had to pass through many levels or steps. Their return was believed to be extremely difficult because these levels were supposedly filled with spiritual obstacles and were inhabited by demonic creatures.

There are also several differences that make Hermeticism unique among gnostic groups:

»   Christian gnostics believed the material world was a mistake from the beginning, the creation of the demented offspring of Sophia. Christian gnostics generally loathed the world, had a pessimistic attitude toward humanity and attempted to control the 'disgusting body' through asceticism. Opposite in its views, Hermeticism generally claimed the material world was the creation of The One and initiates enjoyed its magnificent beauty. They were optimistic about humanity and did not disdain the body, but they did feel that its endless desires played a major role in distracting humanity from truth. However, there was some crossover as *Poimandres*, a hermetic text found in *The Other Bible*, described the body as "a loathsome prison."

Instead of assuming the material realm is reality, oneness gnosis tells us that it's an illusion projected from a portion of consciousness. Since everything, including our illusions, are contained within the Divine, it's still all worthy of our love. Nonetheless, the world of separation we project is a poor substitute for our true Reality in oneness.

» Christian gnostics felt that Source was unattainable and unknowable. Like oneness gnosis, Hermetic teachings proclaim The One is not only knowable, but wants to be known.

» Many Christian gnostics separated humanity into three classifications: Those who were worthy of salvation because they carried the 'divine spark' within them, those who did not have the spark but could possibly be saved, and those who had no chance of salvation. Like oneness gnosis, Hermeticism held out salvation to all, however, practitioners were very careful not to pass on secret information to those who were not fully dedicated to the goal.

While oneness gnosis tells us the Divine "loves all and chooses all," free will dictates that we each have the choice of either accepting or rejecting that love.

» Hermetic teachings describe Source as androgynous, but 'hermaphrodite' may be a more accurate description. The Hermetic texts are unique in claiming that God has both male and female genitals enabling sexual reproduction without a partner. This explanation differs greatly from other gnostic descriptions of a male father figure from whom all life mysteriously flows.

Oneness gnosis bypasses sexual and gender labels when it reveals that all creation takes place when consciousness interacts with energy. The One, being Love, contains all attributes of love, regardless of whether humans label those attributes feminine or masculine. Yes, Source is unique in that all creative thought began with The One, and yet, consciousness, and thereby creativity, is a gift graciously shared with every conscious being in existence.

» Hermetics believed the spiritual realm consisted of many levels that were populated by an assortment of both evil and good immortal spirit creatures. Although humans inhabited the material realm, Hermetics exalted them above all other beings. Why? Humans were thought to be simultaneously mortal (the body) and immortal (the spirit), which meant they were spirits who could procreate sexually. Because Hermetics believed God also reproduced sexually, this meant humans were most like God. Of course this belief brings us right back to duality, separation and specialness.

On the other hand, oneness gnosis (and quantum physics) tells us that physical mortality is an illusion that veils immortal consciousness. In Oneness, all are unique yet equal within the Divine Mind, rather like the different, yet harmonious instruments, notes and rhythms that each play a necessary role in a great symphony.

» Both Hermetic and separation gnosis claim that the soul is judged and either rewarded or punished based on the actions of the body in relationship to man-made laws.

Oneness gnosis describes no laws outside the parameters necessary to sustain life and no rewards or punishments and laughs at the idea that humans can create laws, rules and moral codes, attributing them to Source. We are free to explore all that our creativity allows, including the rejection of our Source. We are also welcomed back to the awareness of our innate oneness whenever we tire of our illusory games.

Unlike other forms of gnosis, Hermeticism included the practice of alchemy, theurgy and astrology which we mentioned earlier. We'll discuss alchemy at length in the following section. For now, suffice it to say that although most of us have been schooled to think of alchemy as a failed attempt at turning lead into gold, far more was involved. Alchemists did work at transmuting a variety of substances, and their experiments served as the foundation of modern chemistry. Nonetheless, at its core, alchemy was a spiritual path.

Theurgy was a type of 'spiritual magic' aimed at conjuring the presence of the gods and invoking them to act on behalf of the practitioner. The goal of these alliances was the ultimate achievement of *henosis*, a reunion with The One. Since it was believed that the brain was unable to interact with the Divine Mind, magic rituals were used to aid practitioners in passing through ten levels that supposedly separated the material and heavenly realms.

Oneness gnosis also recognizes the inability of the brain to interact on its own with the One Mind, but when we bypass intellect and approach Source in consciousness, we find there are no levels to ascend or any magical transformations needed. Regardless, getting the brain out of the way is rather like removing a gigantic rock slide from a highway that's been obstructing the flow of traffic. The 'rocks' are the perceptions, attachments and aversions the little self, and its sidekick the brain, have spent lifetimes piling up to keep us locked in duality.

The short Hermetic text, *Excerpt from the Perfect Discourse* discusses the perils encountered by initiates on the first two of the ten levels. The gods that were said to inhabit both of these levels were not the inert matter they first appeared to be, but were thought of as living beings that had become disconnected from the One Mind. The first level was made up of earthly gods that inhabited statues and temples. Intellectual knowledge and piety were required to get past this level. Astrology became important in Hermeticism because the second level was inhabited by star gods that comprised the boundary between the visible and invisible realms. Like the gods that inhabited statues and temples, these gods were also eternal beings who had become inescapably bound to the stars, doomed to eternally accompany them on their journey through the sky. In fact, the *Discourse* tells us "There is a great demon that the supreme God has appointed as overseer or judge of human souls. God has placed him in the middle of the air between earth and heaven. When a soul comes from a body, it must meet this demon." To pass through this level successfully, an initiate had to be well versed in the patterns and movements of the stars and know what these patterns meant, thus the study of astrology.

Excerpt from the Perfect Discourse also contains an apocalyptic message that closely resembles the *Bible* book *Revelation*. The text foretells a day when Egypt, described as a country more godly than any other, would become impious. When that happened, the gods dwelling there would flee to heaven and the earth would be overrun with evil. When the Father saw what had happened to his glorious creation, he would destroy all evil with fire, flood, plagues and wars so that divine good could be restored. Again we see another variation on the theme of a cosmic struggle between good and evil that culminates in a God-ruled earthly kingdom similar to the one hoped for by apocalyptic Jews and Christians.

Another short text, *The Discourse on the Eighth and Ninth* begins by emphasizing the spiritual focus of Hermeticism when it states, "Trismegistus was concerned about opening a path of spiritual illumination." It explains how humanity became separated from its Source and why 'waking up' was of utmost importance to the hermetic practitioner. In this text, human beings came into existence when the Divine Mind impregnated itself and gave birth to an androgynous human in the spirit realm. This being was reflected in the watery nature of the inferior material world and became both mortal in body and immortal in spirit. On earth, the androgynous body was split into the two sexes, which brought about the beginning of time. As you've seen in all forms of gnostic teachings, 'waking up' is of utmost importance, but for the Hermetic, it meant waking up to the realization of their dual mortal/immortal nature. Ironically, though this dual nature supposedly made them superior to all other beings, their goal of immortality meant the eternal death of their mortal nature and their return to a 'lesser' position.

Like oneness gnosis, Hermeticism taught that intellectual learning was helpful to a point, but the initiate was eventually expected to leave behind the information they had collected and experience the Divine Mind directly. However, *The Discourse on the Eighth and Ninth* tells us this experience was extremely difficult to attain. The text, written as a dialogue between a father (symbolizing Trismegistus) and son (the initiate), explains that an ardent initiate could work through the first nine levels while still in the flesh. If the initiate was successful, they would be rewarded by entering the tenth level after death. But all was not lost if the work was not completed before death since the levels could also be finished in spirit. In *The Discourse on the Eighth and Ninth*, the son had successfully reached the seventh level and sought advice on approaching the eighth, a level where he could expect to be "born again" in the Divine Mind. In this case, the Divine Mind was not The One, but a self-begotten god. Hermetic teachings claimed yet another level existed where The One, who ruled over a plethora of self-begotten gods, existed as the only un-begotten god.

The father advised the son that at the eighth level, he would experience a "rite of regeneration." If the initiate was found to be 'at one' with the Divine Mind, he would be given a kiss symbolizing Divine love which would bring about a series of visions. The initiate was not told in advance what to expect during the visions, but if he recognized his own immortal Self he was then allowed to recover his true nature. At that point, he would also become aware of a tenth level that could only be attained through death. It was believed that the only way the human body could survive these visions was through rigorous spiritual preparation which included prayer, gratitude, ritual, worship and grace.

The Power of Thanksgiving, an epilogue to *The Discourse on the Eighth and Ninth* returns to oneness gnosis when it focuses on the importance of transcendent truth gained through direct experience of the One Mind. This text champions "...the firm conviction that God exists and wishes to be known" and agrees that transcendence results in the awareness of our own divinity.

The Nag Hammadi cache did not include the writings of every early gnostic group, but *The Other Bible* does contain a few fragments written by or about the next two groups. Since the church was so thorough in its destruction of gnostic texts, many groups are known mainly through the scathing denunciations directed at them by church fathers. Of course few of us would believe that an accurate description would be given by a sworn enemy, so these texts must be read with that thought in mind. Although Marcionism, Mandaeism and Manichaeism are barely remembered today, each played a potent part on the gnostic stage.

4. Marcionism

Scholars don't consider the school of thought based on the teachings of Marcion of Sinope (85–160) purely gnostic, but his teachings are an excellent example of early orthodox/ gnostic fusion.

Marcion, a wealthy ship builder, was the son of an orthodox bishop, a position he attained as well. Regardless of his high level of authority within the early church, Marcion was troubled by the fact that he was unable to account for the radical differences between the petty, vengeful and tyrannical God of the *Old Testament* and the more loving and merciful God preached by Jesus. Fearing a schism when the influential Marcion rejected the *Old Testament*, the church fathers excommunicated him, even returning a substantial donation Marcion had made. This was not among the church's wisest moves because the disgruntled ex-bishop immediately used these funds to found a rival institutionalized religion based on his own views. Not only did his group successfully oppose the Orthodox Church during the 1st century, it continued in the west for 300 years, and his ideas continue to influence theology into the present day.

As you've no doubt already noted, Marcion's rejection of the Jewish God shared similarities with many gnostic teachings. Although he did not embrace the complex creation mythologies proposed by many of the Nag Hammadi writers, he did refer to the *Old Testament* God as the demiurge and claimed he was a flawed lesser god who created a defective world that served as a trap for humanity. For that reason, Marcion considered the material world to be evil, rejected it completely, and preached transcendence to a purely spiritual realm of goodness.

Marcion believed Christ had been sent to earth at the behest of a higher God he called "The Stranger God" or "The Alien God." This God, unlike "The One" of oneness gnosis, was a separate entity that did not contain the All. According to Marcion, the Stranger God had held himself aloof from the material world until he sent Christ to intervene in man's affairs. Like many authors of separation gnosis, Marcion believed that although Christ appeared to have a human body, he was completely spirit and therefore had never actually suffered or died on the cross. Since Jesus could not have sacrificed a body to atone for human sin, Marcion reasoned that salvation involved waking up from ignorance rather than putting faith in a sacrifice.

Based on the similarities Marcionism shares with the Orthodox Church, some scholars view Marcion's rebellion as a very early attempt at church reformation rather than a desire to found a new religion. The structure of Marcion's group did closely resemble church hierarchy and rejected the mystery school format favored by most sects that embraced separation gnosis. There were no 'secrets' or 'revelations' to be passed on to a worthy few; 'waking up' came via knowledge gained through diligent study of approved scriptures. All who were willing to learn and adhere to the organization's teachings were considered worthy since The Stranger God's compassion was said to be universal.

Although they probably aren't aware of it, Christians today continue to feel the effects of Marcion's ejection from the church. He is credited with being the first Christian leader to organize a canon of officially sanctioned texts. Made up of eleven texts, Marcion's canon leaned heavily on the writings of the apostle Paul; the only apostle Marcion believed fully grasped Christ's teachings. Marcion's canon caused the church to finally weed through the countless texts it had collected and create a canon of its own that eventually became the *New Testament*. This weeding work also became the Orthodox Church's impetus for identifying some works as heretical and attacking those who clung to them.

The *New Testament* may not have included the writings of Paul if Marcion had not been among the first to value and collect them. Marcion's argument that the God's of the *New* and *Old Testament* could not be the same God still rings true to many *Bible* critics. Thomas Jefferson was so disturbed by the inconsistencies of Jesus' teachings recorded in the *New Testament*; he created his own *Bible* by eliminating any *New Testament* verses that smacked of the vengeful *Old Testament* god. Today, some Christians still follow Marcion's example, rejecting the *Old Testament* and referring to themselves as "*New Testament* Christians."

5. Mandaeism

Mandaeism, which originated around the time of Christianity, is the only sect still in operation that identifies itself as gnostic. In fact, the name of the group is derived from the Aramaic *manda*, which, like gnosis, means knowledge or knowledge of life. However in this case, 'knowing' was obtained through the passing of secret information rather than a direct experience of the Divine. There could possibly be around 60,000 Mandaeans currently living throughout the world, but it is difficult to be precise since this group values separation and secrecy. Like many gnostic groups, the Mandaean community was founded on a mystery school type structure with a strict division between the priesthood and laity. The group claimed to possess the secret laws of God which were guarded by the priests. Once again symbolic language, metaphor and rituals of initiation were used to hide sacred mysteries. Except for a few fragments, none of the group's ancient texts are available for public consumption. If the group has managed to preserve its ancient writings, or added to these works as time went by, they have been hidden by the priesthood.

Mandaean communities were situated by rivers where their most important sacrament, baptism, could be carried out. Like Mormons, they practiced proxy baptisms. And like many other gnostics, their goal was transcending the world of matter. To that end, their sacraments were said to purify the soul and ensure rebirth as spirit. However, unlike some groups who felt certain the world was an evil trap, Mandaeans viewed it as a pleasant prison where family life was encouraged and asceticism discouraged.

This school of thought claimed to be the direct descendants of Noah, which led to their veneration of Noah's family tree, including Adam, Abel, Seth, Enosh, Shem, and Aram. They considered John the Baptist to be the authentic messiah and Jesus a false messiah who had perverted John's true teachings. Mandaeans also claimed Abraham and Moses were false prophets and liars, and they believed the *Bible*'s Holy Spirit was an evil being. Mandaeans had a decidedly dualistic view of the universe, where light and dark continually struggled for supremacy. They called the originator of light "The Great First Life from the Worlds of Light, The Sublime One that stands above all works" or "The Great Life" for short. This was a being similar to "The One," who *is* all and contains all. The evil opposite and ruler of darkness was called Ptahil, a conglomerate of three beings that played a role like that of the Demiurge found in other gnostic texts. The material world was supposedly created by the "Archetypal Man," but it's impossible to know how this took place since the Mandaeans embraced several creation stories, many of them reflecting the influence of outside religions.

6. Manichaeism

Although most people have no idea it even existed, Manichaeism was a major religion that rivaled Buddhism, Christianity and Islam. It spread from the Roman Empire to China, thrived between the 3rd and 7th centuries, and remained dominant in parts of Asia until the Mongolians devastated the group in the 13th century. It's highly organized churches and charismatic leader were so popular, other prominent religions saw them as a threat and persecuted its adherents in several countries. Opposers eventually claimed its Mesopotamian founder, Mani, (216-276) was insane and he was finally martyred by the King of Persia at the urging of his Zoroastrian priests.

Mani's parents brought him up in a small sect known as Elcesaites, but visions he experienced at twelve and twenty-four turned him away from their beliefs. Mani claimed that a spirit he described as his divine twin or true self appeared to him with the knowledge he used to found his religion. As you probably remember from our discussion of *The Gospel of Thomas,* the words twin and Thomas were both derived from the Aramaic word *tauma,* and were used by several gnostic writers to signify the attaining of spiritual awareness. Although none of Mani's original writings have survived intact, the translations and fragments that remain offer a general understanding of his belief system.

Mani was unusual in that he openly claimed to be the reincarnation of Buddha, Krishna, Zoroaster and Jesus. He said that he had been sent to complete and purify their earlier teachings which had been corrupted, misinterpreted or were incomplete. And unlike the limited scope and success of these earlier sages, Mani felt certain his work was meant to be final and universal as he himself served as the messiah who would triumphantly lead humanity to the Light. A highly successful missionary, Mani was also said to be a gifted physician and miracle worker. In China he was called "Buddha of Light" and in Iran "life giver" or "raiser of the dead," but many of his followers simply referred to him as God.

Like Mandaeism (and most other religions for that matter), Manichaeism was based on a dualistic struggle between a spiritual world of light and an evil, material world of darkness. His simplistic view was so black and white, the term 'Manichean' is still applied to simplistic 'moral dualism' that understands the universe only in terms of right/wrong, good/evil, light/dark, spiritual/material etc. Mani named his belief system "The Religion of Light," and his highest deity "The Father of Greatness," but he was unique in that he denied the omnipotence of this God.

Since Mani's dualistic belief system required two opposite forces, the nemesis of Light, a Satan like King of Darkness, wielded equal power. Instead of battling directly with dark forces, the Father of Greatness used a proxy known as "The Original Man" or "Primal Man" to carry out his will. In this system the entire material universe, including the human body, was a battleground influenced by both Light and Dark. Neither the earth nor the flesh was considered intrinsically evil, but particles of Light were understood to be trapped within the dark material realm. Of course the goal was the liberation of Light and its return to the realms of Light.

Once again we return to the gnostic concept of the earth as the flawed construction of an inferior, defective being. Mani claimed that his Father of Greatness had nothing to do with this world, but he reasoned this was because Light and Dark existed in their own separate realms. The cosmic struggle began when the King of Darkness became dissatisfied with his lot, and attacked the realm of Light. The Father of Greatness sent the Original Man to fight on his behalf, but during a series of battles the powers of darkness prevailed. Evil swallowed as much light as possible, including the Original Man. Overflowing with Light, evil beings eventually gave birth to Adam and Eve. At that point the Father of Greatness became involved and sent Jesus in the form of a serpent to wake them up to their divine origin. But instead of waking up Adam and Eve reproduced, trapping the light within their progeny. But Mani did not believe Jesus' visit to earth in the guise of a snake ended his work; rather, he had three identities and purposes:

» Jesus the luminous, who appeared to Adam and Eve as the serpent in the Garden of Eden.

» Jesus the Messiah, whose suffering and death was considered a metaphor for the deliverance of light from the material body of darkness, not as atonement for human sin. Because Mani did not think Jesus actually existed as flesh, he agreed with several other gnostic writers that claimed Jesus could not have been crucified.

» The suffering Jesus, a metaphor for the constant universal suffering of Light-Particles imprisoned in the material universe.

But as we learned earlier, Mani understood himself to be the one who would actually fulfill the identity and complete the purpose of all 'saviors' who had gone before him, including Jesus.

The highly organized Manichean church/ community was secretive yet missionary in nature. Like the organized religions it opposed, it was made up of both clergy (the 'elect' or 'perfect') and laity (the 'hearers'). Among the elect were bishops, elders and 'plain' elect. The elect alone were considered worthy of achieving salvation without going through several rebirths, but they were required to complete several stringent fasts each year as well as abstain from meat, wine, lying, manual labor and sex. Their primary duty consisted of copying and teaching scripture. Women were included in the elect, but could not hold office. The primary duties of the 'hearers' included serving the elect and obeying them without question. Members were taught that procreation only served to bring another soul into bondage, so while sex was permitted; reproduction was thought to help the work of Darkness.

Augustine of Hippo (354-430) was Manichean until the Roman Emperor Theodosius issued a death decree for Manichaeans in 382. After Augustine converted, he became an outspoken enemy of Manichaeism, nonetheless, Mani's ideas continued to influence much of Augustine's Christian philosophy.

V. Later Gnostic Groups

Since the decline of Mandaeism and the destruction of Manichaeism and Marcionism several groups claiming to be gnostic have surfaced that have echoed their belief systems, at least in part. During the 7th century the Paulicians, an ascetic sect founded in Armenia, championed a dualistic system made up of a good spirit realm and a bad material realm. Souls that came from the good were trapped within the bad. In this case, Jesus was an angel sent to preach to these trapped souls, and salvation depended on whether or not one accepted his words. Instead of venerating the cross, the Paulicians revered Jesus' sayings. Paulicians rejected the *Old Testament*, the church and its sacraments, but accepted some *New Testament* texts. Their name means "followers of Little Paul," but it's not known who little Paul actually was.

1. Bogomils

Founded in the 10th century Bulgaria by the priest Bogomil (meaning dear to God), the Bogomils were reformers who pushed for a return to early Christianity. Evidently they were unaware that the diversity of opinion held during the 1st century would make it impossible to discern what early Christianity actually was. However, like many gnostic groups, the Bogomils were dualists who believed the world was created by a flawed Demiurge. They denied the divine birth of Christ and his coexistence within a trinity. Because they openly condemned the church, they became a target for both conversion and persecution. Like many other groups that believed the world was evil, the Bogomils were ascetics who avoided the contamination of the flesh and its desires. They met in private homes and rejected a division between clergy and laity. Unlike most gnostic groups that claimed only a worthy few could attain salvation, the Bogomils taught that instead of following Christ, everyone could become a Christ.

2. Cathars

Since the Cathars have captured the modern imagination in stories connecting them with the legendary Holy Grail, you may already be aware of this 11th to 14th century French group. Whether they thought of themselves as a revival of Gnosticism or a reformation of the Orthodox Church it's impossible to say, but they did attempt to return to beliefs and practices that predated the institutionalization of Christianity. Although the origin of Catharism is not certain, their resemblance to several of the previous dualistic groups we've just discussed argues against their suddenly appearing out of nothingness. In other words, their beliefs testify to an amalgamation of previous beliefs rather than a religion that grew around a sage's direct experience of the Divine.

Like Mandaeism and Manichaeism, the Cathar universe was based on a dualistic struggle between a spiritual world of eternal light and an evil, material world of darkness that existed in time and space. But unlike Manichaeism that denied the omnipotence of the Divine, the Cathars championed an unequal system that gave "The Good God" superior power. In this system, the God of the *New Testament* was the creator of a perfect spiritual realm inhabited by genderless angels. Like many who have questioned the paradox of a loving God and a suffering universe, the Cathars came to the conclusion that "The Good God" could not have created an evil world. Instead, they explained that the *Bible*'s Satan, in a fit of jealous rage, created an illusory material universe that he used to lure and trap angels within physical form. As one might suppose, the Cathars viewed all matter as innately evil and incapable of redemption; therefore, escape back to the spirit realm was the only salvation possible. Trapped spirits were doomed to reincarnate in animal or human form until they had been 'purified' from the material to the point where it was possible to pass through the veil that separated the two realms.

The Cathars were made up of two groups, the "Croyants" or "Believers," and the "Parfaits," an elect group of "Pure Ones." (Men were called Parfaits and women Parfaites.) Unlike a haughty clergy class that was raised high above the laity, the Parfaits lived a lowly life of extreme asceticism. Before taking a deeper look into their practices, let's address the fact that Cathar men and women were considered relatively equal. Since the Cathars believed a spirit would be continually reincarnated as both genders until it was purified, gender distinction became irrelevant until the last reincarnation before spiritual rebirth, which they believed must be male. Women could inherit property, nearly unheard of at the time, and Parfaites were allowed to administer the group's sacrament, the Consolamentum, and act as spiritual leaders. There is no way to know whether or not the Cathars had access to the gnostic *The*

Gospel of Mary that we discussed earlier, but they did hold Mary Magdalene in far higher regard than the apostle Peter, who was openly maligned in that gospel account.

The Croyants/Believers made up the majority of the group who, although living a restricted life, had not disavowed the world to the same extent as the Parfaits/Pure Ones. Unlike the church that wielded a heavy hand, the many rules that governed the Cathars were not intended as discipline, but as practices that would separate them from the evil world. The entire group was vegetarian, avoiding any thing that had come into existence through copulation since it might contain a reincarnated soul. They also rejected procreative sex that might result in trapping another soul in a body. Their acceptance of contraception put them in direct opposition to the church which encouraged its members to "...be fruitful and become many." Since the Cathars did not believe anything of this world could sanctify on a spiritual level, they also rejected the Eucharist and water baptism. On the other hand, the Cathars did respect biblical commands that were in keeping with their views, such as refusing to kill, lie, swear oaths, fight in wars, practice capital punishment or live in wealth and comfort.

Like gnostics who rejected the concept of an ultimate judgment that led either to eternal punishment in hell or eternal bliss in heaven, the Cathars' goal was escape from the mortal body and return to their true eternal Self. For them, this escape meant 'knowing' who and what they truly were. However, their version of 'knowing' was obtained through the intellect, not experiencing the Divine. Rather than seeing Jesus as a savior that atoned for sin or even as a mediator between God and man, they recognized him as an angelic messenger sent by The Good God to share the knowledge they needed to save themselves. Since the angelic Jesus could not actually die, his crucifixion was understood as a brief but transitory satanic victory in the cosmic struggle between good and evil. The most important step a Cathar adult could take on the road to salvation was undergoing the sacrament of the Consolamentum, which signified the transition from Believer to Pure One.

As we've said, the Cathars rejected water baptism, but the Consolamentum was considered a baptism in spirit, fusing the soul trapped in the body with its spiritual counterpart that remained in heaven. The name of the sacrament was based on the idea that Holy Spirit 'consoled' the initiate with the information needed to return to spirit. Since it was believed the body could not receive the spirit without preparation, initiates generally underwent three years of training in an isolated environment. Once qualified, the Parfait spent their life guarding the purity they had attained through asceticism, fasting and prayer. They rejected all sex, worked to provide their own living and traveled about in twos preaching. Only a small minority chose to receive the sacrament while young with many Believers putting it off until death was eminent. In some cases once the believer had taken the sacrament they fasted until death, believing this would keep them pure. If they were successful, they were said to rejoin the spirit world. If they had not reached the required level of purity, they would reincarnate one last time.

Although their enemies associated the word Cathar with the devil, it may have come from the Greek katharoi, meaning 'pur" or "the pure ones." The Cathars referred to themselves as "Good Christians" and to their group as the "Church of the Friends of God." Obviously these titles, along with their rejection of orthodox teachings and sacraments, distanced the Cathars from the institutionalized church, which they believed was an impure, irredeemable part of Satan's defiled material world. As we might imagine, their open condemnation made this popular group a particular target of the church. In 1147, Pope Eugene III did try to persuade the Cathars to return to the church, but the blatant hypocrisy and overindulgence of his envoys made it impossible for them to convince either the Cathars or those living round about who protected and admired them. Eventually Dominic de Guzman established the Dominican Order to try to restore the Catholic priesthood to a level of sanctity that could support their arguments against the Cathars. When Pope Innocent III's attempts at restoration and harassment also failed, he chose a far more violent route. By declaring open war and offering the Cathars' land and possessions to any who would aid in their destruction, the Pope was able to bring about the deaths of thousands of Cathars and their supporters, some of whom were Catholic. Many were murdered during the fighting, and thousands were also burned at the stake. The Catholic Inquisition, which lasted several hundred years and ended the lives of thousands of supposed heretics, was originally established to root out the few Cathars who had managed to escape the initial wave of executions.

VI. Conclusion

Long, long ago when we were children, something called the 'telephone game' was quite popular. Contrary to the name, and consistent with that low-tech era, there were no telephones involved. The game was usually played at a party or in a classroom where there were at least ten children gathered. A line was formed and the first child in line was given a note with a few simple and familiar words written on it such as "row, row, row your boat" or "twinkle, twinkle little star." After reading the note, the first child would whisper the message into the ear of the next child. The whispered message then moved from one child to the next until at the end of the line, the last child spoke the message out loud. Of course by the time the message made it to the last child it was completely garbled and usually quite silly. No matter how many times the game was repeated, and no matter who whispered the message first, it was always garbled at the end. Since children were playing the game and they would get the most fun out of the silliest message, one might suppose that they changed it purposely as it passed down the line.

Years later, we thought it might be interesting to try the game with a large group of adults, assuming they would be able to pass on the message correctly. Our assumption was way off-base, and the message was just as confused and meaningless as it had been after a group of children got through with it. It seemed so odd that adults were no more able to pass on a simple whispered message than children, we tried the game a few more times with different adult groups, but the result remained the same. When we asked each player to repeat the message they had heard when it was whispered in their ear, the message usually deteriorated bit by bit as it passed down the line. But sometimes, the first or second person who passed it on was the one who misheard and unknowingly changed the message dramatically. Much later, when we began to study the way the brain operates, these results began to make sense. At that point, this simple game helped us understand why the unadulterated 'knowing' a sage received during gnosis became a garbled mess after passing through the brains of those who had not experienced for themselves. The meaning is obvious, unless you receive a message directly, there's a very good chance that after it's been filtered through even one other brain, it can be rendered completely inaccurate.

As you can see from examining the Nag Hammadi texts, the vast majority retained the foundation concept of oneness gnosis: "The One" *is all* and *contains all*. Most of the texts we examined also recognize the fact that Source is not involved in the doings of the material world, that this world is an illusion based on a dualistic thought system and that waking up to our true identity is key to our return to Source. But the brain is convinced this world of separation is its reality; it is unable to cope with the paradox of the illusory separation it experiences verses the oneness of Reality that it doesn't. As Ramana Maharshi put it, "How can the reflected and partial light of the intellect envisage the whole and the original Light?" And so, in an effort to remain in its comfort zone, the brain makes up stories that fit what it believes it's experiencing. You see a separate world, you create a separate god. You see the struggle for specialness and it becomes a cosmic war between good and evil. You 'garble the message' until it's palatable once more. But what does the writing of a sage reveal when the message was written by the sage and it has not been treated as roughly as the texts found in the Nag Hammadi collection? In Part Four we'll discover the answer to that question.

Part Four:

Gnosis Outside the Gnostic Gospels

Theologians may quarrel, but the mystics of the world speak the same language—Meister Eckhart

It's obvious to sincere seekers that both religious and spiritual paths overflow with speculation and opinion. But the Indian sage Dadu Dayal (1544-1603) challenged us to, "Ask of those who have attained God." Why? He tells us that when we do, we will find that, "…all speak the same word. All the enlightened have left one message; it is only those in the midst of their journey who hold diverse opinions." Truth cannot help but permeate the universe since all *is* the Divine. But as we've discovered, it is hidden in plain sight and becomes obvious *only* when we're *willing* to see it. Likewise, an endless stream of testimony proclaiming the veracity of gnosis also exists, beginning with the *Upanishad* writers who said, "I have known that spirit who is infinite and in all, who is ever-one, beyond time" and "He can be seen indivisible in the silence of contemplation. There a man possesses everything; for he is one with the ONE." But these words are invisible to eyes not willing to see and mean nothing to hearts unwilling to understand. Nonetheless, texts born out of the direct experience of the Divine exist in such volume, it would be impossible to bind them together in one definitive collection.

Although we will continue to emphasize the fact that *nothing* can compare with your own direct experience, we wouldn't be writing if books were of no value to the heartfelt seeker. Much can be gained by contemplating a sage's writing since the worth of these texts goes far beyond the words or ideas they contain. The 20th century religious scholar Hasan Askari pointed out, "A book written by a sage is like the residence in which he still lives." Whether the author is still projecting a body or has returned to Source, the essence of their deep love and desire to encourage us is woven into their words. While a sage can't experience for us, through oneness the sage can continue to speak to our heart as we grow our own willingness. By reading, we can get an idea of what the spiritual journey means and explore what truth looks like. And in so doing, we can discover what attachments and aversions we may need to let go of that are holding us back from our own direct experience.

Since the Nag Hammadi texts are still fresh in mind, we'd like to begin this section by contrasting them with two texts from the same time period, Plotinus' *Enneads* and *The Hymn of the Pearl*.

I. Plotinus

Strange as it may seem, we can learn far more about gnosis from this 3rd century pagan Greek philosopher who once published a tract entitled *Against the Gnostics*, than we gleaned from most of the texts labeled as gnostic gospels. We could go straight to Plotinus' text, the *Enneads*, but once again, learning something of the context of Plotinus' work will add depth to our understanding. The title of the text means "the nines," and refers to the way Plotinus' student Porphyry arranged the text; six books each containing nine treatises. Although the title is bland, it would be impossible to say the same for the contents.

When the word philosophy, meaning lover of wisdom, was first coined by Pythagoras in the 6th century BCE, its far-ranging subjects of consideration included politics, ethics, logic, biology, aesthetics, rhetoric, ontology (the nature of being) and metaphysics, an exploration of both anthropos (human affairs) and cosmos. Currently, philosophy is considered an intellectual approach to understanding, but at the heart of Greek philosophy was something called *praxis*, from the Greek *prassein*, meaning "to do." Simply put, this was an experiential, lived philosophy, not merely a mental exercise. It would be incorrect to assume that all ancient philosophers were in accord; there were many schools of thought that differed widely and actively argued with one another. Plotinus (204-270 CE) was the last of an impressive line of 'mystical philosophers' that included Pythagoras (570-495 BCE), Parmenides (approx. 515/540 BCE-?) and Plato (approx. 427-348 BCE).

In his book *How Plato and Pythagoras Can Save Your Life*, author Nicholas Kardaras, Ph.D. explains that these mystical philosophers, "...embraced the notion that there was an unseen 'implicate' order of reality that was unavailable to our senses; according to them, our crude senses were limited and able to perceive only the visible 'explicate' yet illusory shadow manifestation...In essence, they believed that the physical world was a quasi-illusion; ephemeral and short lived, and that our senses would often deceive us into believing the illusion was real, when, in fact, it had no permanence. In contrast, the transcendent realm...[is] eternal and everlasting." Yes, this does sound exactly like physicist David Bohm's holographic universe even though these ancient mystical philosophers gained their understanding without the aid of scientific research.

Over twenty-five hundred years ago, Pythagoras realized mathematics was a language that allowed him to see past the explicate order and describe the unseen implicate order. For him, mathematics was a Divine language that expressed universal principles; a living means of communication that had to be approached experientially. After connecting numbers with musical vibrations and inventing the musical scale, he came to the conclusion the universe operated as a vibration. His theory corresponds with the quantum view that what we perceive as matter is really just dense, slowly vibrating information packed energy. This sea of information/energy is interconnected, made from the same subatomic building blocks known as quanta, and only *appears* to have different properties depending on its vibrational frequencies. For Pythagoras, the number one symbolized universal oneness, two stood for the disharmony of duality, and three joined the two extremes together once again and created harmony, like the yin/yang. Not surprisingly, he equated enlightenment with the attainment of universal harmony.

Like Pythagoras, Parmenides taught that the material world was a projection in which the phenomenon of movement and change were no more than an illusory appearance. Currently a few quantum physicists are echoing this view; instead of movement, they feel that everything exists as 'instants' that happen so quickly, we mistake them for movement, rather like the still photos that make up a movie. As Parmenides taught, an eternal Reality served as the unchanging foundation of All That Is, and that universal foundation was "One Being." He also recognized the accurate role of consciousness when he said, "Thought and being are the same." Since quantum research was impossible in his day, how did Parmenides come to these startling conclusions? He claimed to receive this 'knowing' during a state of altered consciousness that could just as accurately be called gnosis.

Working from Parmenides' description of an eternal, unchanging Reality, Plato put forth a concept that revolutionized theological thought: an immaterial, eternal soul that was separate from the human body. At that point, the religions of the world found themselves scrambling to figure out how to fit this new and exciting concept of an eternal soul into their current theologies. Instead of the heavens and hells most theologians concocted to house the soul, Plato claimed the soul was trapped within the mortal body. In *The Republic,* he explained this trapped soul continually reincarnated until it had freed itself of the enticement of material desires, at which point it returned to its original oneness. The parable of "Plato's Cave," in which cave dwellers mistake shadows for reality, illustrates how the senses blind us to Reality. Nonetheless, he saw experiential philosophy as the means of escape. The mystical philosopher, Hierocles of Alexandria (active around 430 BCE) agreed, saying:

> *Philosophy is the purification and perfection of human nature; it is purification, because it delivers it from the temerity and folly that proceed from matter and because it disengages its affections from the mortal body...because it makes it recover its original felicity by restoring it to the likeness of God.*

For Plato, the material world was no more than a shadow of Reality, and only the eternal, which existed on a plane beyond space and time, was real. It becomes evident that Plotinus shared this view; when a painter asked him to sit for a portrait, the sage replied, "Why paint an illusion of an illusion?" Nicholas Kardaras explains that the goal of these experiential philosophers was a "…'mystical union' with the infinite…to break free from the cage of the physical body in order to experience—and join with—the numinous." Yes, these words do sound as if they could have been lifted from several of the Nag Hammadi gnostic gospels. If the goal of the mystical philosophers and the early Christian gnostics was the same, why did Plotinus write *Against the Gnostics*?

As you now know, gnosis originally meant 'knowing' through direct experience and especially the direct, personal experience of the Divine. *This* was the gnosis of Plotinus, and it angered him that the word had been appropriated by the mystery school gnostics who destroyed the word's original meaning. Plotinus was also enraged that those who erroneously claimed the title 'gnostic' had vilified the demiurge. To understand why this was a bone of contention, we need to examine Plotinus' "Three in One" view of the universe. Unlike trinities made up of three distinct beings in one, Plotinus' 'trinity' is composed of three harmonious and unified aspects of the Divine:

1. The One (also called The First or The Self-contained): The foundation or 'ground' of all existence; all energy potentiality without which nothing could exist. Everything emanates from this foundation without its being altered or diminished. Plotinus did not think of The One as *a* Being, but as a light filled *generator of Being*. He said, "We must call The One a sheer Dynamis or potentiality without which nothing can exist… It is precisely because there is nothing within

The One that all things are from It...Think of The One as Mind or as God, and you think too meanly." In other words, there is no either/or concerning The One; it is potential, the energy needed to bring potential to fruition and the consciousness that acts upon it. As you've learned, Plotinus' words, spoken so long ago, are now being echoed by quantum physicists.

2. The Divine Mind (The Good): Consciousness, Being, the Divine Itself, the Thinker and the Thought, the creative aspect of the universe. As to the Divine Mind also being The Good, Plotinus argues, "Cause to all, how can It acquire its character outside of Itself, to know any good outside? The good of its being cannot be borrowed: This is The Good" Like the Divine Being described in *Nasadiya Sukta* that chose to BE love, Plotinus' Divine Mind chose to BE Good.

3. The Soul or All-Soul: An extension of the Divine Mind, which is both one and many. This is where we come in, unique consciousness that is nonetheless one with the Divine Mind. Free will comes into play when Plotinus explained that each Soul has the free will to choose between two aspects, focusing on The One or focusing away from The One. As Plotinus put it:

We always move round The One, but we do not always fix our gaze upon It: we are like a choir of singers who stand round the conductor, but do not always sing in time because their attention is diverted to some external object; when they look at the conductor they sing well and are really with him...but we do not always look towards

> *the One. When we do, we attain...our repose,*
> *and we no longer sing out of tune, but form in*
> *very truth a divine chorus round The One.*

Sharing the creative aspects of the Divine Mind, the soul is able to combine consciousness and energy potential to manifest the material illusion. Yes, Plotinus was accurately pointing out that as the true Self, we all shared in the creation of the material world and sustain it through our continued projection. Rather than the evil work of an insane Demiurge, Plotinus saw only good and beauty in the world itself. However, he explained that it was our identification or "couplement" with our creations that drew our awareness away from the Divine and caused the soul to be trapped in the material realm. He did not infer that this was either sinful or evil, but rather a free will choice that keeps us from our highest Self. Plotinus made it clear that the Self can never be stained, "In all this there is no sin...our concern is not merely to be sinless but to be God."

Although we have lost our way, mesmerized by the virtual reality we create/project, Plotinus accurately maintained that our creations/projections remain Divine since everything ultimately derives from, and remains within, The One. This point is central to the reasoning behind his main argument in *Against the Gnostics*. Plotinus knew through direct experience that the essential oneness of All That Is can never be divided, and The One can never be other than good. His 'knowing' brooked no duality. On the other hand, the self-proclaimed gnostic writers wreaked havoc with oneness by claiming that an evil demiurge had emanated from The One, created a flawed material world that opposed the spiritual and instigated a cosmic war between good and evil. Regardless of the fact that most gnostic writers continued to agree that The One played no part in the material world; the mere hint that evil had come from The Good was a deception Plotinus refused to tolerate.

As we can see from the examples of these pagan philosophers, no religion or spiritual path can claim exclusive access to the Divine. *A key to gnosis is the willingness to let go of our conditioning and accept the truth the Divine wants to show us.* Like the gnostic authors, other philosophers imagined hundreds of levels of beings that stood between humanity and The One, but Plotinus insisted that there are no levels or barriers. Speaking of the person who experiences gnosis, he wrote:

> *We ought not even to say that he will see, but he will be that which he sees, if indeed it is possible any longer to distinguish between seer and seen, and not boldly to affirm that the two are one. In this state the seer does not see or distinguish or imagine two things' he becomes another, he ceases to be himself and to belong to himself. He belongs to him, is one with him....we see ourselves as pure, subtle, ethereal, light: we become divine, or rather we know ourselves to be divine.*

Although gnosis was not a new concept in the East, Plato was one of the first in the West to hint that *henosis* (union with The One) was possible. It's interesting to note that Plotinus had studied for eleven years with Ammonias Saccus (200-250), a philosopher known as "The God Taught," a title which also hints at gnosis. Unfortunately he left no written works, so it's impossible to know what he shared with Plotinus. Nonetheless, Plotinus openly declared his own first-hand experience stating, "The One is by which, in which, and from which All That Is proceeds. It may also be KNOWN. The knowledge of The One has always been, and continues to be revealed by those who have the experience." How is the experience attained? Plotinus answers:

> *There is a returning impulse, drawing all... towards the center from whence all came...Along the same road by which it descended, the soul must retrace its steps back to the supreme Good. It must first of all return to itself...one must become "God." Thought cannot attain this...thought is a mere preliminary to communion with God...You ask, how can we know the Infinite? I answer, not by reason...You can only apprehend the Infinite by a faculty superior to reason, by entering into a state in which you are your finite self no longer — in which the divine essence is communicated to you. It is the liberation of your mind from its finite consciousness.*

Although Plotinus admitted, "The vision baffles telling...For how can one describe, as other than oneself, that which, when one saw it, seemed to be one with oneself?," he added, "I am striving to give back the divine in me to the divine in all." Like so many who have experienced gnosis, it became his purpose to share the fact that Source *can* be known and *wants* to be known. Like other sages who knew that they could not experience *for* anyone Plotinus states, "That which is divine is ineffable, and cannot be shown to those who have not had the happiness to see it." Yet Plotinus lovingly shares the simple means by which others can also experience:

Shut your eyes and wake another way of seeing, which everyone has but few use…How then can this come to us? Strip yourself of everything… that it may receive The One alone, as The One is alone…It is impossible for one who has in his soul any extraneous image to conceive of The One while that image distracts his attention…the soul must forsake all that is external, and turn itself wholly to that which is within…and so it will come to the vision of The One and will be united with it; and then, after a sufficient converse with it, it will return and bring word, if it be possible.

Jesus' words recorded in *The Gospel of Thomas* may come to mind while reading this except from the *Enneads* :

God, as Plato says, is not far from every one of us; he is present with all, though they know him not. Men flee away from him, or rather from themselves. They cannot grasp him from whom they have fled…But he who has learnt to know himself will know also whence he is…For we are not cut off from our source nor separated from it…but we breathe and maintain our being in our source which does not first give itself and then withdraw, but is always supplying us, as long as it is what it is…For our present life, without God is a mere shadow and mimicry of the true life.

Before going on to *The Hymn of the Pearl*, let's take a few moments to consider the deep understanding of the universe that Plotinus acquired through gnosis:

» Quantum consciousness is our Reality; the material world is projected from consciousness:

We do not pass through the material world; the material world passes through our eternal consciousness... We must then pass on upward, removing all that is other than God until...we behold the source of life, Consciousness, Being.

External objects present us only with appearances...Our question lies with the ideal reality that exists behind appearance.

» We are Soul/Consciousness, which is the creative force of All That Is:

Let every soul recall, then, at the outset the truth that Soul is the author of all living things, that it has breathed the life into them all...they gather or dissolve as Soul brings them life or abandons them, but Soul, since it never can abandon itself, is of eternal being.

Consciousness is the sole basis of certainty.

» We have become lost in our projections:

Murders, death in all its guises, the reduction and sacking of cities, all must be to us just such a spectacle as the changing scenes of a play...for on earth, in all the succession of life, it is not the soul within but the shadow outside...the doing of man knowing no more than to live the lower and outer life, and never perceiving that, in his weeping and in his graver doings alike, he is but at play.

» Reality is holographic/non-local:

The authentic and primal Cosmos is the being of the Divine Mind of the truly Existent. This contains within itself no spatial distinction and has none of the feebleness of division...Every part that it gives forth is the whole...for here is no separation of thing from thing, no part standing in isolated existence estranged from the rest... Everywhere one and complete.

» The little, false self is a deluded, conditioned portion of consciousness, the result of free will:

At the source, it is one, eternal, unconditional; at the other end of the projection it is a multitude of souls, all intricately conditioned. Soul has, therefore, two aspects, two identities: in its origin it is eternal Divinity; in its temporal display, coupled with matter, it is still Divine, but it is also a thing limited and burdened by conditions. Yet, even in its limited projection, it maintains its 'higher' identity — just as light, however it may be refracted into a multicolored spectrum, remains pure light, or as the ocean, however lashed into multiple waves, remains the ocean. The soul, however hemmed in by conditions and delusion, is always unconditioned at its core, always ultimately restorable to its eternal unity, above all conditionality...it is bound, but it is free; it is the projected image, but it is also the Exemplar.

» The Nature of Love:

Love is God's magnetic attraction, drawing us to His presence. Its pull is felt the stronger as we inwardly approach the source of that attraction.

Love...has of necessity been eternally in existence, for it springs from the intention of the soul towards its best, towards the Good. As long as soul has been, Love has been.

» Awakening:

> *I am not this thing I appear to be, I am the eternal One… to real Being we go back, to all that we have and are. To That we return as from That we came. Of what is There we have direct knowledge, no images or even impressions. And to know without image is to be; by our part in true knowledge we are those supernal beings…We are they while we are also one with all: therefore we and all things are one…It is important to have intellectual knowledge of The Good…this is the grand learning. We come to this learning by analogies, by abstractions" but then we experience, and see that we are Identical with Being and Divine Mind and the entire living All, we no longer see the Supreme as an external…Here, we put aside all learning. The vision floods the eyes with Light, but it is not a light showing some other object; the Light is itself the vision…when we attain to this state…we are Life itself, having entered into That which contains no admixture but is purely Itself. Our way takes us beyond knowing…Such is the life of…blessed men, a liberation from all earthly bonds…a flight of the alone to the Alone.*

The *Enneads* makes the obvious point that slapping labels such as 'pagan,' or 'gnostic' on a text is not an accurate indicator of what might be found inside. How would the one who has not experienced the Divine recognize the words of the one who has? On the other hand, a label can occasionally be correct, and that is certainly true of our next selection.

II. *The Hymn of the Pearl*

The Hymn of the Pearl is a gnostic poem that reads like an action/adventure story while still capturing all the essential elements of the perennial philosophy. Also known as *The Song of Deliverance*, *Hymn of the Robe of Glory*, or *The Hymn of the Soul*, this allegory is easily one of the most appealing examples of Gnostic writing. Although the poem may be pre-Christian, it's often attributed to Bardaisan (154-222 AD), an Assyrian gnostic who was also a scientitst, astrologer, philosopher and poet. If he is the author, his early life in a noble and wealthy family may have served as the inspiration for the poem. The Manicheans also claimed the *Hymn* and used it to glorify their founder Mani, who they connected with the poem's protagonist. Surprisingly, the poem survived intact on the shelves of orthodox archives tucked inside the Greek apocryphal *Acts of Judas Thomas the Apostle*, a text it had no connection to, either in style or content.

Like many gnostic writings, the *Hymn* is presented in symbolic language. The surface story alone is entertaining, but until we're willing to look deeper, we'll easily miss the most significant parts of the adventure. If you've read our book *The Beginning of Fearlessness: Quantum Prodigal Son*, there's little doubt that you'll be struck by the similarity between *The Hymn of the Pearl* and Jesus' parable of the prodigal son. Although Jesus' parable is found in the *New Testament* gospel of *Luke* (15: 11-32), and most Christian religions consider it to be no more than a charming story about God's forgiveness, it is our contention that Jesus' parable is also an allegory that originated in gnosis. Both stories feature a wealthy father and two sons, and in each case, the younger son journeys to a distant land where he forgets his true home. Eventually each young man 'comes to his senses' and returns. Both of these stories focus on the central theme of gnosis: our journey away from Source and our need to return. As we examine the *Hymn*, we'll also compare and contrast it with a few of the main points found in Jesus' parable. A translation of the *Hymn* by Willis Barnstone (1927-) is included in *The Other Bible*, and several older translations can be read or downloaded on the internet. We've taken the liberty of offering the poem in a modern English prose version, but the contents remain the same. Following the *Hymn*, you'll find a copy of Jesus' parable of the prodigal son:

> When I was a little child living in my kingdom, in my father's house, comfortable in the wealth and luxuries of my family that nurtured me, my parents equipped me with abundant provisions and sent me forth from the East, our home. From the wealth of their treasure they gathered up a bundle for me that was abundant, yet light enough that I could carry it myself. It held gold, silver, rubies, opals and adamant which can crush iron. And they removed my magnificent robe of glory which they had woven for me out of love, and took away my purple toga, which was made to fit my stature. They made a covenant with me which was written on my heart so that it would not be forgotten. They promised, "If you go down to Egypt and come to us with the One Pearl which is guarded by a snarling serpent who lies in the midst of the sea, you will once again wear your robe of glory and your toga, and

with your older bother you will be heir to our kingdom.

I left the East with my two royal guardians, since the way was dangerous and difficult and I was quite young to be traveling it alone. I passed the borders of Maishan where merchants of the East met to trade, reached the land of Babel and entered the walls of Sarbug. When I arrived in Egypt, my companions left me. Without hesitation, I went to an inn close to the serpent and waited for him to fall asleep so I could take my pearl from him. Since I was all alone I was a stranger to others in the inn, yet I saw one of my own people there, a young nobleman from the East, and we became close friends. I shared my belongings, confided the purpose of my mission and warned him against becoming involved with the Egyptians or those who were unclean. Since I was afraid the people would realize that I had come to take the pearl and they would set the serpent upon me, I disguised myself in native garb so no one would suspect that I was not their countryman.

Somehow, my secret was revealed and the people connived to harm me. They gave me food to eat that caused me to forget that I was a son of kings. I served their king and I forgot the pearl that my parents had sent me to retrieve. Their poisonous food and their oppression caused me to fall into a deep sleep. Nonetheless, my parents were aware of all the trials that befell me, and they grieved for me. They proclaimed that all the kings, princes and nobles should meet at the gates of our kingdom and weave a plan that I might be freed from Egypt. They wrote me a letter and everyone in attendance signed their name. It read:

"From your father, the King of Kings, your mother, the Mistress of the East, and from your brother, our second in authority, to our son in Egypt, greetings: Awake and hear the words of our letter! Remember that you are a son of Kings and see the slavery of your life. Remember the pearl for which you were sent to Egypt! Remember your magnificent robe of glory and your splendid toga that will adorn you when your name has been read from the book of life and the list of heroes, when you and your bother inherit our kingdom."

The letter was sealed by the King with his right hand to protect it from the evil ones of Babel and Sarbug. And the letter flew up in the form of an eagle, the king of all birds; and it flew until it alighted beside me, and it began speaking. The sound of its voice woke me, and I rose from my sleep. I took it, kissed it, broke its seal and began to read. And the words that I read were the words that had been written on my heart and I remembered that I was a son of Kings and my free soul longed to return to its own kind. Now I remembered the pearl that I had come to acquire, and I began to enchant the terrible, snarling serpent. By chanting the names of my Father, my mother and my brother, I caused the serpent to fall into a deep sleep. I seized the pearl and turned back toward the house of my Father.

I immediately stripped off their filthy and impure garments, left them laying in the fields, and directed my way toward the light of our homeland in the East. The letter, whose voice had awakened me was going before me on road and was leading me with its light. Its voice soothed my fears and its love encouraged me to go on. I retraced my journey, but this time I hurried past Sarbug and Babel and arrived in Maishan, which lay next to the sea. My robe of glory which I had taken off and the toga, which was wrapped with it, had been sent here by my parents and been entrusted to the safekeeping of their faithful treasurers. Since much time had passed since I had seen the robe, I had forgotten its splendor. As I beheld it, the garment suddenly seemed to become a mirror of myself. I saw in it my whole Self, and in it I also saw myself apart, for we were two entities, yet one form.

And I saw the treasurers who brought me the robe in the same manner; they were like two entities yet one form, and the seal of the King was written on them both. They restored my wealth, and my brightly colored robe which had been skillfully worked with gold and beryl, with rubies and opals and sardonyx. Its seams were fastened with diamond clasps, and the image of the King of Kings was embroidered on it with sapphires of many colors. I saw the robe quiver all over with the understanding of gnosis, and realized that it was preparing to speak. As it moved toward me, I heard the tones of its song: "I am the active in deeds, whom they reared for him before my father; and I perceived myself growing in stature according to his labors."

With kingly movements the robe approached me, urging me to take it. And love urged me to run to meet it and accept it, so I stretched forward and clothed myself with the beauty of its colors. I also wrapped myself in my exquisite toga and thus adorned, ascended to the Gate of Salutation and Adoration. I bowed my head to the majesty of my Father who had sent it to me, for I had fulfilled his commandments and he had kept his promises to me, and at the gate of his princes I joined his nobles. My Father rejoiced in me and received me in his kingdom and all his servants praised him. And he promised me that we would quickly journey together to the Gate of the King of Kings, and with my gifts and my pearl I would appear with him before our King.

Parable of the Prodigal Son

And [Jesus] said, There was a man who had two sons, and the younger of them said to his father, "Father, give me the share of property that falls to me." And he divided his living between them. Not many days later, the younger son gathered all he had and took his journey into a far country, and there he squandered his property in loose living. And when he had spent everything, a great famine arose in the country, and he began to be in want. So he went and joined himself to one of the citizens of that country who sent him into his field to feed the swine. And he would have gladly fed on the pods that the swine ate, and no one gave him anything. But when he came to himself he said, "How many of my father's hired servants have bread to spare, but I perish here with hunger. I will arise and go to my father, and I will say to him, 'Father, I have sinned against heaven and before you, I am no longer worthy to be called your son, treat me as one of your hired servants.'" And he arose and came to his father. But while he was yet at a distance, his father saw him and had compassion and ran and embraced him and kissed him. And the son said to him "Father, I have sinned against heaven and before you, I am no longer worthy to be called your son." But the father said to his servants, "Bring quickly the best robe and put it on him and put a ring on his finger and shoes on his feet, and bring the fatted calf and kill it, and let us eat and make merry." For his son was dead and is alive again, he was lost and is found. And they began to make merry. Now his elder son was in the field; and as he came and drew near to the house, he heard music and dancing. And he called one of the servants and asked what this meant. And he said to him, "Your brother has come, and your father has killed the fatted calf, because he has received him safe and sound." But he was angry and refused to go in. His father came out and entreated him, but he answered his father, "Lo, these many years I have served you, and I never disobeyed your command; yet you never gave me a kid that I might make merry with my friends. But as soon as this your son who ate up your living with harlots arrived, you slaughtered the

> *fatted calf for him." And he said to him, "Son,*
> *you are always with me and all that is mine is*
> *yours. It was fitting to make merry and be glad*
> *for this your brother was dead, and is alive; he*
> *was lost and is found."* — Luke: 15: 11-32

Each tale opens with a young man living very comfortably in a wealthy family home. In Jesus' parable, the Father symbolizes the Divine. In egalitarian gnostic fashion, the *Hymn* portrays both the young man's father and mother acting in tandem for his benefit. The Father symbolizes truth, the mother, wisdom, and both share equal glory as the mother is referred to as both "The Mistress of the East" and "The Mistress of Heaven." This was not written to promote separate male and female gods, but to confirm, like the yin/yang, that all qualities, those considered both feminine and masculine, are contained within the Divine. Although the mother and father are divine, they are not *the* Divine. At the end of the story the father and son take the pearl to the King of Kings who symbolizes The One. In both stories there is also an older brother. In the *Hymn*, the older son remains in oneness with Source. In Jesus' parable, the older son takes a more subtle journey away from the Father by claiming that he is doing his father's will while he is actually carrying out his own. Although both sons in the *Hymn* return to Source, it's interesting to note that the parable of the prodigal son remains open ended, with the older son symbolizing those of us who have still not completed our journey back to Source.

The family palace stands for our natural dwelling in oneness with Source, but we can no longer think of it as a separate 'heaven,' or for that matter, a separate place at all. The gnostic view agrees with quantum physics in that the Divine ground *is* our Reality, and we *are* the consciousness that permeates it. So instead of literally traveling from one location to another, both tales feature a figurative journey of consciousness. Since it would be impossible for us to literally leave our Source, this 'journey' is really no more than a shift in awareness from Reality to illusion and back again. The words 'journey' and 'path' describe a spiritual process, a transition, not the act of going from one place to another. Thus the young man's spiritual journey takes place 'in place' and urges us to open our hearts to the realization of what that 'place' actually is.

While the prodigal son openly rebels and leaves home at odds with his father, the young man in the *Hymn*, who we'll refer to as 'the prince,' *appears* to be sent away. However, considering the spiritual danger involved in the journey, it seems more likely that the parents are, like the father of the prodigal son, doing the best that they can to support the success of a dangerous journey the son insists on making. (Keep in mind that accurately translating every nuance of an ancient manuscript is impossible.) In each case, the young man leaves home with provisions he has received from his family. In the *Hymn*, the son's bundle is large, but it remains light enough for him to carry himself. Burdens are often a symbol for sin, but here the lightness of the bundle tells us that while his parents would rather that he remain at home, they are not judging his choices or considering his journey away from them a sin, but rather a free will choice.

Both stories emphasize the fact that the son is young, informing us that the decision to leave is likely the result of immature thinking. In both cases, the young traveler is allowed to discover the error in his thinking through his own direct experience. It also stands to reason that no parent would willingly give provisions to a headstrong adolescent and send him into a dangerous situation unless they were certain no real harm could occur, and in both stories we see that that is true. Like the young men, we've also been given the opportunity to compare the value of separation vs. oneness via a harmless illusion. The *Hymn* tells us that before the prince left, he and his parents made a covenant for their kingdom that was written on his heart so that he could not forget. This is similar to the "cord of light between your heart and Source" that Rumi promises us "nothing can weaken or break, and it is always in His hands." Like the covenant, this cord rests lightly in our heart, but contains the knowledge of our true identity. We can focus on this bond of remembrance at any time, no matter how far we stray from home.

As you'll remember from *The Gospel of Thomas*, garments were regularly used to symbolize the physical body, but the *Hymn* uses a very different garment, the "magnificent robe of glory" as a symbol for the true Self. Jesus taught that it would be impossible to return to Source unless we were willing to let go of the body, or as he put it, undress and trample our clothing under our feet. But in the *Hymn*, we have a reversal. When the prince says, "They took off my bright robe of glory which they had made for me out of love," he is forsaking his true identity, an identity that was the result of Source's desire to express love. However, the prince is assured that not only can he put on his glorious robe any time he wishes; he may also don a "purple toga." This garment is a symbol of royalty that assures him he will remain in his original position of honor as heir to his parent's kingdom. Although the prodigal son did not receive these assurances when he left, they are implied by what happened when he returned.

The parable gives this beautiful description of the prodigal son's return: "But while he was yet at a distance, his father saw him and had compassion and ran and embraced him and kissed him." This could not have happened unless his father was constantly watching for his child's return. It also assures us that the Divine will 'run out to meet us' whenever we choose to return. His father also immediately gave him a kiss (a symbol of acceptance and friendship), sandals (the footwear of a free man), the best robe (a symbol of high honor and rank), a ring (a seal ring that gave the wearer power to act on behalf of the master) and a 'welcome home' party (an indication to all onlookers that the son was not to be rejected). These particular gifts proclaimed the position and authority of the wearer, and signified that not only was he accepted back into the home, he was once again a recognized heir to his father's kingdom, just as we all are.

In the *Hymn*, the young man travels to Egypt. Except in the case of Hermitic gnostics who revered Egypt, that country was often used by gnostic writers to symbolize our illusionary world of form, and in Jesus' parable, the "the far country" fills that role. To become part of the world, it was necessary for both young men to begin identifying with a physical body. In the *Hymn*, this identification is made clear when the prince says, "I disguised myself in native garb so no one would suspect that I was not their countryman." The garment/body that he began to identify with not only allowed him to blend in with everyone else living in the illusion of form, it caused him to deceive himself and forget who he was. This robe was far inferior to the dazzling garments he had removed, just as the body is an extremely poor substitute for the true Self. In Jesus' parable, the prodigal son lost everything his father gave him in "loose living," a phase that may lead us to believe he wasted his money on debauchery, as his older brother falsely claimed. However, "thoughtless living" is actually a more accurate translation, which is confirmed by the fact that his father never judged him, mentioned the word sin or expected any form of apology or atonement. In this case, the term "loose living" reminds us that even the most innocuous desires of the body can easily cause us to forget the Self.

Although the parents in the *Hymn* appear to send the prince out into the world on a risky mission for a pearl they don't seem to need, symbolism makes it clear that this trip was not their idea. As you know, a pearl is an oyster's attempt to protect itself from an irritating grain of sand that has worked its way into the mollusk's tender belly. Because the pearl is something valuable that comes from something valueless, it was often used to symbolize transcendence. The pearl is our clue that the young man's spiritual state is at the crux of his journey. Like the prodigal son, the prince would have nothing to transcend if he had remained in oneness, but he chose to throw away everything to gain the nothingness of separation and specialness. The trials each young man experiences are like the sand that creates the pearl. Awakening to their own foolishness, they both return home bearing this priceless gift. This is not to say that the Divine tests us or sends us to an 'earth school' to evolve; we unknowingly put our own inevitable series of 'cause and effect' tests into motion the moment we chose our dualistic system. At this point we can remain asleep or we can choose to learn when we're confronted with the suffering we've created for ourselves.

Although they're represented by different symbols, both young men faced several similar obstacles. Early on, they each dealt with the influence and conditioning of others who were steeped in illusion. The *Hymn* tells us that the prince had companions, but when he made the choice to reside in illusion, symbolized by entering the serpent's inn, they wisely decided to stay behind. While there, he befriended a "young man of my own people" who appeared on the surface to be a worthy companion but did nothing more than accept a share of his belongings. Similarly, the prodigal son easily found companions who were willing to help him enjoy the wealth his father had given him, but they were nowhere to be found once it had all been spent. In both cases these 'friends' highlight the fact that those who are drowning in illusion can do nothing more than pull us down with them, no matter how powerful they many appear to be.

When the "Egyptians" in the *Hymn* realized the prince wanted to recover the pearl (transcend) they poisoned him with their food (conditioning) and caused him to fall into the deep sleep of spiritual blindness. The prince naively believed that he would be able to steal the pearl when the serpent fell asleep, but instead, he's the one that's asleep. As you've learned, gnostic writers regularly used sleep, nightmares and drunkenness to describe our confused state of mind within the illusion. This sleep is so deep; it causes us to forget who we actually are and is so convincing, we rarely question whether or not this world is our reality. Once the prodigal son's wealth was gone, "a famine arose in the country, and he began to be in want." Although the far country is always in a state of spiritual famine, when the prodigal son was no longer distracted by the desires his wealth could fulfill, he began to feel the lack. Unfortunately, he sought sustenance from an empty source.

The prince, like most who are mired in illusion, placed the blame for his plight on others, claiming the Egyptians 'cunningly' slipped him drugged food. In the same way, the prodigal son believed that someone else should take responsibility for his pitiful condition, so he went to a wealthy and powerful "citizen" looking for help. This citizen sent the prodigal son out to tend his herd of swine, but the young man is not even allowed to share the pods he is told to feed them. Rather than symbolizing the greed of the citizen, his actions demonstrate the impossibility of finding a savior outside ourselves; an illusion cannot save us from another illusion. Someone may offer us something that could temporarily help the body, but no one else can carry us back to the Divine. We can endlessly blame others for the predicaments we find ourselves in, but we chose to enter this illusion and we each make hundreds of choices each day that keep us here and project the world we see. No matter how much we might protest, each of us is personally responsible for the state of affairs we find within the illusion. Until we take responsibility for our mistake, we will be unable to correct it. The prince complained about the 'heaviness' of the food the Egyptians gave him while the prodigal son starved, but in each case, the food (or lack of it) signified the fact that there is nothing in the illusion that can satisfy our spiritual hunger or begin to compare with our Reality. All our desires, regardless of whether they're overindulged or denied, are pitiful substitutes for our deep-seated yearning for Source.

Although the *Hymn* tells us the pearl was guarded by a snarling serpent, this beast did not represent an evil entity. However, it does symbolize the only thing that stands in the way of transcendence: the little, false self that does its very best to keep us mired in spiritual darkness. Although many confuse the ego and the false self, the ego is attached only to the body, and the body's sense of self. As you've learned, the false self is the small portion of consciousness that we've willfully closed off from the One Mind of God. Though consciousness cannot detach from Source, the false self has confined itself to the darkness of subjective perception that it filters through the brain and senses. It is not a separate entity, but exists within a thought system that was born out of our desire to experiment with separation and specialness. It survives exclusively on our continued willingness to support it with polarized dualistic thinking. It does, however, use the body's ego to establish the separate identity/ personality associated with each body it projects. Although the false mind uses each's body's desires to serve its own ends, it isn't attached to any specific personality or body.

Even in its closed off, unaware condition, the little self remains a part of the immortal One Mind. As it continues to project one lifetime after another, it can easily afford to disengage itself from any lifetime that's nonproductive from its point of view. Within its deepest recesses, the false mind is aware that 'waking up' is the first step towards its demise so it's quite appropriate for its terror to be symbolized by a hissing serpent that's desperate to keep us from "coming to ourselves."

Just when it appears that all is lost, the prince receives a letter from his parents stating, "Awake and hear the words of our letter! Remember that you are a son of Kings and see the slavery of your life. Remember the pearl for which you were sent to Egypt! Remember your magnificent robe of glory and your splendid toga that will adorn you when your name has been read from the book of life and the list of heroes, when you and your bother inherit our kingdom." In this way, the *Hymn* assures us that no matter what circumstances we find ourselves in, Source is aware and willing to assist us. The gnostic *Gospel of Philip* also reminds us, "When the pearl is cast down into the mud, it does not become greatly despised...but it always has value in the eyes of its owner." In Jesus' parable, the father runs out to meet the prodigal son and physically supports him as they finish the journey together and enter their home. This meeting on the road could not have taken place unless the father was continuously anticipating and watching for his son's return. As Rumi said, "In every event of your life, the Beloved is whispering to you exactly what you need to hear and know." In this case, the letter symbolizes that whispering, but the Divine will never force us to listen, so the message is always subtle. Regardless, it's always there, written on our hearts, should we decide to listen.

As you'll remember, provisions had been given to both young men before they set out. We can liken these provisions, letters and covenants to a safety net. Although we chose to project this illusion because we thought that separation could work as well as oneness, we must not have been so certain of the result that we were willing to completely turn our backs on Source. The provisions we all still carry with us are like a GPS that guarantees we'll find our way back home. Rumi put it this way, "The second you stepped into this world of existence a ladder was placed before you to help you escape." Just as the letter reminded the young man of his slavery, the prodigal son also compared his miserable situation to the freedom he had once experienced in his father's house and he found it wanting. In his case, he felt that his error was so great; he would have to earn his way back into his father's favor. Since his father ignored his pleas for forgiveness when he confessed his 'sins' and begged to be treated as a slave, we learn that it's grace, not atonement or works, that carry us back to the Beloved. The joyful message we can all take away from these parables is the assurance that our current 'slavery' has in no way changed our Reality.

There is a statement in each of our stories that point to the moment of enlightenment. In the *Hymn*, the young man says, "I remembered that I was a son of Kings and my free soul longed for its own kind" and in Jesus' parable we find that the prodigal son, "came to himself." In both cases these statements epitomize the realization that we are not the body or the personality. In that instant, we *know* that we are something far greater, something that is not of this world. Our eyes are open to the futility and emptiness of separation, the pursuit of specialness and the illusory birth/death cycle. We long once again to live as the eternal Self, to restore our Oneness with All That Is. Many mistake this instant for the end of the journey, but as our two stories demonstrate, it's actually the beginning. The prodigal son understood that his realization would have no value if he continued to lie in the pig sty thinking about it. Instead of wasting time trying to 'purify' himself, he began the long trudge home just as he was. Why? He remembered his father's loving heart and believed that no matter what condition he was in, he wouldn't be turned away. The prodigal son's journey home retraced the steps of his original route, but this time he was stripping off the veils of illusion instead of putting them on.

The prince's return began when he enchanted the serpent. How did he do this? He says, "Now I remembered the pearl that I had come to acquire, and I began to enchant the terrible, snarling serpent. By chanting the names of my Father, my mother and my brother, I caused the serpent to fall into a deep sleep. I seized the pearl and turned back toward the house of my Father." For the prodigal son, the walk back home represented the deconstruction of the little self. For the prince, it was the remembrance of truth. The little self is nothing that we can fight or overpower since any attention it receives strengthens it, but we can starve it into nonexistence. Since it feeds on dualistic thoughts of separation and specialness, if we exchange those thoughts for love and oneness, it shrinks. Just like a vine that's deprived of the sun and water it needs to flourish, it withers and once again becomes part of the soil that it originally sprang from.

Putting the serpent/false self to sleep signifies gnosis. Although the prince was still projecting a body, he had freed himself from the limited sense perception of the body and opened to the 'knowing' available through the One Mind. His body would continue until its natural death, but he would use it merely as a means to navigate the illusion until he was once again in his parent's home. He was now able to understand that in comparison to the Self, the human body is a mere rag, which he willingly strips off and leaves in this world. Remember that in *The Gospel of Thomas,* Jesus used the symbol of a field to stand for this world, a field where his mature followers would strip off their garments/ bodies, leave them and give the field to those who still wanted to inhabit it. So we learn from these words that we strip off the garment of flesh twice, once figuratively when we are still "in the world but no part of the world," and once literally, when we stop projecting the life/death cycle and return to Source. Likewise, in the parable of the prodigal son, the full return to Self is not complete until the son once again steps over the threshold and enters his father's house.

Like the father who met the prodigal son on the road and lovingly placed a robe of honor around his shoulders, the prince's parent's sent his robe of glory to him. When it appeared, he said, "As I gazed on it suddenly the garment seemed to be a mirror of myself. I saw in it my whole Self, and in it I saw myself apart, for we were two entities, yet one form. The treasurers brought me one robe: they were two of the same shape with one kingly seal." Here the *Hymn* highlights an extremely important point in gnostic understanding, a point that is continually made throughout the long history of the perennial philosophy: *We are our own savior.*

The robe the young man had taken off to enter illusion was his true Self. That Self had remained with his parents and was kept in safety. It was unaltered no matter what the young man had done as he masqueraded as the little, false self. Although he thought that he had been divided from the Self, *his sleep had not caused any actual division, only the illusion of division.* As you've learned, sages equate sin, not with wrong doing, but with the ignorance of the little, false self. Others may be able to show us that the door to the Self is open, but we are the only ones that can walk through it. As the Buddha said, "No one saves us but ourselves. No one can and no one may. We ourselves must walk the path." Remember that in the Gnostic *Dialogue of the Savior* Jesus said, "Light the lamp within you…Knock on yourself as upon a door and walk upon yourself as on a straight road." By opening our hearts to the Self, we literally become our own savior.

Embroidered on the robe, the prince found an image of the King of Kings, reminding him that the true Self was not just the image of Source, it is *one* with the Divine, it itself *is* Divine. Not only that, but the robe also "quivered all over with the understanding of gnosis." Since the robe signified the Self, we see that it remained in a state of direct, personal communion with the Divine. Gnosis/knowing is our indivisible connection with the infinite field of truth encompassed by the One Mind. Truth, like gnosis, is not something that can be either taught or learned, but something that *must be experienced.* When we stop limiting our thinking to the brain and reconnect with the infinite intelligence of the One Mind, we don't learn new things; we *remember* them because these truths always have been, and always will be, what we are. In fact, the robe/

Self speaks, letting the prince know that while he slumbered in illusion, the Self had not slept, but had continued "growing in stature." This fact allowed the prince to wake up and resume the position he always had as if no interruption had taken place. The same was true of the prodigal son. Although his older brother falsely accused him of behavior he personally judged to be sinful, his father did not agree with this assessment. He restored his younger son to the same position and rights of inheritance he had enjoyed before he left regardless of the fact that he had already wasted his share of the inheritance. How could that be? The quantum field of potentiality has no limits. We can draw from it eternally and it will remain forever full! While we play at virtual reality, the greatest percentage of our consciousness remains at one with Source and we will return as if nothing has happened, because in fact nothing actually has.

As the *Hymn* comes to a close, the little self has dissolved into the Self and reunited with Source. The prince will not project another useless life in illusion. As the Self, he will once again enter his rightful home where his return completes the Oneness of All That Is. Just like the young men in these stories, we rejected our true nature and its inherent Oneness to play in the world of separate forms and pursue our own specialness. No matter what drama we chose to project in this virtual reality of illusion, the Self remains safe and secure. Through gnosis we are all free to access the Self and the One Mind at any time we wish. It is the will of our royal family that we each snatch the pearl of transcendence from the serpent of illusion as quickly as possible.

(For a detailed verse-by-verse quantum/gnostic reading of Jesus' parable of the prodigal son, and more about the gnostic Jesus, please read *The Beginning of Fearlessness: Quantum Prodigal Son*.)

III. Alchemy

The oldest known books on alchemy were written early in the 4th century by Zosimos of Panaopolis (around 300), an Egyptian who claimed to be both an alchemist and gnostic mystic. That may appear to be an odd combination, but there was far more to alchemy than turning base metals into gold or discovering a formula for a 'philosopher's stone,' or 'elixir of life' that had the power to restore health and confer immortal human life. Zosimos claimed that alchemy originated with the priests of the Pharaohs and played a part in the magic that was practiced in ancient Egypt, but that claim is impossible to prove. However, the practice has a known history of at least four thousand years and spread throughout China, India, the Islamic world, Egypt and medieval Europe.

Alchemy was ubiquitous throughout Europe from the 13th to the 18th century, and was viewed as a legitimate science of distillation. Books and pamphlets on alchemical topics were readily accessible, and were eagerly read by both the intellectually elite and the middle class. Doctors, apothecaries and housewives all concocted healing substances by means of distillation. Even churchmen embraced the quest for the 'elixir of life,' which they thought would literally return humans to the perfection of a second Eden.

The processes of alchemy were based on the theory of transmutation, which proposed that all matter consisted of four basic elements; earth, air, fire and water (a theory of Aristotle), and that these elements were all mutable or interchangeable. While this seems preposterous now, it must be remembered that during this period empirical evidence validated the theory; water could be transformed into ice and steam, acorns became mighty oak trees and caterpillars became butterflies. Also, a strong belief in transubstantiation (the belief that the wine and bread of Holy Communion literally become Christ's body and blood) no doubt strengthened these theories. From this point of view, it would not be a tremendous leap to believe that base metals could be turned into gold or an elixir of life could be distilled from plants. (Note: Using particle acceleration, scientists are currently able to turn small amounts of lead into gold, but the cost far exceeds the result.)

When Robert Boyle wrote a treatise entitled *The Skeptical Chemist* in 1661, his words fueled a chain reaction of doubt that eventually led to the rejection of the transmutation theory. As alchemy's scientific credibility declined, it gained renewed popularity when it was associated with the supernatural and occult. Currently, it's common to stamp anything that's even remotely transformative with the alchemical label and a wide variety of artists and New Age gurus of all types currently claim the title of alchemist. In the face of this gross misunderstanding and cheapening of alchemy's deepest meaning, Terrance McKenna pointed out, "Alchemy, as I'm sure many of you know, is really the secret tradition of the redemption of spirit from matter." When we put the magical and pseudo-scientific elements aside, we find there is a deeply spiritual aspect to alchemy that deserves our consideration. Ali Puli (aka Alipili) was the name associated with several

17th century alchemical texts. Whether he existed or not is unknown, but one of the texts attributed to him explained the spiritual element this way:

> *The highest wisdom consists in this, for man to know himself…therefore let high inquirers and searchers into the deep mysteries of nature learn first to know what they have in themselves, and by the divine power within them let them first heal themselves and transmute their own souls… I admonish you, whosoever you are, that desire to dive into the innermost parts of Nature, if you do not find what you seek within you, you will never find it outside you.*

In line with this quote, it's important to note that during alchemy's medieval heyday, the work done in the laboratory often served as a symbol, and/or a cover, for the real work of spiritual transformation. In some cases the deeply esoteric symbolism, steps and formulas were just another mystery school type ploy used to seek specialness through coopting and controlling information. But for others, alchemy became a spiritual necessity. The dense symbolism and difficulty of gaining admittance into the inner circle hid the actual intentions of many sincere spiritual seekers from the prying and dangerous eyes of an institutionalized church that wielded the power necessary to ruin, and/or end, lives. Many who were not content with the meager spiritual food the church was willing to parcel out, secretly sought their own experience of the Divine, and here we find the alchemical connection with gnosis.

On a spiritual level, alchemy was a metaphor that stood for the reunion of the lower self that identified with the human body and the higher/

true Self that identified with the Divine. Base metals symbolized the lower self, gold the true Self. Since it was thought that the qualities of gold were present in lesser metals, it followed that the true Self was hidden within the lowly human self. The point was to refine the metals (the human self) until everything that was base and incompatible with gold (the true Self) was removed. This process was symbolized by a series of cycles that were repeated again and again, but on increasingly more subtle levels, until the goal of returning to Self was achieved. Just as Jesus taught that the end would be found in the beginning, the alchemist's work began and ended with *prima materia* (primal material), the seeming chaos that makes up the foundation of the universe. In other words, it was thought that the Self originated in this primal sea of energy, was somehow divided from it, and would only be in its proper state when it returned to the primal realm. Quantum physics has shown us that we can identify these states with the implicate and explicate orders of our holographic universe. The common alchemical motto: "*solve et coagula,*" or "divide and unite" describes this journey into duality and our return to unity.

Most alchemical books contain a staggering array of pictures and symbols that outline the process of transmutation, but the four basic steps of the *Opus Magnus* (Great Work) that were repeated until transformation took place are, *nigredo* (blackness), *albedo* (whiteness), *citrintas* (yellowing) and *rubedo* (redness). On a strictly spiritual level, *Nigredo* symbolized the alchemist's journey into darkness. This occurred when the beginner realized there must be a greater reality beyond the material world, and an identity that had nothing to do with either the body or personality. The alchemist was in darkness because s/he was shocked by this startling revelation, recalling Jesus' words in *The Gospel of Thomas*, "When one finds, one will be astonished." Although the alchemist was becoming aware of the *prima materia*, s/he did not yet understand their own relationship to it and still felt separate from it. *Nigredo* can also be likened to the state of despair that can hit before full spiritual awakening takes place or an odd sense of displacement one may feel as the 'reality' of the material world begins to fall away.

In the second step, the whiteness of *albedo* shed light on the alchemist's growing awareness that the self and the Self are at odds with one another. Since harmony could not be achieved if this dichotomy remained, the alchemist was charged with bringing about a resolution of opposites. The third step, where *albedo* changes to *citrinitas* was symbolized by the transmutation of silver into gold. It signified the realization that the Self is pure light, or the understanding that a 'soul light' is inherent in one's being. Since the philosopher's stone was usually thought of as red, it was fitting that the final step would be *rubedo*. Why? The stone (or egg) was considered to be both an integral agent of alchemical transmutation and a vessel within which that transformation could take place, but it also symbolized the ultimate goal of the work. Carl Jung discovered that throughout the history of alchemy this stone symbolized, "something that can never be lost or dissolved, something eternal… a mystical experience, a symbol of something that can be found only within man."

Like Jung, many sages have described the

Divine/Truth/Reality (also symbolized by the philosopher's stone) as something that we are unaware of even though it is always within us. The 17th century alchemist Barclus wrote that the stone was, "…familiar to all men, both young and old, is found in the country, in the village, in the town, in all things created by God, yet it is despised by all. Rich and poor handle it every day. It is cast into the street by serving maids, children play with it, yet no one prizes it." In *The Gospel of Thomas* Jesus used similar symbolism when he said, "The kingdom is like a person who had a treasure hidden in his field and did not know it. And when he died, he left it to his son. The son did not know about it. He took over the field and sold it. The buyer went plowing, discovered the treasure, and began to lend money at interest to whomever he wished." Although the treasure was right under their feet, the first two owners were oblivious to its existence. The third owner, obviously interested in the field, put out the energy needed to 'plow' and was rewarded for his desire to know what was below the surface. This treasure, like the philosopher's stone, is the key to the resolution of opposites. Like the yin/yang that resolves all opposites in harmony, the philosopher's stone is the restored, harmonious Self. No longer divided between the material and the spiritual, no longer trapped in a dualistic thought system; the Self manifests in wholeness and is one with the Divine *prima materia*.

Hermes Trismegistus, who we met earlier in our discussion on Hermeticism, was also a central figure in alchemy. As you'll remember, the name was derived from the Egyptian god Thoth and the Greek god Hermes. Hermes was also a generic term for any Greek deity and was represented by a plain stone pillar with a carved head atop it. The stone was thought to be a place where one could communicate with the deities and eventually Hermes was associated with knowledge. Ironically, the term 'hermetically sealed' comes from the ancient belief that Hermes Trismegistus invented a magic seal that rendered vessels impervious to external influence. It's likely that the term also referred to how tightly ancient secrets were guarded.

The writings attributed to Hermes Trismegistus probably passed through many hands during the long hermetic, alchemical and pagan gnostic traditions. One of these texts, known as *Poimandres* (*Shepherd of Man*) highlights many of the spiritual ideas included in both alchemy and gnosis. As the text opens, the writer begins to realize there is something within him that exists beyond his physical form. A vista beyond the material opens up and he sees, "All was light, a soothing and happy light." Later he reveals, "Light and life are God...and if you learn that you are also made of Light and Life, you will return to light and life." Logically, the writer then asks the question, "Why have you accepted death when you have been given the power to enjoy immortality?"

The work also includes a description of gnosis with the author experiencing the Divine as infinite Light, "...that which is unpolluted, which has no limit, no color, no form, is motionless, naked, shining, which can only be apprehended by Itself, the unalterable Good, the Incorporeal...this Light is I, Myself." Not only does he discover that he is one with the Divine, "The energies which operate in [the universe] are parts of God. Whether you speak of matter or bodies or substance, know that all these are the energy of God, of the God who is All. In the All there is nothing which is not God."

The author discovers how to resolve the conflict between the material and spiritual when he's told, "First, with the dissolution of your material body, you yield your character…your image vanishes… the bodily senses…become part of the cosmos, and , combined in new ways, do other work…the body's sleep becomes the soul's awakening." As the text informs us, the writer follows the instructions, letting go of his identification with the body and senses, and his willingness is rewarded by "the soul's awakening." He goes on to say, "The closing of my eyes became the true vision…I became God-inspired, God-Minded, and came with the Truth." He prays, "Let me not be removed from Gnosis… with your grace, let me bring Light," because, "This is the good, the aim of those who have gnosis: to become God." As you can discern from these words, the Divine is the whole, the foundation or *prima materia* and the goal is a return to oneness with All That Is.

This story of gnosis and transformation brings to mind the alchemical symbol of the snake swallowing its tail; the Ouroboros (which may also be spelled Oroborus, Uroboros or Uroburus). You may have noticed that we've named our publishing company "Oroborus Books." This symbol was first seen in Egypt in the 14th century BCE and has been used throughout the world ever since, with a slightly different meaning in each culture. For alchemists, the drawing symbolized the cyclical alchemical process of destruction and regeneration that's a necessary part of letting go of the little, false self and returning to the Divine Self. Some have likened this cyclical process to climbing a spiral staircase within a tower. We keep passing the same truths over and over again, but each step up takes us to a higher level of understanding.

Like the phoenix that rises from its own ashes, the ouroboros also reflects the cyclical nature of the universe and the constant exchange between energy and matter. Spiritually speaking, the phoenix and Ouroboros picture the mortal self returning to the eternal and immortal Self. Alchemists also used the unbroken circle of the snake's body as a symbol for the oneness and interdependence of everything in existence. Some early Christians used the inside of the serpent to symbolize the confines of the material world and the outside to symbolize the unlimited nature of spirit. Gnostics sometimes painted one half of the serpent black and the other white, symbolizing the dualistic plane of physical existence. But for them, the Ouroboros also symbolized a continuum or integration of those dualistic opposites which culminates in our return to the whole. In a 2nd century alchemical text the words *hen to pan*, literally 'one, the all' or 'All is One,' were written inside the Ouroboros.

1. *The Kybalion*

Although we've had to condense and simplify our coverage of alchemy, we would be remiss if we failed to mention *The Kybalion*, a small book originally published anonymously in 1908 by the "Three Initiates." Although scholars feel certain Hermes Trismegistus represented a group rather than a single person, the authors of *The Kybalion* claim this slim volume contains the direct wisdom of that ancient sage:

The original truths taught by [Hermes] have been kept intact in their original purity by a few men in each age, who, refusing great numbers of half-developed students and followers, followed the Hermetic custom and reserved their truth for the few who were ready to comprehend and master it. From lip to ear the truth has been handed down among the few...There have always been a few Initiates in each generation, in the various lands of the earth, who kept alive the sacred flame of the Hermetic Teachings...Even to this day, we use the term "hermetic" in the sense of "secret," sealed so that nothing can escape...the followers of Hermes always observed the principle of secrecy in their teaching.

As you can see, *The Kybalion* clings to the *prisca theologia*, the mystery school structure and defines gnosis as receiving secret knowledge or 'being in the know.' However, the book also focuses on something it calls "mental alchemy" and claims "true Hermetic transmutation is a mental art," because "The ALL is Mind; the universe is mental... The Underlying Reality of the Universe is Mind; and the Universe itself is...existing in the Mind of THE ALL.... The infinite Mind of The All is the womb of all universes." These lines fit nicely with our quantum understanding of the Divine as consciousness that contains the oneness of everything in existence. On the other hand, many devotees of *The Kybalion* confine "mental alchemy" to the material plane and consider it to be the art of transmuting one's own mental states as well as manipulating the minds of others. For that reason, it should come as no surprise *The Kybalion* is currently credited with inspiring a wide range of New Age mysticism, including the law of attraction, visualization, power of intention and self-help psychology. However, the "mental alchemy" of *The Kybalion* also appears to fall near the fundamental definition of gnosis when it says:

> *The universe is in the nature of an illusion, a dream, a phantasmagoria as compared to THE ALL in itself...Anything that has a beginning and an ending must be, in a sense, unreal and untrue.*

> *From the Absolute point of view, there is nothing Real except THE ALL...to mortals this Universe of Mentality is very real indeed...but not until THE ALL finally withdraws us into itself does the vision actually vanish.*

> *Do not feel insecure or afraid — we are all held firmly in the infinite mind of THE ALL, and there is naught to hurt us or for us to fear. There is no power outside of THE ALL to affect us.*

> *All are on the Path, whose end is THE ALL...All progress is a returning home.*

IV. Carl Jung

A name that became synonymous with both alchemy and gnosis during the 20th century was that of the Swiss psychiatrist Carl Jung. Although the Nag Hammadi library was not available to him, Jung was completely enamored of the few Gnostic writings that were accessible. Unfortunately, many of these texts were inaccurate accounts written by early church fathers attacking gnosis. Based on these texts, Jung questioned whether Gnosticism was a religion or an early form of psychology. He concluded it could be both, and as such, he believed that each could complement the other. However,

Jung was frustrated by the apparent lack of a bridge that could span the gap between ancient gnostic secrets and the modern world. Intuitively, he began to feel that the link might be found in alchemy. He believed that his hunch had been vindicated when a colleague sent him *The Secret of the Golden Flower*, a treatise on Chinese Taoist alchemy. This writing linked the alchemical quest for the golden flower, similar to the the philosopher's stone, with personal/spiritual transmutation. In Jung's opinion the 'metal' needed for this alchemical transformation was modern psychology and the alchemical process was a symbol for psychoanalysis.

Jung called his psychological/alchemical process "individuation." As the word implies, the process focused entirely on the integration of the evident and hidden aspects of the human being. Like the alchemist who released gold from base metals, Jung believed the psychologist would release the whole, healed individual from a shattered psyche, reconciling opposites and bringing meaning out of chaos. As we've learned, alchemy and gnosis associated with the perennial philosophy concentrated on refining or melting away anything that was not part of the immortal Self, which included identification with the mortal body and personality. Jung, on the other hand, felt that God would handle the final transmutation that took place at death, while psychiatry concentrated on personal transformation by healing the human psyche. Since Jung failed to appreciate the illusory nature of the material portion or the universe, he applied the words 'spiritual' and 'Self' on a purely material level, using the first to describe psychoanalysis and the second the healed individual/personality.

As we've learned from quantum physics and the sages, there is one consciousness, the One Mind of the Divine. The Divine and our true Self think with the One Mind. When we have divided off a portion of consciousness that no longer thinks from the whole, we're operating from the little, false self. Jung did not share this view; he equated consciousness with the brain's thought process but also identified something he called the unconscious mind. He divided this into two parts, the personal (which is individual and private) and the collective (which is shared by all). He felt that both forms of the unconscious mind directed a large percentage of human behavior, especially 'archetypes, a set of inherited thought patterns and symbolic images that evolved from past collective experience and continue to influence each of us.

You may also be familiar with two other concepts that Jung made popular, the persona and the ego. Jung explained that the persona was a mask that we all wear that allows us to connect with society without revealing who we are. He claimed the persona helps us to act in a manner that society accepts while hiding the desires, ideas or behaviors that it would not. However, Jung felt that this split was not without consequences and could cause serious mental problems. For Jung, the ego ordered each person's psychological qualities and allowed them to make sense of themselves, distinguish themselves from others and retain a sense of unique individuality.

As you read the last paragraph, you may have realized that Jung's ideas have permeated much of what we might label 'New Age' thinking and have been commonly misunderstood and misused.

Most spiritual teachers today confuse the ego with the little, false self. They counsel their students to overcome the ego, not realizing that it is a natural and necessary component of the human being that gives the body a sense of self and the will to preserve that self. In doing so, they fail to recognize the split that has actually taken place on a conscious level between the true Self/One Mind and the little, false self. Although the emotional trauma experienced by the body may also need attention, it's the split between the true Self/One Mind and the little, false self that requires the focused attention of sincere spiritual seekers.

Like Jung, most New Age spirituality focuses on improving every level of the human experience, equating 'having it all' on the material plane with spiritual development. As gratifying as having an enjoyable career, a fulfilling relationship and/or material comforts might be, they all remain transitory and we are still left with the question of who and what we actually are and whether or not there is more to life than what appears on the material plane. And sadly, this focus has also led us to combine 'body, mind and spirit' as if they were the same thing and accept the belief that they can be healed simultaneously if we take a yoga class, drink green tea or spend a day at the spa. Although it appears that we're experiencing a renaissance of spiritual interest, due to Jung's influence, much of it leads seekers in the opposite direction of the sages, enslaving us to the body rather than liberating the Self from it. It's impossible to know how Jung would have felt about that outcome, especially since he also made several comments that hint at an understanding of gnosis and alchemy apart from his psychological interests. Here are a few of those quotes:

The world is a kind of illusion...like a dream which seems a reality as long as we are in it... I know things and must hint at things which others apparently know nothing of, and for the most part do not want to know.

The only events in my life worth telling are those when the imperishable world erupted into this transitory one.

Although the Self is my origin, it is also the goal of my quest.

The way is within us, but not in gods, nor in teachings, nor in laws. Within us is the way, the truth, and the life...The knowledge of the heart is in no book and is not to be found in the mouth of any teacher...It is the inner work that reveals divine light...Who looks outside dreams. Who looks inside awakes.

I simply believe that some part of the human Self or Soul is not subject to the laws of space and time...They are only an illusion – time and space. And, so in a certain part of our psyche time does not exist at all.

One of the main functions of formalized religion is to protect people against a direct experience of God.

V. Mysticism

Mysticism is the art of union with Reality. The mystic is a person who has attained that union in greater or less degree; or who aims at and believes in such attainment — Evelyn Underhill (Christian mystic 1875-1941)

As we've emphasized throughout the book, the Divine experience is not the possession of any group and has not been limited to any time period. Our language and thought system encourages us to categorize and label, but doing so limits our understanding. As you've seen, if we limit ourselves to the gnosis defined by scholars we would miss the point; the same would be true of the label 'mystic.' Like the word gnosis, the word mystic has taken on several different meanings, one that's relevant to our discussion and several that are not.

The words mystic, mysticism and mysterious came from the Greek root *mu*, which meant 'silent' or 'mute,' and the adjective, *mystikos*, meaning 'to conceal.' In this context, the word was used to refer to the mystery schools and their practice of hidden secrets, steps and rituals. During the Middle Ages, the word was used to describe both religious and occult secrets and symbols. The *Stanford Encyclopedia of Philosophy* currently describes mysticism as "a constellation of distinctive practices, discourses, texts, institutions, traditions, and experiences aimed at human transformation, variously defined in different traditions." In that context, the definition is so abstract; it's open to virtually any usage. However, another of the original meanings, the one that's pertinent to our discussion, was "consciousness of the transcendent/ ultimate reality/God" and/or "union with the Absolute/Infinite/God." These definitions bring us to the point where the experience of gnosis and that of the mystic are interchangeable.

Those mystics fitting our last definition have existed on the fringes of virtually every established religion and, at times, at the center. During human history there has often been nowhere to go outside of state or institutionalized religion. In those cases, seekers of the Divine experience have not allowed their circumstantial or forced religious affiliations to stand in their way. Because they understand the illusory nature of the world and the insignificance of human rules, those who experience the Divine have rarely felt the need to martyr themselves in the name of belief. When many early Christians were martyred for refusing to burn a pinch of incense to the deified Roman Emperor, gnostic Christians complied in recognition of the fact that all are Divine. Nor should we ignore the words of a mystic/sage merely because the truths they speak are couched in religious terms. When we strip away the cultural and religious connotations, all their words, symbols and stories end up reflecting the same truths. As French philosopher and mystic Louis Claude de Saint-Martin (1743–1803) stated, "All mystics speak the same language, for they come from the same country." This is also the case when mystics have no religious or spiritual affiliation but come to gnosis through an overwhelming willingness to know truth, no matter where that may lead them. Richard Maurice Bucke (1837-1902) the author of *Cosmic Consciousness: A Study in the Evolution of the Human Mind* was just such a seeker.

Bucke, who was an adventurer in his youth, eventually studied medicine and psychiatry which led to his work in reforming the care of the mentally ill and the introduction of what is now known as occupational therapy. For some time, Bucke adhered to the positivist philosophy of Auguste Comte who professed that religion had been outmoded by science, the repository of all genuine knowledge. Despite his atheistic attitude, at the age of thirty-five, in a sudden and unexpected flash, Bucke experienced the Divine. Writing as if he were describing someone else's experience, Bucke explained what he experienced:

Into his brain streamed one momentary lightning-flash of the Brahmic Splendor which has ever since lighted his life; upon his heart fell one drop of Brahmic Bliss, leaving thence-forward for always an aftertaste of heaven...he saw and knew that the Cosmos is not dead matter but a living Presence, that the soul of man is immortal, that the universe is so built and ordered that without any peradventure (doubt) *all things work together for the good of each and all, that the foundation principle of the world is what we call love and the happiness of every one is, in the long run, absolutely certain. He learned more within the few seconds during which the illumination lasted than in previous months or even years of study, and that he learned much that no study could ever have taught. The illumination itself continued not more than a few moments, but its effects proved ineffaceable; it was impossible for him ever to forget what he at that time saw and knew; neither did he, or could he, ever doubt the truth of what was then presented to his mind.*

Because Bucke was both shocked and deeply affected by gnosis, he spent several years studying others who had similar 'cosmic' experiences. He came to several conclusions that ring true for mysticism/gnosis. The following is a list of these concepts accompanied by a complimentary quote from a sage:

» The experience always feels more real than life.

Like the appearance of silver in mother of pearl, the world seems real until the Self, the underlying reality, is realized — Shankara

» The foundation truths are the same for all experiencers even though they may be presented differently.

Theologians may quarrel, but the mystics of the world speak the same language — Meister Eckhart

» The experience moves you to good, to love and unity.

The consciousness in you and the consciousness in me, apparently two, really one, seek unity and that is love — Nisargadatta Maharaj

And some validation from the scientists:

Quantum physics says that everything is entirely connected, that underlying all of our physical reality as we understand it is an energy matrix of harmony and order, and honestly in the end –one physicist in particular, David Bohm said, we could call it "love." The energy that literally underlies all of physical reality is one of love — Dean Shrock, Ph.D

» Those that have experienced agree with and support one another's words.

In all ten directions of the universe, there is only one truth. When we see clearly, the great teachings are the same — Ryokan Taigu (Japanese Zen master (1758–1831)

Speaking of sages, there are no differences. It's only the bodies that are different. The Realization is the same — Satchidananda Saraswati (Indian sage 1914 – 2002)

Bucke also identified several key sensations and understandings that are innate to the divine experience. We'll find these same identifiers in the words of the mystics we'll examine in the remainder of this section:

» A feeling of being either within something infinite or that something infinite is within them.

There is no reality except the one contained within us. That is why so many people live such an unreal life. They take the images outside them for reality and never allow the world within to assert itself — Hermann Hesse (Nobel Prize in Literature 1877 – 1962)

The first peace, which is the most important, is that which comes within the souls of people when they realize their relationship, their oneness with the Universe and all its powers, and when they realize that at the center of the Universe dwells the Great Spirit, and that this center is really everywhere, it is within each of us — Black Elk (Medicine man/mystic of Oglala Lakota Sioux 1863-1950)

» An overwhelming feeling of peace and joy.

The Self is of the nature that is peaceful. The Self is of the nature of Existence-Consciousness-Bliss — Ribhu Gita

That which cannot change remains. The great peace, the deep silence, the hidden beauty of reality remains. While it cannot be conveyed through words, it is waiting for you to experience for yourself…The Self does not need to be put to rest. It is peace itself, not at peace. Only the mind is restless — Nisargadatta Maharaj

» The assurance that salvation comes from within.

Light the lamp within you…knock on yourself as upon a door and walk upon yourself as on a straight road. Open the door for yourself that you may know what is…Whatever you will open for yourself, you will open — Dialogue of the Savior

If you bring forth what is within you, what you have will save you — The Gospel of Thomas

» Sin does not exist.

God…said: "There is no man on this earth who needs a pardon from Me for there is really no such thing as sin — Hafiz

"What is the sin of the world?" Jesus replied, "There is no such thing as a sin…This is why you get sick and die; because you love what deceives you." — The Gospel of Mary

» Gnosis is an instantaneous intellectual illumination; a thought bundle of 'knowing' that does not involve language, the brain or senses. It offers a clear and sudden understanding of the meaning and purpose of the universe.

And while I stood there I saw more than I can tell and I understood more than I saw; for I was seeing in a sacred manner the shapes of all things in the spirit and the shape of all shapes as they must live together like one being — Black Elk

You cannot mistake light coming from the Source, for it comes with complete understanding — Peace Pilgrim (mystic and peace activist Mildred Norman 1908-1981)

A single understanding, "I am the One Awareness," consumes all suffering in the fire of an instant. Be happy — Ashtavakra Gita

Just as knowing a rope to be a rope destroys the illusion it's a snake, Maya is destroyed by the direct experience of the Divine — Shankara

6. Knowing that everything is alive, and the universe itself is a living presence.

Nature is a living system, so sacred that those who use it profanely will surely lose it; and to lose nature is to lose ourselves — Lao-Tzu

All things are living, even stones. It has to be that way...since all are part of the Omnipresent Living Being — Hafiz

» The feeling of universal Oneness.

We are but one thread...Whatever we do to the

web, we do to ourselves. All things are bound together. All things connect — Chief Seattle (Duwamish tribe 1780-1866)

We do not inhabit detached residences, but are parts of a vast spiritual organism — Evelyn Underhill

Constantly I think of the Universe as one living creature, embracing one being and one soul; how all is absorbed into the one consciousness of this living creature; how it encompasses all things with a single purpose, and how all things work together to cause all that comes to pass, with their wonderful web and texture — Marcus Aurelius (Roman Emperor, philosopher and author of *Meditations* 121 — 180 AD)

And something from a scientist/mystic:

We are held together like the stars-in firmament with ties inseparable — these ties cannot be seen but we can feel them — each of us is only part of a whole — Nikola Tesla

» Consciousness is the foundation of the Universe.

At the innermost depths there is one Consciousness, unchanging and the same... We do not pass through the material world; the material world passes through our eternal consciousness — Plotinus

You are...the pure unchanging consciousness, which pervades everything. Your nature is bliss, your glory without stain — Shankara

When I say "I am," I do not mean a separate entity with a body...I mean the totality of being, the ocean of consciousness, the entire universe of all that is and knows — Nisargadatta Maharaj

You are only dreaming that you have a body of flesh. Your real self is light and consciousness... Our native land is omnipresence — Paramahansa Yogananda

Those who see the consciousness within themselves is the same consciousness within all beings attain eternal peace — Katha Upanishad

And something from the scientists:

Consciousness is a singular of which the plural is unknown...There is only ONE Thing, and what seems to be a plurality is merely a series of different aspects of this One Thing — Erwin Schrodinger

As far as this world is concerned, everything is structured in consciousness...consciousness is...the only absolute, unquestionable truth...the faculty of consciousness...is a primary quality of the cosmos, an intimate aspect of all existence.... consciousness is omnipresent — Peter Russell

Consciousness is the ground of all being, and quantum physics makes this as clear as daylight — Amit Goswami

» Knowing that everything *is* the Divine.

Like the waves in the ocean, the worlds arise, live and dissolve in the Supreme Self, the substance and cause of everything — Shankara

This spirit has poured himself out into everything, even into inorganic matter; he is present in metal and stone — Carl Jung

Can there be anything not known to That Who is the One in All? Know the One, know all — Katha Upanishad

» The realization that we cannot be anything other than the Divine.

Like can only apprehend like; when you thus cease to be finite, you become one with the Infinite. It is in the reduction of your soul to its simplest Self, its Divine essence, you realize this union – this identity — Plotinus

Everything is the undifferentiated Absolute Supreme Being which is not different from the Self and oneself — Ribhu Gita

When the mysterious Unity between the soul and the Divine becomes clear, you will realize that you are none other than God. You will see all your actions as His actions; all you features as His features; all your breaths as His breath — Ibn al Arabi (Sufi mystic/poet 1165-1240)

» Knowing that everything is Love.

There is no movement in the universe which is not a movement of love — Ibn al Arabi

Everything has being because of God's love... God is all love and wants to love all... We have always been in God's foreknowledge, known and loved without beginning...We were made for love — Julian of Norwich (Christian mystic and author of *Revelations of Divine Love*, the first English language book known to have been written by a woman 1342—1416)

The Lord of Love dwells in the hearts of all— Taittiriya Upanishad

The Supreme is Love itself—Plotinus

» Realizing there is no death.

This place is a dream only a sleeper considers real then death comes like dawn and you wake up laughing at what you thought was your grief— Rumi

What is birth and death but the beginning and ending of a stream of events in Consciousness— Nisargadatta Maharaj

When you become clear that you are not this body, but that it is your instrument, then worries about death dissolve. In essence, death dies— The Lost Writings of Wu Hsin (2nd to 4th century BCE)

In all creation, be assured, there is no death – no death, but only change...What we people call birth is but a different new beginning; death is but to cease to be the same— Pythagoras

Death is not extinguishing the light. It is only putting out the lamp because dawn has come— Rabindranath Tagore (mystic/poet, Nobel Prize for Literature 1861—1941)

» The experiencer is radically changed by the experience and can no longer live as they once had. This change can appear shocking, leading some to believe the experiencer has become god-like while others decide (s)he has gone crazy.

Jesus was a prime example of someone completely changed by gnosis/mysticism. He had been raised in a legalistic culture bent on judgment, a society that lived by the law of "an eye for an eye." How shocking it must have been when he began teaching his followers to love their enemies and to offer mercy rather than sacrifice! At one point Jesus may have hoped for a cosmic judge/savior and a literal kingdom, but as we can see in both *The Gospel of Thomas* and in the *New Testament* gospels, he came to know that God's kingdom is everywhere and that we each must act as our own savior. Since he understood that rules and sin were both human concepts, he had no problem breaking religious laws when they stood in the way of love. Its little wonder that his family believed he had lost his mind and tried to stop his preaching work or that religious and political powers feared his liberating message. Regardless of how inspiring we find Jesus' teachings, it's important to remember that he was only one of a countless multitude who have experienced the Divine and dedicated the remainder of their projected life in the material realm to encouraging others to do the same. As we said earlier, it would be impossible to create a book that could contain all their words, and it would be far better for you to have your own experience than to spend your life reading about theirs. Nonetheless, they would not have bothered to speak or write if they did not feel that their experience could be an inspiration for yours.

1. Sufi Mystics

For the remainder of this section, we'll take a closer look at several seekers whose lives were dramatically changed through gnosis/mysticism. We'll begin with the Sufi mystics Hafiz, Hakim Sanai, Rabia, Attar, and Rumi. It should be mentioned that while most Westerners think of Sufism as a branch of Islam, but this is not a description Sufis would embrace. Daniel Ladinsky, who has expertly translated many of Hafiz's poems explains, "Sufis themselves say their 'way' has always existed, under many names, in many lands, associated with the mystical dimension of every spiritual system" As you can see, we're continually drawn back to the perennial philosophy, and in turn, to gnosis. For Sufis, gnosis (*marifa*) connotes attainment, union, 'knowing' that illuminates and ultimately God-knowing (*marifa Alla*) that takes place in union with the Divine. This progression was called Unveiling *(kashf)* for the veils are lifted from one's eyes until one beholds Reality. The sage Ibn al Arabi spoke of four 'stages' many seekers experience on the spiritual path:

1. *Shariah*: Belief has its foundation in religious law; the seeker sees things in terms of separation and "yours *or* mine."

2. *Tariqah*: Stepping away from religion, the seeker enters the mystical path and sees things as "yours *and* mine."

3. *Haqiqah*: Truth enters the seeker's life; detached from the world, (s)he realizes all things are from the Divine. There is no "mine and/or yours."

4. *Marifah*: Gnosis reveals that there is "no me and no you" since nothing can be separate from the Divine. As Rumi so elegantly put it, "I used to think that love and beloved are different. I know now they are the same. I was seeing two in one."

As you read the following accounts, you'll quickly see that the Sufi 'path' has always been love. As

Rumi confirmed, "A step toward your own heart is a step toward the Beloved...Be drunk in love, for love is all that exists, without the commerce of love there is no admittance to the Beloved."

Hafiz: Divine Drunkard

Shams ud-Din Muhammad, a 14th century Persian Sufi, was known as Hafiz, a name that means "one who can recite the entire Koran." Although 500-700 of Hafiz's poems have survived, it's said that these comprise only ten percent of his work. As Daniel Ladinsky explains, "The vast majority of his work is said to have been destroyed by clerics and rulers who disapproved of the content...Hafiz was viewed as a great threat, a spiritual rebel, whose insights emancipate his readers from the clutches of those in power — those who exploit an innocent with insane religions propaganda." At times his poems were 'blacklisted' and he was exiled for several years by fundamentalists who claimed it was impossible to approach or experience the Divine. But as Ladinsky shares, "Hafiz reveals a God...that would never cripple us with guilt or control us with fear...To Hafiz, God is Someone we can meet, enter, and eternally explore."

Hafiz is considered one of the world's greatest mystic poets, and a grandmaster of wit and symbolism. The symbols he used served not only as a teaching tool, but a way to keep his true meaning secret from the prying eyes of fundamentalist fanatics. (Note: using symbols to escape persecution has no connection to the symbolism used by mystery schools to create secrets and confer specialness.) In his poems, Hafiz portrayed himself as a scandalous drunk who spent most of his time in taverns. In fact, he invited everyone to join in the revelry. His fellow seekers, who were forced to meet together in secret, understood the symbols and were happy to take part in his 'sins.' You'll see why in the following excerpts from several of his poems:

> *Come, let's get drunk, even if it is our ruin; for sometimes under ruins one finds treasure...Like Hafiz, drink your wine to the sound of harp-strings...Bring your cup near me, for I am a sweet old vagabond with an infinite leaking barrel of Light and Laughter and Truth... I am Blissful, and Drunk and Overflowing.*

Some religions do use wine as part of their worship, but Hafiz is clearly not speaking about religious services. And considering the fact that Islam forbids the use of wine or any other intoxicants, these word pictures could be very confusing if we took them literally. Instead, Hafiz used these symbols to describe his own personal experience of the Divine. After meeting the Divine, Hafiz was intoxicated by the love he had experienced, and his poetry bubbled over with that love:

> *Now all Hafiz wants to do is open a beautiful tavern where this Sacred Wine of God's Truth, Knowledge and Love is forever and ever freely offered to you...With a wonderful God...why isn't everyone a screaming drunk?*

In Hafiz's poems, wine symbolizes the 'knowing' that came out of gnosis. In contrast, it's interesting to note that in *The Gospel of Thomas*, Jesus called those who *had not* experienced the Divine drunkards. This may seem to be the opposite of what Hafiz is saying, but the important point is that both masters are observing a distinct difference in awareness between those who have experienced the Divine and those who haven't. Each master used symbols to tell us that separation from the One Mind alters consciousness and the direct experience of the Divine returns it to its original state. Whether we compare gnosis to sobering up or getting drunk doesn't matter as much as the recognition of the undeniable change that takes place.

On the surface, Hafiz's references to the wine shop or the tavern appear to symbolize the secret meeting places of those escaping rabid fundamentalists. But more importantly, he was calling attention to a meeting of the minds that takes place between all who have experienced the Divine. The wine seller can be understood two ways, as either the Divine, or as a symbol for the spiritual master who is dispensing truth. Although Hafiz was clearly a master, he often portrayed himself as a student. He is correct in claiming both roles, since learning in an infinite universe doesn't stop when one has attained mastery over the little self.

The wine symbolized the 'knowing' that can come only though gnosis because it's impossible to become drunk on Divine love until we actually drink it. As Hafiz explained, "If you think that the Truth can be known from words...someone should start laughing, someone should start wildly laughing — Now!" Of course we can't really say that the seeker is imbibing, or taking in, the Divine since we are already one with our Source. Instead, the seeker imbibes the wine of the Divine by waking up to this forgotten truth. Anyone who enjoys wine knows there is a difference between new and aged wine. For Hafiz, aged wine symbolized those who had attained mastery over the illusionary self and lived in constant awareness of their oneness with everything in existence. The cup also symbolized the Divine experience because it held everything the seeker desired.

Hafiz regularly spoke of the Divine in the words of a lover. This familiarity certainly offended the fundamentalists of his day, but it may also sound far too intimate for Christians who have been taught that God is a separate being who should be feared, obeyed and held in awe. However, Hafiz pointed out that we are already intimately connected with the Divine when he said, "I do not want to touch any object in this world without my eyes testifying to the truth that everything is my Beloved…Because there is nothing outside of my Master's body, I try to show reverence to all things."

Hafiz asks us to abandon the restraints of conventional religion and surrender to the infinite and absolute beauty of Divine love and oneness. He said, "I run to kiss our beautiful Friend and I dissolve in the Truth that I Am." Hafiz also used the symbolism of physical ecstasy to entice us into gnosis. Like so many sages, he used something that we can already understand to draw us toward something we do not yet understand. What appears to be a description of sexual union represents the mystic's ecstatic absorption into Source:

Let thought become the beautiful Woman. Cultivate your mind and heart to that depth that it can give you everything a warm body can. Why just keep making love with god's child— form when the Friend Himself is standing before us so open-armed? My dear, let prayer become your beautiful Lover and become free, become

free of this whole world like Hafiz — translation
by Daniel Ladinsky

Like many other Sufi poets, Hafiz likened the absolute beauty of the Divine to a rose, and awareness of the presence of the Divine to entering a rose garden. Instead of using a title that kept Source at a distance, Hafiz addressed the Divine as the Friend or the Beloved. Any misery involved in this relationship appeared only when Hafiz felt that he was the one who had distanced himself. At those times, he spoke of himself as a nightingale that was hopelessly in love with the rose or used the symbol of a reed that had been pulled from the reed bed and carved into a flute. The flute can only make a sound because it is hollow, a sound that replicated the hollow feeling of separation from the Divine.

Although we're centuries apart, Hafiz's words sound as if they were written yesterday. He stands as a surety that we can, and must, meet the Divine directly. Hafiz cried out to each of us, letting us know that The Beloved is not separate or far off. He invited us to make that discovery and join him in the ecstasy of oneness:

We have not come here to take prisoners, but to surrender ever more deeply to freedom and joy. We have not come into this exquisite world to hold ourselves hostage from love. Run like hell my dear, from anyone likely to put a sharp knife into the sacred, tender vision of your beautiful heart. For we have not come here to take prisoners or to confine our wondrous spirits, but to experience ever and ever more deeply our divine courage, freedom and light! — translation by Daniel Ladinsky

If you are interested in reading more of Hafiz's poetry, we recommend translations by Daniel Ladinsky, who has a lovely talent for bringing Hafiz's brilliant wit to life. For example:

We all sit in God's classroom. Now, the only thing left for us to do, my dear, is to stop throwing spitballs for a while.

Learn to recognize the counterfeit coins that may buy you just a moment of pleasure but then drag you for days...behind a farting camel.

No one but a rebel can get their mitts on God. At some point you will have to wean yourself from the pack.

Hakim Sanai: *The Walled Garden of Truth*

Imagine attending a concert performed by one of your favorite bands or symphonies. You've been anticipating the music they're about to play but when the first notes are sounded, it's obvious something is very wrong. Each of the instruments the musicians are playing is missing a string, a key or some other essential part. Although you're hearing many of the notes the group was supposed to play, the result is jarring and unsatisfying. Now picture each of us as a note in a Divine, universal instrument. If some of the notes are missing, the sublime harmony of universal love cannot be expressed as a satisfying whole. Based on the personal experience that changed his life, Hakim Sanai explained that Divine music is played within a walled garden. Until we choose to enter the garden and join in, our essential notes cannot be heard.

Sanai, like all other sages and mystics, began his spiritual journey in the world outside the garden. He had gained fame as the court poet of the Sultan of Ghazni. As such, it was his duty to write poetic histories that sang the praises of the Sultan and immortalized his victories. In this exalted capacity, Sanai accompanied the Sultan and his army on a mission of conquest across India. As the great caravan passed a walled garden Sanai heard a melody so sweet; it pierced his heart with an ecstasy he had never known before. Although he felt compelled to investigate, the rest of the vast company was disinterested and irritated by the 'horrible racket' they heard.

When Sanai saw the musician responsible for the glorious music, he appeared to be an incorrigible drunk. Although it's considered a sin for Muslims to drink alcohol, the tipsy musician called for wine so he could toast the passing Sultan. Of course the Sultan expected high praise; after all, who would offer anything less to one who could so easily end their life? But this was no ordinary drunk; it was Lai-Khur, a renowned, yet notorious, Sufi mystic. Instead of praise, Lai-Khur toasted the Sultan's blindness in going off to attack India when Ghazni itself contained infinite beauty. If that were not enough, he called for a second toast to the "even greater blindness" of Hakim Sanai!

Before we discover what happened next, it's important that we look past the surface of the story. The meeting between a 'crazy' mystic and two great men could easily be written off as dead history, but Sanai's symbolic language recalls the timeless story of spiritual awakening. As we already learned in our discussion of Hafiz, the walled garden symbolized something far greater than a few flower beds inside a fence. Even the English word paradise evolved from old French, Latin and Greek words that described an 'enclosed park.' Many use the words heaven and paradise interchangeably, but for Sufis, this walled 'paradise' garden symbolized gnosis; the sublime spiritual state of oneness with the Divine.

It's common for us to think of a wall or enclosure as something that's been constructed to keep others out, but in this case there's an opposite meaning. This wall is a barricade the little self constructs to confine the Divine music and keep it from reaching our heart and luring us back to join in the Divine song. The stones of the wall are made up of all the strategies the little self uses to convince us that we'll be happier outside the garden independently playing our own music. The wall also signifies the fact that we must each make a conscious free will choice to enter or remain outside.

As you've probably already figured out, Lai-Khur was drunk, not on literal wine, but on gnosis. In the book *Essential Sufism* edited by James Fadiman and Robert Frager, they tell us this experience "…transports [the sage] to a higher, distinctly different level of consciousness" that "dissociates them from the ordinary world." Although the body Lai-Khur was projecting continued on, he had let go of the little self and was living fully as the Divine Self. From the standpoint of those who were outside the wall still enmeshed in this world, he appeared to be a raving lunatic and his music sounded discordant and unbearable. When Lai-Khur raised the cup of truth to 'toast' the Sultan and his poet, he wasn't condemning them for 'sinful' actions, but was pointing out their spiritual blindness. When Lai-Khur spoke of the Sultan's planned invasion of India, he was not condemning his greed. Rather, he was alluding to the fact that the Sultan had missedthe point when he set his heart on conquering what was outside him instead of realizing the real prize was already within.

Sanai may have secretly agreed that the Sultan was greedy and foolish, but he certainly wasn't prepared to have Lai-Khur accuse him of being even worse! The Sultan was well aware of his own greed for power and riches, but Sanai was fooling himself. Sanai took great pride in his own godly devotion and virtuous behavior, but that was the problem. His religious obedience was based on his desire to establish his own righteousness and gain the admiration of others. Regardless, he had allowed Lai-Khur's exquisite music to enter his heart, and his spiritual eyes were opened. He suddenly saw that he had been as deeply asleep as the Sultan, and just as attached to the world of separation and specialness. He realized that if he were to enter the garden, he would have to be the one to tear down the wall of separation that he had erected to keep himself from Oneness with All That Is.

Without delay, Sanai resigned his position as court poet. The Sultan, who couldn't imagine what insanity had suddenly overtaken his friend, offered Sanai his daughter and half his kingdom if he would stay. But what had once held great value for Sinai now was completely valueless. After leaving the Sultan, Sanai set off on a pilgrimage that was both literal and spiritual. He continued to open himself to one insight after another until he had mastered the little, false self. When he returned to Lai-Khur, he was living as the Divine Self and he was ready to permanently enter the garden. As he discovered:

Being famous, or being a disgrace, who's ahead or behind, these considerations are rocks and clogged places that slow you.

My friend, everything existing exists through him; your own existence is a mere pretense. No more nonsense! Lose yourself, and the hell of your heart becomes a heaven.

When the path ignites a soul, there's no remaining in place. The foot touches ground, but not for long…The real road is found by polishing, polishing the mirror of your heart.

Hakim Sanai did not return to Lai-Khur empty handed. He had poured his experience of gnosis into a book, *The Walled Garden of Truth*. He joined his note to the music that continually drifts from behind the walls of the garden. Do you hear it? Will you join in?

We tried reasoning our way to him: it didn't work; but the moment we gave up, no obstacle remained. He introduced himself to us out of kindness: how else could we have known Him? Reason took us as far as the door; but it was His presence that let us in. But how will you ever know Him, as long as you are unable to know Yourself? Once one is one, no more, no less; error begins with duality; unity knows no error. The road your Self must journey on lies in polishing the mirror of your heart…Break free from the chains you have forged about yourself; for you will be free when you are free of clay —excerpt from The Walled Garden of Truth

Attar: *Conference of the Birds*

The works of the Sufi sage Abŭ Hamîd bin Abŭ Bakr Ibrâhîm (1145-1221) were relatively unknown until the 15th century. He was Hafiz's spiritual mentor, and as you'll recall, during that time mystics were forced to keep a low profile and veil their words in symbolism to avoid the wrath of religious authorities. But how did this highly educated son of a wealthy pharmacist go from operating his own pharmacy to becoming the sage known as Attar? Although many feel that attar means herbalist, druggist, perfumer or alchemist and the name connects him to his profession, it also means 'oil or essence of the rose.' Recall that Hafiz regularly used the rose to symbolize the absolute beauty of the Divine. In this usage, Attar chose this penname as a testimony to the fact that he had come to understand that he was one with the Divine. To more fully appreciate this change; let's go back to the story of his awakening.

Like Hakim Sanai, Attar was shocked into spiritual wakefulness. One day one of the successful pharmacist's ragged customers shocked Attar by accusing him of being more attached to his own prestige and the things the world had given him than he was to God. Attar, who had felt quite comfortable with his material and religious status, was stunned by the truthfulness of this unexpected revelation. He temporarily closed his shop to travel and contemplate his situation and when he returned, he was a changed man. Yes, it is possible that a literal journey may help us get away from the known and contemplate the unknown, but as every sage knows it's the 'travel' from sleep to wakefulness, from self to Self that matters. This is certainly the case in Attar's exquisite allegory *Conference of the Birds*.

As the story opens, the birds of the world have congregated to discuss the fact that they have no king. The flamboyantly crested Hoopoe bird suggests that the Simurgh, a bird so old it had risen from the flames of world destruction three times, would be a worthy candidate. Not only that, the Simurgh was said to possess all knowledge and contain the essence of the Divine. The Hoopoe explained that all birds are one with the Simurgh and if they find it, they will be immersed in its glorious presence. With those words, the search for a king was transformed into spiritual transformation through Divine gnosis.

Since the birds had congregated for the express purpose of finding a king, one might have expected them to set out immediately. But like humans who find many reasons to put off seeking the Divine, many of the birds offered objections and excuses. The Hoopoe warned his companions, "...so long as we identify with someone or something, we shall never be free. The spiritual way is not for those wrapped up in exterior life...If while living you fail to find yourself, to know yourself, how will you be able to understand the secret of your existence when you die?" Unfortunately, his words fell on many deaf ears and the vast majority chose to remain where they were. Those birds that did choose to accompany the Hoopoe on the quest would have to cross seven valleys, each valley representing a challenge to the little self:

1. The Valley of Quest: Anyone who sets out on a quest necessarily leaves much behind. In this valley, the birds freed themselves of whatever had once appeared to be precious to them, but now seemed valueless when compared to their goal. As we've learned, Sufis use wine to symbolize gnosis, and here the birds asked for wine so that the beliefs and dogmas that had ruled their lives might be dulled.

2. The Valley of Love: Here the birds began to understand that love is a state of being, not an emotion or anything that could possibly result from the brain's reasoning. Since Divine love has no exceptions or conditions, their love would have to widen out to include All That Is.

3. The Valley of Understanding: Instead of leaning on knowledge that resulted from the brain's collection of information, the birds begin to value the wisdom and understanding that came to them through the One Mind.

4. The Valley of Independence and Detachment: At this point, the birds realized that to finish the quest, they needed to let go of their attachments, aversions and preconceived notions. Instead of looking outside themselves, it was time for each of them to be their own savior.

5. The Valley of Unity: Here, the Hoopoe explained that the eyes deceive us by showing us a world of separation. In contrast, the heart's true vision reveals there is only One. The birds came to understand that separation and dualistic thinking could never take them to their goal, but only unity and oneness could.

6. The Valley of Astonishment and Bewilderment: The birds that dropped their dualistic thinking began to experience the oneness that has always existed beyond the illusion of separation. Unexpectedly they found themselves in the same condition as Jesus did when he said, "When one finds, one will be astonished."

7. The Valley of Deprivation and Death: The name of this valley can be deceptive since the only thing that 'dies' here is the little, false self and any potential future lives it may have projected. The birds that embraced unity were given an astonishing glimpse of oneness in the Valley of Astonishment but now those who were willing could choose to permanently drop the little self and enter into the Whole of Reality.

Of the thousands of birds that originally set out on the quest, only thirty reached their destination. Assuming they would be immediately, and triumphantly, ushered into the presence of Simurgh, they were stunned when a servant left them waiting outside. After all the birds had gone through; we might agree that their chagrin was justified. However, the significance of this wait becomes clear when we consider the symbolism that would have been understood by Attar and his readers. As Rumi wrote:

> *There came one and knocked at the door of the Beloved. And a voice answered and said, "Who is there?" The lover replied, "It is I." "Go hence," returned the voice; "'there is no room within for thee and me." Then came the lover a second time and knocked and again the voice demanded, "Who is there?" He answered, "It is thou."*

> *"Enter," said the voice, "for I am within." You must know...That the Beloved you seek is none other than you. Hold onto this truth and don't be afraid.*

Sages often pictured seekers standing outside a door as if they have been denied admittance, but this is not a door that has been constructed by the Divine. The seeker may wait some time for the door to be opened before they realize they had constructed the door themselves and barred it with the belief that they are different and separate from the Divine. Attar made the point clear when the birds were left to stand outside until it dawned on them that *they are Simurgh!*

This is the ultimate realization of oneness, when our own Divinity is accepted. The birds have annihilated the little self in the Oneness of Simurgh, but instead of being swallowed up, they now 'know' the infinite expanse of truth because they realized they *are* truth.

Here are a few more of Attar's observations exploring the connection of love and oneness:

> *Let us drown ourselves in the ocean of nonexistence and come out cloaked with the garment of divine existence...In Love no longer 'Thou' and 'I' exist, for self has passed away in the Beloved... Now will I draw aside the veil from Love, and in the temple of my inmost soul behold the Friend, Incomparable Love.*

> *He who would know the secret of both worlds will find that the secret of them both is Love... The Eternal wisdom made all things in Love. On Love they all depend, to Love all turn...What is*

the end of love? O simpleton, love has no end. Why? Because the Beloved has no end.

Tear apart the veils of all you see in this world, and you will find yourself in solitude with God. If you draw aside the veils of stars and spheres, you will see that all is one with the essence of your own pure soul. If you will but tear aside the veil, you will see nonexistence, and you will see the true meaning of God's purpose. When you have cast aside the veil, you will see the Essence, and all things will be shown forth within the Essence. If you draw aside the veil from the Face of the Beloved, all that is hidden will be made manifest, and you will become one with God, for then will you be the very Essence of the Divine.

Rumi and Rabia: The Love Mystics

There are as many paths to the Divine as there are seekers, but the Sufi path has always been one of love. But even among all those who seek in love, the ecstatic poetry of Rumi (Jalâl ad-Dîn Muhammad Rűmî, 1207-1273) usually comes to mind. First, let's travel back 500 years before Rumi's birth to meet Rabia (Rabia al-Adawiyya al-Qaysiyya, 717-801), a Sufi mystic poet who was one of his inspirations. Why was Rumi so drawn to Rabia's writings? It could have been the fact that Rabia was female, courageous and quite eccentric, but it's far more likely it was her radical view of love.

Although Rabia's name sounds beautiful to our ears, she was not so much named as numbered. Rabia literally means 'fourth' and designated her place as the fourth daughter in a poor family. Some tales claim that her family became so desperate they sold her into slavery. Others say that she left her family in Basra, Iraq when a famine hit and still others claim that she was stolen from her home. Most agree that a caravan she was travelling with was attacked by robbers, and she was sold to a brothel. Regardless of which story is accurate, the poverty, abuse and slavery of her body did nothing to dampen the spiritual fire blazing in in her heart.

When Rabia was about fifty years old, a wealthy man bought her freedom from the brothel. One story tells us that Rabia's patron was in love with her, but he was also well aware of her love for the Divine. When he offered her the choice of marriage and a fine house or freedom to follow her spiritual longings, he was not at all surprised that she chose freedom. Although her fame grew and both students and renowned religious leaders were drawn to her, she bucked the traditional religious tide. Like most of us, Rabia had been taught that God was to be feared. Unlike the religious leaders who used this fear as a tool of control, she courageously taught that God was not to be worshiped because of the fear of punishment in hell or the hope for a heavenly reward, but for love alone. To make her point, it is said that she once ran through the streets carrying a bucket of water and a torch, the water to put out the fires of hell and the torch to burn down concepts of rewards in paradise.

While religious leaders referred to their sacred books, Rabia said openly that her words carried more authority because she had experienced the Divine directly. She explained:

> *Speech is born out of longing, true description from the real taste. The one who tastes, knows; the one who explains, lies…When I entered God,*

my vision became like His, it flooded out over existence. I knew no limits…Until we know that God lives in us and we can see Him there, a great poverty we suffer.

Through gnosis Rabia had experienced the Divine as pure love and realized that we were created to share that love. Like Jesus' teachings on love, Rabia's words were revolutionary for their time, and are equally relevant today. And, like Jesus, Rabia accepted holy books only so far as they aligned with the Ultimate Reality she knew. One story tells us that a visiting Sufi wanted to read from Rabia's *Koran*, but was shocked to see that many of the verses had been altered. When the incensed visitor asked what had happened, Rabia explained that after she had experienced the Divine, she had to remove the words and verses that were not truthful. Although the visitor was furious over the sacrilege she had supposedly committed, Rabia retorted that the Divine was nothing but love, and that her own love had grown to the point that there was no longer room for hate, fear or even a need for hope. While many around her continued to believe that the things outside them could make them happy, Rabia remained joyful for a very different reason, saying, "My Beloved is always with me."

Once, when Rabia was asked for the secret of her understanding, she explained, "You know of the how, but I know of the how-less." Instead of relying on the 'how' of religion, Rabia willingly let go of her conditioning and preconceived notions so the Divine could instruct her firsthand. She made it clear that it was her direct, loving relationship with

Source that was of paramount importance when she said, "In my soul there is a temple, a shrine, a mosque, a church that dissolve, that dissolve in God."

Since hundreds of volumes have already been written about Rumi, it may appear redundant to add more. There is however, one important point to be made. Although most authors make the point that Rumi's life changed forever once he met the wandering sage Shams i-Tabrizi (1185 – 1248), few recognize the true impetus for that change. For several generations, Rumi's family had been Islamic scholars and preachers, so Rumi was educated to take part in the family business. When his father died, the twenty-five year old Rumi stepped into his place as the head of a religious school and went on to become an Islamic jurist and popular preacher in the mosques. When Rumi was a young man he had met Attar, who immediately recognized his sincere spiritual interest, but Rumi remained committed to his very conventional, prestigious and prosperous, religious vocation.

Shams is usually pictured as a wild dervish (ascetic), but he had studied religious law and he earned his living as a teacher. Author/translator of *Me & Rumi*, William C. Chittick, explains why Shams and Rumi's meeting had an irrevocable impact on both of them. Unlike his contemporaries, Shams "...certainly looked with contempt on the superficial learning and the pretensions of the *ulama* (scholars). In his view, they were traitors to their calling because they employed religious learning to make a living rather than to find God." And how did Shams think they should find God? Chittick tells us that Shams taught "...Students and seekers should be striving to achieve 'realization' (*tahqiq*), which is to know the reality of God for oneself and see all things as they actually and truly are." Rather than filling Rumi with more knowledge, Shams introduced him to gnosis.

There are several different stories about Sham's and Rumi's initial meeting, but the important point is that it caused Rumi to walk away from his prestigious religious and scholarly vocation. Rumi and Shams then entered a mystical retreat of oneness with the Divine that transfixed them for several years. This radical change was, to say the least, extremely unpopular with Rumi's family and religious community. They were determined to return Rumi to his previous life, even if it meant murdering Shams. When Shams went missing, Rumi mistakenly thought that he had lost Shams because the body Shams had projected was no longer present. Rumi was devastated by the loss until gnosis woke him to the fact that he could not be parted from Shams any more than he could be separated from the Divine. He immediately stopped mourning and said, "Why should I seek? I am the same as he. His essence speaks through me. I have been looking for myself!" From that time until his death, poetry and prose poured from Rumi's lips, much of which he attributed to Shams.

As we've found with all the Sufi writers, it's important to understand the system of symbols that they used. This is true of Rumi as well, but to capture the depth of his work we also need to realize that unlike spiritual authors who have not experienced the Divine, *none* of Rumi's words originated from the little, false self. Many associate his work with the glories of romantic love and the passions of the body, but Rumi's works come from the Self that has experienced the ecstasy of union with the Divine. Like Rabia, Rumi cautioned his many followers "Don't pretend to know something you haven't experienced."

Coleman Barks, one of Rumi's well-known translators, points out that Rumi's writings are grounded in *fana* and *baqa*, Arabic words that describe two phases of the ecstatic experience. The first, *fana*, is the ultra-orgasmic melding with the Divine. There is no place for the little self in this 'act of gnosis' that allows us to know beyond all doubt that the Self and the Divine are one. But as long as the body we have chosen to project continues on, it would be impossible to sustain *fana* indefinitely. This is where *baqa* comes in; when consciousness turns once again to the physical world, there is no need for the little self to regain control. In the state of *baqa*, which means 'living within;' the body continues as a shell, but the true Self is now the navigator. If we want to understand the poems as Rumi spoke them, it's helpful to keep these two states in mind. However, in both states Rumi's focus was always Divine love. As Rumi explained, "Love is beyond any condition. Love is fearless in the midst of the sea of fear. Love is the energizing elixir of the Universe, the cause and effect of all harmonies. Love said to me, 'There is nothing that is not me. Be silent.'" Let go of everything that is not love and cultivate a willingness to let the Divine instruct you directly and personally. Then you too can be a 'love mystic.'

2. Tao Mystics

The spiritual philosophy known as Tao dates back to sometime during the 4th to 6th centuries BCE. The first written text, the *Tao Te Ching*, may also be that old. It's not known whether the author Lao-tzu (meaning old master) was one person or many. The title was added some time after the text was written and literally translates as Tao (way) Te (virtue, divine power, inner potency) Ching (great book, classic, cannon). We can scramble those words around and come up with several variations, but the meaning boils down to 'The Great Book of the Way to the Divine.' This title could easily lead us to conclude that this 'way' is either a specific path or set of practices, but John Blofield (1913 – 1987), author of *Taoism: The Road to Immortality*, explained, "The Tao is just a convenient term for what can best be called the Nameless. Nothing can be said of it that does not detract from its fullness." In other words, the path, the one walking the path *and* the goal are one and the same. How can that be?

We know that Western religion endorses a God that's separate from creation, restricting humans to obedience and worship from a distance. But for many Eastern philosophies, separation is no more than a human delusion. Everything in existence is understood to be a manifestation of the Tao itself, and therefore, one with it. In that case, worship and obedience have no meaning while union with the One means everything.

Pottery decorations dating from the 5th century BCE illustrate sages who were said to leave their bodies in flights of vision. Following such a flight, the sage would be 'reborn,' fully transformed from self to

Self. The Tao reminds us that gnosis and a return to Source is something we are all capable of because we're all united by a 'drop of spirit' that dwells in the heart. This 'precious jewel' is not an individual possession, but is innate in all that exists. The *Tao Te Ching* asks, "Can you coax your mind from its wandering, keep to the original Oneness and not let go?" Like Jesus' words from the *Dialogue of the Savior*, "enlighten your mind...Light the lamp within you...knock on yourself as upon a door and walk upon yourself as on a straight road," Lao-tzu tells us:

> *The Way...is as deep as the source of all things... Use your own light and return to the source of light. This is called practicing eternity...The origin of the Great Way is the heavenly heart... the heavenly heart will spontaneously manifest itself...Since before time and space were, the Tao is. It is beyond is and is not. How do I know this is true? I look inside myself and see...Why is the Tao so valuable? Because it is everywhere, and everyone can use it. This is why those who seek will find...It is not up to another, but up to oneself; it is not up to anyone else. When one attains it, everything is included...Approach it and there is no beginning; follow it and there is no end. You can't know it, but you can be it.*

Like virtually all other truths that originated with gnosis, Tao eventually became an institutionalized 'ism' with sects and deities. Alchemical and yogic branches veered far from the original goal of throwing off illusion and focused instead on attaining immortality of the body. When Taoist teachings were bastardized, an unknown number of sages went underground and remained true to gnosis. In the writings of the Taoist master Chuang tzu, the golden threads of the perennial philosophy are obvious:

Gnosis:

All things become one, whatever their state of being. Only he who has transcended sees this oneness…Don't listen with your ears but with your heart…don't listen with your mind but with your spirit…The perfect man…carries his mind back to before the beginning. Content…in nowhere…merged in the infinite.

Onenss:

The sage…achieves simplicity in oneness. For him, all the ten thousand things…enfold each other…Those who, being completely unified with the Creator Himself, take delight in the realm of the original Unity before it is divided into Heaven and Earth…He who regards all things as One is a companion of nature.

Duality:

There is right because of wrong and wrong because of right. The best thing to do is look beyond right and wrong…When there is no more separation between 'this' and 'that,' it is called the still-point of the Tao. At the still-point in the center of the circle one can see the infinite in all things… When we understand, we are at the center of the circle – and there we sit while yes and no chase each other around the circumference… When the heart is right, 'for' and 'against' are forgotten.

Illusion:

> *Your preciousness lies in your essence; it cannot be lost by anything that happens...Someday there will be a great awakening when we know that this is all a great dream...Forget the years, forget distinctions. Leap into the boundless and make it your home.*

Quantum Reality:

> *That which gives life to all creation, yet which is, Itself, never drawn upon — that is the Tao... All things come from nowhere! How vast, how invisible. No way to explain it!*

Return to Source:

> *The wise flow with Tao in life and in death merge with the Oneness of all things.*

Most of the Tao sages wrote in the 'sayings' format we discovered in Q and several of the gnostic gospels, but as you discovered earlier Chuang tzu often taught with parables, some serious, many humorous, but all constructed to reach the heart. He illustrated the difference between the false self and true Self by comparing them to two frogs. The first frog had lived his entire life in a well. The well provided all the frog's needs; rain and light entered the opening at the top of the well and enough curious bugs flew in to keep the frog fed. Comfortable in his own little kingdom, the well frog had never imagined that anything existed outside it, or needed to. One pleasant afternoon, the well frog was shocked to see another frog peering over the edge of the well. The visiting frog, amazed by the narrow life of the well frog, tried to entice him from the well with a vivid description of the infinite and glorious ocean where he lived The well frog, who had never heard of a lake or a river, let alone an ocean, dismissed the wild ravings of the 'crazy' ocean frog and refused to give it another thought Of course Chuang tzu was making the point that this world, symbolized by the well, hides what lies beyond it. Like the well frog, we're content to live from the little self, mesmerized by what the body's senses tell us is real. When an ocean frog (a sage) comes along and tells us there's something more, how will we respond? The sage confronts each of us with the choice of deciding the sage is delusional or taking a look over the edge of our own little self-made well.

Lao-tzu wrote, "To become whole and return to the Source, one must be ever in accord with nature." Although most of the Tao sages did live as close to nature as possible, Lao tzu's words are better understood when we remember that the terms nature and Tao were used interchangeably. Anything that was not harmonious with Tao/nature was considered part of the illusion of the little self. By letting go of anything that was not in accord with Tao, the little self would eventually have no choice but to yield to Self. Lao tzu explained this method of waking up when he said, "Learning consists in adding to one's stock day by day. The practice of Tao consists in subtracting day by day." To that end, one of Tao's most important concepts became wu wei, the 'action of non-action,' 'going with the flow of Tao,' or as Alan Watts explained it, "getting out of our own way" and trusting Tao. Chuang tzu explained, "Easy is right. Begin right and you are easy. Continue easy, and you are right." The little self (and its sidekick, the brain) love complexity and struggle, but the sages recognized that truth is always the simple/easy/joyful/peaceful/loving course. Instead of struggling aligning oneself with the Tao completed the transformation to Self. In this state of being, the sage could not help but experience gnosis and at death the return to Source. As Lao Tzu stated, "Caught in desire, you see only the manifestations. Free from desire, you realize the mystery."

Some claim that the *Wen Tzu* (*Wenzi* or *Book of Master Wen*) was written by Lao-tzu, others say it's the product of one of his students. Initially scholars dismissed the text as a forgery but they could no longer deny its authenticity when archeologists found a copy while excavating a tomb dating to the 5th century BCE. If you read the *Wen Tzu*, it's helpful to keep in mind that it, like many of the gnostic gospels, displays the signs of an author who knew a sage that experienced gnosis but did not personally experience the Divine. Regardless, it does appear to be a commentary on, or expansion of, the *Tao Te Ching*, and thus contains several verses that point to gnosis. The *Wen Tzu* is also striking for the simple fact that the writer sounds as if he/she is describing the overwhelming problems of our day. Considering the fact that it was written before the 5th century BCE, it testifies to the fact that the problems caused by separation and specialness have existed continually throughout human history and cannot be solved as long as we cling to their cause.

A collection of sayings entitled *The Lost Writings of Wu Hsin*, is dated somewhere between the 4th and 2nd centuries BCE. Wu Hsin is literally translated 'no-mindedness' and probably describes the state of the anonymous sage who wrote it or the goal proposed by the text. Unfortunately, many take the concept of no-mindedness quite literally and feel that they must force the brain to stop its incessant chattering. Alan Watts described something quite different when he defined Tao no-mindedness as "a state of mind in which there is no sensation of a separate mind or separate thinker." From this standpoint, 'no-mindedness' necessitates living from the One Mind since the brain is programmed for duality/separation/illusion. Rather than wasting our energy on the impossible task of wresting the brain into submission, it's far easier and more effective to heed Wu Hsin's advice, "Thoughts intrude, like unwelcome guests at a party. Ignored and unfed, they depart...The solution to problems begins with the cessation in believing in the content of one's thoughts...Thoughts are not the problem...The goal is not cessation of thought, the goal is cessation of identification with thought." Or as Zen master Shunryu Suzuki put it, "Leave your front door and your back door open. Allow your thoughts to come and go. Just don't serve them tea."

Before we leave the Tao sages, let's take a brief look at the mark of gnosis evident in the *Wen Tzu* and *The Lost Writings of Wu Hsin*.

You are not the body:

The entire world is merely a play performed on your stage while you are seated in the front row...Identification with a body is the birth of the person, the individual. The personality then acts to protect the body from that which is other than itself. When this false identification is seen through, that which one truly is manifests and shines...When you become clear that you are not this body, but that it is your instrument, then worries about death dissolve. In essence, death dies — Wu Hsin

The physical body may pass away, but the spirit does not change. Use the unchanging to respond to changes — Wen-tzu

Duality:

In the cessation of duality, oneness is revealed. There can be no being one with...There is only being — Wu Hsin

Everything is mysteriously the same; nothing is wrong, nothing is right — Wen-tzu

Everything happens within consciousness:

When you can so readily create a world when you dream, why do you believe the impossibility of your creating another world when you are awake...There is no such thing as "out there." Just as a spider spins a web out from itself, so does each man spin his world out from himself. Seeing this is the beginning of the end — Wu Hsin

What gives birth to life is not itself born...what produces change does not itself change. This is... the path of quintessence — Wen-tzu

We are our own savior:

To know what one is requires a diving into the depths of one's own being. The pearl rests on the bottom — Wu Hsin

With the spirit, anything that is sought can be found... If you know the great and precious, where can you go and not succeed? — Wen-tzu

The true Self:

The world is a collection of objects. That which perceives the objects cannot itself be an object. You are That...Giving attention to What-Is and not giving attention to what appears to be, is the key to opening the prison door — Wu Hsin

Comprehending the fundamental, embracing the spirit...the sage roams the root of heaven and earth...beyond the dust and dirt — Wen-tzu

All is One:

What is the world other than numberless mirrors reflecting the light from a single source? From the One comes the many. As a baby nurses at its mother's breast, one must nurse at the Source of life's sustenance so that one may discover the essence of being — Wu Hsin

Those who are known as Real People...regard ten thousand differences as of one Source...The Way is so high there is nothing above it, so deep there is nothing below it. It is evener than a level, straighter than a plumb line, rounder than a compass, squarer than a ruler. It contains the universe but has no outside or inside; it is hollow like an overturned bowl and has no obstruction — Wen-tzu

Separation:

There is a belief of separateness, that you are separate from the rest. There is nothing you can

311

> *do to rid yourself of this belief because "you" is the belief...All individuals die. Only those who are no longer individuals live forever...The reconciliation of the feeling of separateness with the reality of unity is the enlightened view* — Wu Hsin

We return to our beginning:

> *There is no journey as such. It may not seem so, but we are always back where we started. What we were in essence, and what we will be in essence, is what we are in essence* — Wu Hsin

Gnosis:

> *Communion with the Way is like the axle of a carriage, which does not move itself yet enables the carriage to travel thousands of miles, turning on an inexhaustible basis* — Wu Hsin

3. Buddhist and Zen Mystics

Sometime between 563 and 400 BCE a prince, Siddhartha Gautama, left a life of ease determined to discover the cause of suffering, and more importantly, the means of liberating oneself from it. When he examined religion, he witnessed the unrelieved suffering of many devout worshippers and concluded it was pointless to search for a savior god. And in a collection of his sayings known as *The Dhammapada,* he exclaimed, "Gripped by fear men go to the sacred mountains, sacred groves, sacred trees and shrines," revealing that religion is itself a source of much suffering. After years of inner struggle, he came to the realization that "All that we are is the result of our thoughts. We are made of our thoughts; we are molded by our thoughts." If suffering began in the mind, then liberation also was of the mind. His philosophy of detachment (the Middle Way) proved effective and he became known as the Buddha, or 'awakened one.' Siddhartha's original teachings are strictly a nontheistic philosophy, but over time some have raised Buddha from teacher to god and turned his philosophy into a religion. However, it's important to note that although Buddha chose not to speak of either a personal or abstract god; his teachings do not prohibit or impede the spiritual seeker. As you've probably already realized, detachment from the brain's dualistic thinking is an important step toward reconnecting with Self. And in fact, many of Buddha's teachings echo the perennial philosophy:

Be a lamp to yourself. Be your own confidence. Hold to the truth within yourself, as the only truth...No one saves us but ourselves. No one can and no one may. We ourselves must walk the path...Work out your own salvation. Do not depend on others.

We are shaped by our thoughts; we become what we think. When the mind is pure, joy follows like a shadow that never leaves...Happiness does not depend on what you have or who you are, it solely relies on what you think.

Freed from illusion...they have renounced the world of appearance to find reality. Thus have they reached the highest...When one sees that everything exists as an illusion, one can live in a higher sphere than ordinary man.

All beings are already enlightened! It is only because of their delusions that they don't realize this.

Develop a power of love so strong that the mind becomes like space that cannot be tainted...You are far from the end of your journey. The way is not in the sky. The way is in the heart. See how you love.

Those who experience the unity of life see their own Self in all beings, and all beings in their own Self.

Jianzhi Sengcan (6th century), the Third Chinese Zen Patriarch also known as Seng-Ts'an or Sosan, was the author of *XinXin Ming* (*Hsin Hsin Ming*). The title of this text is usually translated "Faith in Mind," but some translators argue for something that hints at the difference between the brain and consciousness, "Verses on the Perfect Mind." Seng-Ts'an does support the Buddha's teachings on suffering, but he also points out that letting go of duality is a necessary step in discovering truth:

Indeed it is due to our choosing to accept or reject that we do not see the true nature of things...If you want to realize truth, don't be for or against. The struggle between good and evil is the primal disease of the mind...The great way has no impediments. It does not pick and choose. When you abandon attachment and aversion you see it plainly.

Why?

To return to the root is to find the meaning, but to pursue appearances is to lose their Source...

When no discriminating thoughts arise, the old mind ceases to exist...To seek Mind (the One Mind of God) *with the discriminating mind* (the brain) *is the greatest of all mistakes.*

Seng Ts'an went past the Buddha's teaching and came to know that the self/mind/brain and the Self/Mind/Consciousness are not the same. He saw that it's impossible to find the Self/consciousness with the brain since the brain itself is a projection of consciousness, and when we try; we miss Source/ One Mind. Obviously he spoke from his own direct experience since he came to know the One that exists behind all appearances:

Asserting that the world is real, you are blind to its deeper reality...The changes that appear to occur in the empty world we call real only because of our ignorance...As long as you remain in one extreme or the other you will never know Oneness...If the mind makes no discriminations, the ten thousand things are as they are, of single essence...One is all; all are one...One thing, all things: move among and intermingle without distinction. To live in this realization is to be without anxiety.

The Chinese Zen master Huang Po's (Huangbo Xiyun, 8th century) teachings also smack of gnosis. Although it was common to diligently study the words of Buddhist masters, Huang Po declared, "'Studying the Way' is just a figure of speech...In fact, the Way is not something which can be studied. You must not allow this name (The Way) to lead you into forming a mental concept of a road." Although Huang Po knew the Buddhist texts, when his students sought enlightenment within books he pointed them toward direct experience advising, "If it can be understood in this manner, then it isn't the true teaching. If it can be seen in paper and ink, then it's not the Essence." Like Seng Ts'an, Huang Po taught that the brain's dualistic thinking veils truth:

> *If you could eliminate all conceptual thinking, Source would appear, like the sun rising through the empty sky...Indulging in various practices...can't be compared to the elimination of conceptual thinking...So just discard all you have acquired...rid yourself of the whole gamut of dualistic concepts.*

He also spoke of the difference between the brain and consciousness and proclaimed that we are all of the One Mind of Source:

> *Most think that the mind is just the faculty that sees, hears, feels, and knows...they don't perceive the radiance of the Source...There exists just the One Mind. Truly there are no multiplicities of forms...The pure mind, which is the source of all things, shines forever with the radiance of its own perfection...Our True Nature...fills the Void everywhere and is intrinsically of the substance of the One Mind...The Buddha and all sentient beings are nothing but expressions of the One Mind. There is nothing else...The One Mind is the Buddha, and there is no distinction between Buddha and everyone else...How can there be Buddhas who save or ordinary beings who must be saved if the true nature of all things is the same?*

Through gnosis Huang Po discovered the difference between illusion and Reality:

> *Your true nature...was never born and can never die. It shines through the whole universe... Your true nature...contains not the smallest hairbreadth of anything that exists objectively... Your true nature...is all-pervading, radiant beauty: absolute reality...Every grain of matter, every appearance is one with Eternal and Immutable Reality!*

Before we move on, let's take a quick look at what the Zen philosopher, Nishida Kitaro (1870-1945) had to say about Ultimate Reality and the true Self:

> *At the base of the world, there are neither the many nor the one; it is a world of absolute unity of opposites...At the base of consciousness is a transcendent unchanging reality apart from time...God is not something that transcends reality; God is the base of reality...God is that which dissolves the distinction between subjectivity and objectivity and unites spirit and nature.*
>
> *If we know the true Self we...fuse with the essence of the universe...Our true Self is the ultimate reality of the universe.*

4. Gems from India

Throughout the book we've quoted extensively from the oldest known texts proclaiming the perennial philosophy, *The Upanishads*. As you'll quickly see, the next sages we're about to discuss were influenced by *The Upanishads* and another ancient, yet well-known work, *The Bhagavad Gita,* that dates from the 5th to the 2nd centuries BCE. Since gita means song, the title can also be rendered as *The Song of Bhagavan*. In this case, 'song' may be quite literal since it was a popular oral story that was passed around for untold generations before it was finally written down. The text is attributed to the revered Hindu figure Vyasa, but like many of the gnostic gospels that were falsely credited to apostles; this attribution was probably made to add weight to the words. Like many of the gnostic gospels, it was written as a dialogue between a questioner, the prince Arjuna, and the master, the god-king Krishna, who poses as Arjuna's charioteer. As the text opens, Arjuna is understandably upset by the fact that he is about to go to war against his own relatives. Instead of commiserating, Krishna draws his attention back to the illusory nature of the drama he's involved in and the Reality he needs to focus on:

> *Fear not. What is not real never was and never will be. What is real always was and cannot be destroyed...That which is not, shall never be; that which is, shall never cease to be. To the wise, these truths are self-evident...There has never been a time when you and I have not existed, nor will there be a time when we will cease to exist... The Self is unmanifested, beyond all thought, beyond all change. Knowing this, you should not grieve...Beyond this creation...there is an Invisible, higher, Eternal; and when all things pass away, this remains forever and ever...I am the Self...seated in the heart of every creature. I am the origin, the middle, and the end that all will come to.*

How can Arjuna live as Self? Krishna explains:

> *To the extent that a well is of use when there is a flood...to the same extent are the scriptures of use to an enlightened one...The Self cannot be known by the senses, nor thought by the mind, nor caught by time...When one can see eternity in things that pass away and infinity in finite things, then one has pure knowledge...However men try to reach me, I return their love with love; whatever path they may travel, it leads to me in the end.*

Shankara

The legends surrounding Adi Shankara (686-718) are reminiscent of the mythology that evolved around Jesus. He was said to be an exceptionally intelligent child who had a strong interest in spirituality. He spent time with the holy men, had read the sacred texts and had written commentaries on many of them. Still, Shankara felt an emptiness books and teachings could not fill. He was disgusted by the hypocrisy of the materialistic interests of society so when his father died when he was ten, he begged his mother to let him take a monastic vow. He quickly mastered everything his guru taught him, and as a teenager he set out to teach on his own. Like Rumi, Attar and Hakim Sanai, a 'chance encounter' and a challenge changed his life.

Shankara, a *Brahmin* (the highest caste in India), was walking to the Ganges River when his way was blocked by a *Chandala* (an untouchable of the lowest caste) and his dogs. Upset by this supposed insult, Shankara ordered the man to get out of his way. Instead of moving, the *Chandala* asked, "If there is only one God, how can there be many kinds of men?" These words not only shocked and embarrassed Shankara; they jolted him into a far deeper understanding of Reality. Shortly after this encounter he wrote, "He who has learned to see the Existence everywhere, He is my master — be he Brahmin or Chandala." Like Rumi, Shankara was a prolific author. One of his best known works is *The Crest-Jewel of Discrimination*, a piece that reestablishes and reinvigorates the essential meaning of the *Upanishads*. The unmistakable thrust of this dialogue between master and student is the impossibility of anything real existing outside the Divine:

> *I am Brahman* (Ultimate Reality); *Like space, I pervade everything. I am within and without. Never affected by the manifestation of forms, I am eternal, unattached, motionless and pure, the same in all...The name "universe" is superimposed on Brahman but what we call the "universe" is really nothing but Brahman.*

Regardless of this truth, Shankara pointed out, "The fool thinks, 'I am the body.' The intelligent man thinks, 'I am an individual soul united with the body.'" However, Shankara went on to explain that *neither* of those assumptions is true:

> *But the wise man, in the greatness of his knowledge and spiritual discrimination sees the Self as the only reality and thinks, "I am Brahman." You are pure Consciousness, the witness of all experiences. Your real nature is joy. Cease this very moment to identify yourself with the body.*

Although the material portion of the universe has its foundation in Reality, Shankara clarified that in comparison to Reality, the material portion of the universe is a mere shadow. Much like the characters in Plato's cave, our problem is born from our desire to cling to the shadows we believe are real rather than *know* the substance that is Real. Shankara proposed that only the true Self, veiled by the illusion of the body, is capable of recognizing Reality. Why? Because that Self has always been Brahman/Reality:

> *Like the appearance of silver in mother of pearl, the world seems real until the Self, the underlying reality, is realized. You are the Self, the infinite Being, the pure unchanging Consciousness, which pervades everything. Because you identify yourself with the body, you are tied to birth and death. Your bondage has no other cause...The entire universe is truly the Self. There exists nothing at all other than the Self. The enlightened person sees everything in the world as his own Self...Liberation never comes, even at the end of a hundred eons, without the realization of the Oneness of Self.*

Although his contemporaries promoted scriptures, practices, asceticism and rituals as the paths to the Divine, Shankara was adamant that there is absolutely no substitute for direct experience. He proclaimed, "Teachers and scriptures can stimulate spiritual awareness, but the wise disciple crosses the ocean of ignorance by direct illumination, through the grace of God." As he pointed out, we can all understand on an intellectual level that there is a difference between illusion and Reality but, "Just as knowing a rope to be a rope destroys the illusion it's a snake, Maya is destroyed by the direct experience of Brahman...Sickness is not cured by saying the word medicine. Liberation does not come by saying the word God. The Divine must be experienced."

We can continue to search and wonder, or as Shankara invites us, we can experience the Real for ourselves:

> *The Self is eternally present. It is revealed by transcendental experience, which is not dependent on place, time or rituals...The Self is the witness, beyond all attributes, beyond action. It can be directly realized as pure Consciousness and infinite bliss...A clear vision of Reality may be obtained only through our own eyes, when they have been opened by spiritual insight...When the vision of Reality comes, the veil of ignorance will be completely removed.*

The Avadhuta Gita

(aka *The Song of Avadhut* or *The Song of Dattatreya,* 9th or 10th century)

We can learn quite a bit about this text directly from the title. The alternate title, *The Song of Dattatreya,* attributes the work to Dattatreya, a legendary sage also called The Avadhut. This title was used in India to describe a particular type of sage that existed, in the most literal sense, without attachment to the world. Although they roamed naked without a home or name, it would not be accurate to label them ascetics or renunciates. Why? They embraced everything in existence, knowing its Divine nature. *The Avadhuta Gita* explains:

> *I am the Essence, the all-pervading Essence; I have no form of my own. I'm beyond the division*

of subject and object; how could I possibly be an object to myself? The subject and object are unseparated and inseparable. That undivided One is you.

The Avadhut identified with pure consciousness, not the material illusion projected by it:

I am the infinite and immutable One; I am pure Consciousness, without any form. I am One; I am all of this! Yet I am undifferentiated, beyond all forms. How, then, do I regard the Self? As both the Unmanifest and the manifest world… The one Reality is ever the same; this is what all the wise men say. Whether you embrace or renounce desires, the one Consciousness remains unaffected…Here, everything is eternal; everything is Consciousness. Here, only the Immutable exists; everything is Consciousness. Without any exception, everything is Consciousness. Why lament, then, O mind? I'm the same Self in all.

Although it's not known who actually penned the text, it's obvious that the work is based on direct experience:

It was said that a seeker asked [Dattatreya], *"Kindly tell us what guru has given you the great knowledge which has made you perfect in wisdom, full of peace, and devoted to the good of all living beings." He answered, "One's own Self is one's chief Guru. By knowledge of Self communion one gets the great bliss."*

There are no divine scriptures, no world, no imperative religious practices. There are no gods, no classes or races of men, no stages of life, no superior or inferior. There is nothing but...the Supreme Reality...The practice of yoga will not lead you to purity. Silencing the mind will not lead you to purity. The Guru's instructions will not lead you to purity. Purity is your Essence. It's your very own Consciousness! I have neither Guru nor initiation. I have no discipline and no duty to perform...I'm the self-existent Purity.

When a jar is broken, the space that was inside merges into the space outside. In the same way, my mind has merged in God.

The Avadhuta Gita has one message only; *You are That.* Although this truth is repeated in a slightly different way in virtually every verse, it's a beautiful and inspiring way to use repetition as a teaching tool. Here are a few examples of the hundreds of ways to express *You are That*:

All that exists in this world of forms Is nothing but the Self, and the Self alone...To whom, then shall I bow my head? I, myself, am the stainless One! Truly, all this universe is only my Self; It is neither divided nor undivided. How can I even assert that it exists? I can only view it with wonder and awe! What, then, is the heart of the highest truth, the core of knowledge, the wisdom supreme? It is, "I am the Self, the formless One; by my very nature, I am pervading all."

All forms, understand, are only temporary manifestations; only the formless Essence eternally exists. Once this truth is realized, there's no more necessity to be reborn.

Neither birth nor death pertains to you. You have never been a body...There is no such thing as infinite form...You are That which is both inside and out; you're everything everywhere. Why, then, are you so deluded? If ice and water are mixed together, there is no difference between one and the other. It is the same with matter and spirit – translations by Swami Abhayananda

Ashtavakra Gita

Like all the other texts in this section, The *Ashtavakra Gita* focuses on Self-realization, but it takes an interesting twist. Written around 500-400 BCE, it's presented as a dialogue between the sage Ashtavakra and King Janaka, who is also mentioned in *The Bhagavad Gita* and was said to be a disciple of one of the *Upanishad* writers. Given Janaka's spiritual background, the reader is not surprised when the king instantly recognized the truth in Ashtavakra's teachings. And just as quickly, Ashtavakra recognized an issue that Janaka is stumbling over and is unable to perceive. After experiencing Oneness first hand, the king was convinced of his own enlightenment. Nevertheless, it was clear that he remained attached to "I," continuing to think and live in terms of separation and the pursuit of specialness. The little self has continued to make use of this 'slight-of-hand' trick down to our day.

Since we currently have the luxury of quantum research, many understand and accept the concept that All is One. And, on the basis of intellectual understanding alone, many currently assume they are enlightened. This issue has also overtaken some seekers who have directly experienced the Divine but were so overwhelmed by the gnosis of Oneness; they assumed this experience rendered them spiritually complete. Like Janaka, they are confident in their 'knowing' and feel no need to let that knowing change their lives. Nonetheless, the shift from knowing *of* the Self to *being* the Self virtually always involves a process that takes time. Some translators of this *Gita* have failed to see the importance of this point, offer the entire *Gita* as if it were one speech rather than a dialogue that focuses on important corrections. Reading the text in dialogue form highlights the give and take; Janaka waxes poetic about his blissful state of enlightenment while Ashtavakra points out his continued attachments to separation and specialness. When Janaka's words finally reveal that the little self has melted into nothingness, Ashtavakra is satisfied. Here are a few of Ashtavakra's 'corrections' that can prove helpful to each of us:

> *For he who thinks knowledge is things and ideas, how can there be Self-knowledge? For how many lifetimes have you done hard and painful labor with body, mind and speech? It is time to stop... Having seen for certain that this universe and body is without form or substance, I am revealed as Awareness alone.*

> *The fool tries to control the mind with the mind — what folly! The wise one delights in Self alone... Give up the idea that you are separate, a person, that there is within and without...I am not the body. I do not have a body. I am Awareness, not a person.*

> *My child, you may read or discuss scripture as much as you like, but until you forget everything, you will never live in your heart...The body is strained by practices. The mind numbs with meditation. Detached from all this, I live as I*

am...A single understanding, "I am the One Awareness," consumes all suffering in the fire of an instant...Abide in Awareness with no illusion of person. You will be instantly free and at peace.

Attraction to the world's offerings is the suffering of bondage. This is the truth. Now do as you please...Look upon friends, lands, wealth, houses...and all apparent good fortune — as a passing show, as a dream lasting [a few] days.

As waves, foam and bubbles are not different from water, so the universe emanating from Self is not different from Self...I am not other than Light. The universe manifests at my glance.

Having seen for certain that this universe and body is without form or substance, I am revealed as Awareness alone...Having realized yourself as One, being serene and indestructible, why do you desire wealth? Having realized yourself as pure Awareness, as beautiful beyond description, how can you remain a slave? I am Awareness alone. The world is a passing show. How can thoughts arise of acceptance or rejection?

I see no differences or separation. Even the multitudes appear as a single formless desert. To what should I cling? Just as the same space exists both within and without a jar, the timeless, all-pervasive One exists as Totality.

Not seeing Self, the world is materialized. Seeing Self, the world is vanished...The universe is but a thought in Consciousness. In Reality it is nothing. One who sees the true nature...never ceases to exist...That which has form is not real. Only the formless is permanent. Once this is known, you will not return to illusion…The body is made of worldly stuff. It comes, it lingers, it goes. The Self neither comes nor goes, yet remains. Why mourn the body? The body exists only in imagination, as do heaven and hell, bondage, freedom, fear. Are they my concern? You are pure consciousness – the substance of the universe. The universe exists within you. Don't be small-minded.

5. Christian Mystics

Meister Eckhart

Eckhart von Hochheim (1260-1328), commonly known as Meister (Master) Eckhart, was a celebrated Dominican theologian, teacher and speaker until he began preaching a "radical panentheism." Unlike pantheism, which teaches that "all is God," Meister Eckhart went further by proclaiming, "All are in God, and God is in all." Those two statements may sound similar on the surface, but there is a subtle, yet significant, difference.

Pantheism tells us God *is* the universe, meaning that all things are equally God, and only God. Panentheism describes the Divine as the life-giving foundation of All That Is; a force that permeates and sustains everything in existence because everything exists within it and is part of it. However, panentheism also allows for beings that are one with the Divine yet are not the elemental foundation. This means that we are not only God; we also remain unique beings that share the Divine's life force, consciousness, free will, creativity and love. Once again, since Source chose to *be* love, other unique, individual beings must exist who are able to receive and give in a Divine love exchange. Meister Eckhart explained:

> *The divine nature is Oneness, and each Person is One, the same One in [God's] nature....Since we find God in oneness, that oneness must be in him who is to find God....Be therefore that One so that you may find God. And of course, if you are wholly that One, you shall remain so, even where apparent distinctions are. Different things will all be parts of that One to you, and you will no longer stand in your way...To look for unity short of God is to be self-deceived.*

> *The eye through which I see God is the same eye though which God sees me...one seeing, one knowing, one love...It is your destiny to see as God sees, to know as God knows, to feel as God feels...With the same enjoyment with which God enjoys the Godself, God enjoys all creatures, not as creatures, but as God.*

For Eckhart, God was entirely beyond all and yet still completely within all, both the ground of all being and a personal God that loves us:

> *Divine love cannot deny it's very Self. Divine love will be eternally true to its own being, and its being is giving all it can...God lies in wait for us with nothing so much as love.*

Although Eckhart's words clearly align with the perennial philosophy and fit the quantum model, when he boldly stated, "God and I are One" he pushed the church too far. He was subsequently brought before the Inquisition in 1326 and accused of heresy. In turn, Eckhart accused the inquisitors of stupidity and appealed to the Pope for a hearing.

Unfortunately, Eckhart passed away before he could defend himself and he was posthumously condemned.

Meister Eckhart's teachings were buried by the church and relatively unknown until they were revived during the 19th century. As we study the content of his words, it's helpful to keep in mind the context. To the modern reader, Eckhart's regular use of puns, jokes and hilarious comparisons sound inventive and highly entertaining, but his style and the concepts he was sharing, rocked the establishment of his day. Nonetheless, he was exceedingly popular among the common people, mainly because he assured them that God was with them and could be approached directly by all:

> To get at the core of God at his greatest, one must first get into the core of himself at his least, for no one can know God who has not first known himself. Go to the depths of the soul, the secret place of the Most High, to the roots, to the heights; for all that God can do is focused there.

For people who had been taught they were unworthy sinners whose duty was to obey and fear God, it may have felt both impossible and terrifying to meet God in one's own soul. Nonetheless, Eckhart assured his followers the tyrannical god they had been taught to fear and the God of love were mutually exclusive:

> A god that could frighten is not a god – but an insidious idol and weapon in the hands of the insane…A god who talks of sin is worshipped by the infirm…How long will grown men and women…keep drawing in their coloring books an image of God that makes them sad? I find nothing

more destructive to the well-being of life than to support a god that makes you feel unworthy and in debt...It is a lie – any talk of God that does not comfort you.

Eckhart also seriously undercut the church's 'one size fits all' methods and the need for mediators when he explained how the Divine reaches each willing heart individually:

All people are not called to God by the same road...God never tied man's salvation to any pattern....We must see that all good ways belong together in the One Way...God does not work in all hearts alike but according to the preparation and sensitivity He finds in each.

Like so many sages, Eckhart made it clear that we cannot be pawns in a war between good and evil. Based on our own deluded belief in duality we use free will to project the world of separation that we see:

God is at home, it is we who have gone for a walk... It was when we left the All we once were that the agony began, the fear and questions came...and tears I had never known before...When we cannot be who we are, our divine senses become mute and sick from the insanity of judging what He made Immaculate...Your essential nature is not at all in time or place, but is purely and simply in eternity...Great harm comes of feeling that God is distant. For let a man go away or come back: God never leaves.

And, as we have found so often in our discussion, Eckhart echoed the key to gnosis when he said:

> *God is not found in the soul by adding anything but by process of subtraction...Think of the soul as a vortex or whirlpool and you will understand how we are to sink eternally from negation to negation into the One...A person can hardly know that he knows God when he does not know himself! True prayer...isn't to plead for a particular benefit—it is to heighten your awareness of your union with God.*

Evelyn Underhill

> *Mystics do not write for the purpose of handing on a philosophical scheme, but in order to describe something which they have themselves experienced; something which they feel to be of transcendent importance for humanity*—Evelyn Underhill

A prolific writer (39 books and 350+ articles), a lifelong student and gracious teacher, Evelyn Underhill (1875-1941) was also a bit of a paradox. Initially agnostic (some say atheist), she had also been involved in the pseudo-gnostic hermetic group called Society of the Golden Dawn, collaborated with the sage Rabindranath Tagore, was fascinated by Catholicism and intrigued by Plotinus, a member of many Anglican groups and a mystic. Although she worked for British naval intelligence during World War I, she eventually became an outspoken pacifist, writing a pamphlet that openly denounced the church's role in war.

Although we may like to think of our time as a unique period of spiritual evolution, Underhill's day was also a time of spiritual revival mixed with the psychic, occult, psychology and science, much as it is today. Contrary to popular spirituality, Underhill repeatedly declared mysticism to be entirely practical; purely spiritual rather than magical and anchored in Divine love rather than the pursuit of ecstatic experiences. In her view (one we agree with wholeheartedly), it had always been mystics rather than religionists, who held aloft the light of spiritual understanding. And yet, as Underhill explained, "We are all the kindred of the mystics...Strange and far away from us though they seem, they are not cut off from us by some impassable abyss...[they are] our guarantee of the end to which immanent love, the hidden steersman...is moving us on the path toward the Real."

It is Underhill's grasp of the practical aspects of the mystic's life that stand out in her writing. As she explained, ecstatic experience may or may not take place in the life of the mystic, but their presence does not prove gnosis, nor does their absence deny them. Instead, the mystic's life is:

> ...An 'ordered movement,' an awakening of the self to God, by which the self is purified, illuminated, and finally united to God...Mysticism is no isolated vision, no fugitive glimpse of reality, but a complete system of life carrying its own guarantees and obligations...It is the name of that organic process which involves the perfect consummation of the Love of God...Mysticism is the art of union with Reality. The mystic is a person who has attained that union in greater or less degree; or who aims at and believes in such attainment."

In the book *Evelyn Underhill Essential Writings*, Editor Emille Griffin outlined several of Underhill's observations on the characteristics of a mystic that are helpful to any sincere seeker on the spiritual path:

» The One is not only the foundation of All That Is, but also a living, personal object of mutual Love. Above all, mysticism is centered in love:

We do not inhabit detached residences, but are parts of a vast spiritual organism...A harmony is set up between the mystic and Life in all its forms.

The Absolute of the mystics is lovable, attainable, alive.

The business and method of mysticism is love.

The only question asked about the soul's use of its...gifts...will be: "Have you loved well?"

» Oneness with the Divine requires stripping away of everything that is not real and aligning with the Real. This is an organic process, "the art of establishing a conscious relationship with the Absolute."

Spiritual life, which is profoundly organic, means the give and take...of the little human spirit with the Infinite Spirit.

Nothing can happen until...the involved interests and tangled motives of the self are simplified, and the false complications of temporal life are recognized and cast away.

The heart outstrips the clumsy senses, and sees —

perhaps for an instant, perhaps for long periods of bliss – an undistorted and more veritable world…this cleansing of the doors of perceptions, is surely what we might expect to occur as man moves toward higher centers of consciousness.

» Mysticism is not for the isolationist or ascetic but one who participates in and "accepts life in its wholeness":

The mystic is a realist…mysticism is an invitation to the soul to attain that fullness of life for which we were made.

Distinction between the spiritual life and the practical life is false. We cannot divide them. One affects the other all the time. A spiritual life is simply a life in which all that we do comes from the center, where we are anchored in God.

Sweetly, it is true, the illuminated mystic may live; but not, as some think, placidly. Enlightenment is a symptom of growth and growth is a living process, which knows no rest. The spirit, indeed, is invaded by a heavenly peace; but it is the peace, not of idleness, but of ordered activity, "A rest most busy" The urgent push of that indwelling spirit, aspiring to its home in the heart of Reality, is felt more and more, as the invasion of the normal consciousness by the transcendental personality – the growth of the New Man – proceeds towards its term.

» The 'mystical life' is within the reach of all:

I have merely attempted to put the view of the universe and man's place in it which is common to all mystics in plain and untechnical language:

and to suggest the practical conditions under which ordinary persons may participate in their experience…Mysticism is seen as the "one way out" for the awakened spirit of man, healing that human incompleteness which is the origin of our divine unrest.

The spiritual life is not a special career, involving abstraction from the world of things. It is a part of every man's life; and until he has realized it he is not a complete human being, he has not entered into possession of all his powers.

When we read Underhill's words, we see once again that while technology has changed very quickly, people have not:

The people of our time are helpless, distracted and rebellious…largely because they have lost this sure hold on the eternal…The practical life of a vast number of people is not…worthwhile at all. It's like an impressive fur coat with no one inside it…Most men prefer to dwell in comfortable ignorance upon the lower slopes, and there to make of their obvious characteristics a drapery which shall veil the naked truth.

We mostly spend our lives conjugating three verbs: to Want, to Have and to Do. Craving, clutching and fussing on the material, political, social, emotional, intellectual — even on the religious — plane, we are kept in perpetual unrest: forgetting that none of these verbs have any ultimate significance, except so far as they are transcended by and included in, the fundamental verb, to Be: and that Being, not wanting, having and doing, is the essence of a spiritual life.

6. Peace Pilgrim

Although the sages we've discussed have been associated, however loosely, with a religion or a spiritual philosophy, that is certainly not a prerequisite to waking up. Mildred Norman, more widely known as Peace Pilgrim, was born in 1908 to a family of 'free thinkers' who taught their children to rely on intellect and reason rather than religion. Mildred excelled at school and as a young adult found that she also had a talent for making money easily. Although this would make most young people happy, Mildred felt an intense emptiness in the meaningless cycle of self-centered earning and spending. Her relentless self-questioning ultimately led her to an inner knowing that God not only existed, but is an "ever-present, all pervading spirit — which binds the universe together and gives life to everything."

After this awareness came to her, Mildred, like so many others, once again became engulfed in the cares of everyday life. Eventually, when she entered a particularly difficult period of her life, her thoughts returned to Source. Since she had always found solace in nature, Mildred walked through the woods one night praying for Divine direction. Soon she was overwhelmed by a feeling of complete willingness that caused her to dedicate her life to the service of peace. But Mildred had no interest in becoming a peace protester; hers was a quest to spread the truth that the only real foundation for external peace was inner peace. As she pointed out, "You are within God and God is within you. You could not be where God is not. The sanctuary of peace dwells within…When you find peace within yourself you become the kind of person who can live at peace with others...Be a sweet melody in the great orchestration, instead of a discordant note." But how is this imperturbable inner peace found and embraced?

Mildred explained in a radio presentation entitled *Steps toward Inner Peace* (KPFK radio talk, Los Angeles, 1964) that there is a great chasm between the *idea* of being peace and actually attaining that state. She candidly admitted that it took her fifteen years of inner work to resolve what she called the "two selves or two natures or two wills with two different viewpoints" that exist within each of us. She eloquently described the schism between the little, false self and the true Self when she said:

> *The body, mind and emotions are instruments which can be used by either the self-centered nature or the God-centered nature. The self-centered nature uses these instruments, yet it is never fully able to control them, so there is a constant struggle. They can only be fully controlled by the God-centered nature. When the God-centered nature takes over, you have found inner peace....The self-centered nature is a very formidable enemy and it struggles fiercely to retain its identity. It defends itself in a cunning manner and should not be regarded lightly. It knows the weakest spots in your armor....During these periods of attack...be intimate with none but the guiding whisper of your higher self.*

As we've discovered, the little, false self is not a separate or evil entity but rather a small part of our consciousness that resists What Is. It is this resistance to oneness and the insistence on specialness that created the "hills and valleys" Mildred experienced.

But as we've discussed, once we've decided on the goal of return we can be side-tracked but never derailed:

> *So there were hills and valley — lots of hills and valleys. Then in the midst of the struggle there came a wonderful mountain-top experience, and for the first time I knew what inner peace was like. I felt a oneness — oneness with all my fellow human beings, oneness with all of creation. I have never felt really separate since...I knew that for me the struggle was over, that finally I had succeeded in...finding inner peace. Again this is a point of no return. You can never go back into the struggle. The struggle is over now because you will do the right thing, and you don't need to be pushed into it.*

Although it may appear that such an experience would mark some sort of spiritual pinnacle, Mildred made it clear that we can expand our understanding as long as the body continues:

> *However progress is not over...it's as though the central figure of the jigsaw puzzle of your life is complete and clear and unchanging, and around the edges other pieces keep fitting in. There is always a growing edge, but the progress is harmonious. There is a feeling of always being surrounded by all of the good things, like love and peace and joy.*

Although these quotes were drawn from a radio presentation that highlighted steps toward inner peace, Mildred recognized that each of us comes to Self in our own way. She emphasized "the steps toward inner peace are not taken in any certain order. The first step for one may be the last step for another. So, just take whatever steps seem easiest for you." Among the steps she listed was the need to "Stop being an escapist! Stop being a surface-liver who stays right in the froth…get down beneath the surface of life where the realities are found." Like the other sages we've studied, Mildred recognized that we can all be "our own worst enemies" and for that reason we need to live "according to the highest light" we currently have. When we do that, we open ourselves to receiving even greater light, a cycle that will continue to repeat until we return to Source. As part of her 'steps,' Mildred spoke extensively of relinquishment, but her meaning has nothing to do with sacrifice. Instead, relinquishment meant letting go of whatever burdens us down, whatever no longer serves us. It may be our entanglement with the materials things of the world, our attachments, aversions, thoughts and emotions that are not in line with love, and of course the will of the little self; all things that may have appeared valuable to us at one time, but are ultimately recognized as valueless.

When Mildred was forty-four, she hiked 2,050 miles of the Appalachian Trail. During the hike, she decided to "remain a wanderer until mankind has learned the way of peace, walking until given shelter and fasting until given food." Although her pilgrimage covered over 25,000 miles and lasted 28 years, she walked with only the clothes on her back, a comb, map, toothbrush and a small supply of pamphlets explaining her mission which were handed out only when they were requested. Although Peace Pilgrim 'walked her purpose' in a state of imperturbable peace until her death in a car accident at the age of 73, very few have followed her example of *being* peace.

If asked, nearly everyone would say they want peace, but in the last 5,600 years, there have been only 292 years of peace, 14,550+ wars and over 4 billion dead as a result! Evidently what many of us really mean is peace on our terms, peace that will serve our interests. This doesn't mean that we necessarily have any conscious intention to harm others for our own benefit. It can be as simple as thinking only from our own perspective, harboring the belief that our way of life is superior; wanting to keep the lifestyle we enjoy or fear that our loved ones won't be safe. These thoughts may seem harmless, but they all contribute to the lack of peace we see in the world. How do we move from thinking about peace in terms that would serve our interests and start thinking in ways that would benefit everyone? As Peace Pilgrim came to understand, no one can be at peace externally until they have quieted the conflict within; to offer peace, we must *be* peace.

Few find inner peace but this is not because they try and fail; it is because they do not try...I wish I could help [everyone] in their spiritual growth but, as I pointed out before, it is a do-it-yourself project, and really, there is little I can do except say, "Of course you can find inner peace; if I can do it so can you." When you find peace within yourself, you become the kind of person who can live at peace with others...To attain inner peace you must actually give your life...When you at last give your life – bringing into alignment your beliefs and the way you live then, and only then, can you begin to find inner peace.

As she walked through the city streets, Peace Pilgrim observed the endless array of items that were being displayed and offered to the thousands of people "hurrying in rather orderly lines to and from their places of employment." Sadly, it was the valueless, rather than the valuable that was offered; the freedom, truth, love, peace, joy, security and comfort of knowing Source were all missing. Peace Pilgrim's advice, "To obtain these my friends, you too may need to escape from the orderly lines and risk being looked upon disdainfully."

Part Four: Gnosis Outside the Gnostic Gosples

Part Five:
Your Gnosis

*I say only what I have seen with my own eyes – and you keep quoting the scriptures. Experience, O seeker, is the essence of all things—*Kabir

*The attitude of faith is to let go, and become open to truth, whatever it might turn out to be—*Alan Watts

Have you ever moved a long distance from someone you hold dear, or had a loved one move far away from you? As little as a hundred years ago, a long-distance move could very possibly have meant that you might never see your closest friends or relatives again. Now, with cell phones, skype and email, we can easily stay in contact. But great as those conveniences are, they can't substitute for holding someone in your arms or experiencing something significant with them by your side. Few of us would be content with continuous separation from the ones who are dearest to us, yet most of us have no difficulty keeping our Divine Source at arm's length.

I. Change

Without change, something sleeps inside us and seldom awakens. The sleeper must awaken — Frank Herbert (author and Zen Buddhist 1920-1986)

Our willingness to distance ourselves from the Divine may stem from the prevailing world view of an aloof, unknowable God who must be obeyed and is usually feared. But once we've dismissed such immature views and realize the Divine is pure love, what continues to hold us back from a direct experience? Why do we cling to a second-hand version of the Beloved when we can experience the Reality of Oneness first-hand? Vietnamese Zen monk, Thich Nhat Hanh (1926 –) shed light on this issue when he said, "People have a hard time letting go of their suffering. Out of a fear of the unknown, they prefer suffering that is familiar."

Of course our dualistic thought system continually reinforces the erroneous belief that our creator must be both good and bad, but there is more to it than that. Like the prodigal son, most of us harbor a deep-seated but unjustified guilt, a feeling that somehow we've betrayed our Source and deserve punishment. And, like that young man, we fear what could take place if we tried to return. Ritual, worship, obedience, sacrifice — and religion itself — sprouted from that foundation of fear. Considering the fact that we've spent untold hundreds or thousands of lifetimes in the "far country" in the thrall of the little self, our conscious and subconscious fear should come as no surprise. Like the prodigal son's scheme to work his way back into favor, we mistakenly believe we must pacify Source or come up with a scheme of our own to regain the Divine's good graces. Nothing could be further from the truth, but our fears have made us feel safer and more comfortable in our suffering than we feel when we begin to contemplate returning to our forgotten home.

As an example, we recently caught the last bit of an intriguing radio interview. The speaker was describing what many might consider a 'perfect spiritual situation. For several years he had lived within the walls of an ashram that had been purposely designed to create an ideal atmosphere for accelerated spiritual growth. The group that founded and lived in the ashram were free of all but the most minimal outside influences. They ate an organic, vegetarian diet and were all focused on sustaining a healthy, peaceful and supportive atmosphere that included several hours of meditation and various spiritual practices each day. They also held regular gatherings where they could share their insights. Most of us would assume that this lifestyle would produce tremendous results and we might wonder how we could sign up.

Sadly, a few years into the project, it began to dawn on the participants that despite all this work, they hadn't changed; they were virtually the same people they had been when their mission began. Why? When they were honest with each other they had to admit that at heart, they really hadn't wanted to change. As theoretical physicist Brian Greene (1963–) wrote, "The boldness of asking deep questions may require unforeseen flexibility if we are to accept the answers." They were forced to come to the conclusion that the ashram had merely served as a means of isolating them from a world they no longer enjoyed. Although they relished going through the motions of a spiritual seeker, they were actually terrified of what might happen if they went deeper. They responded to their fear by guarding the inner status quo despite the meditation, spiritual discussions and practices they had engaged in for years. As a popular Buddhist teacher, Adyashanti (1962–) deals with this issue on a regular basis. He explains:

> *In my experience, everyone will say they want to discover the Truth, right up until they realize that the Truth will rob them of their deepest held ideas, beliefs, hopes, and dreams. The freedom of enlightenment means much more than the experience of love and peace. It means discovering a Truth that will turn your view of self and life upside-down. For one who is truly ready, this will be unimaginably liberating. But for one who is still clinging in any way, this will be extremely challenging indeed. How does one know if they*

are ready? One is ready when they are willing to be absolutely consumed, when they are willing to be fuel for a fire without end.

The ultimate source of this fear is captured in a quote from spiritual author Ram Dass (Born Richard Alpert, 1931–), "*Who you think you are* will always be frightened of change. But it doesn't make any difference to *who you really are*." [Italics ours] Without a doubt, gnosis *is* change; change of the most dramatic sort. The little self has feared and fought this change for eons while the true Self has desired nothing else.

Ralph Waldo Emerson made this observation, "Whenever a mind is simple and receives a divine wisdom, old things pass away—means, teachers, texts, temples fall." There's no way around it; deciding that you do want to experience Reality will begin a chain reaction of ever expansive change. Although our outer life may change in response to the inner, the changes we need to make all occur within consciousness. Since its continued existence is on the line, the little self feels abject terror, and will let us know via the body and brain. On the other hand, the true Self welcomes its release and supports our willingness to expand. Although it's impossible, the little self will still try to convince us that it can remain in power while we pursue spiritual interests. The mystic poet Hazrat Inayat Khan shares this truth, "There can be no rebirth without…a total annihilation of all that you believed in." This includes the belief that you *are* the body and this world is your reality.

Plotinus made it clear that the finite (consciousness that's filtered through the brain and therefore limited to time and space) cannot know the infinite (Boundless Divine consciousness), so a change in consciousness, one that taps into the level of the true Self, is absolutely necessary:

> *You ask, how can we know the Infinite? I answer, not by reason...You can only apprehend the Infinite by a faculty superior to reason, by entering into a state in which you are your finite self no longer – in which the divine essence is communicated to you. It is the liberation of your mind from its finite consciousness. Like can only apprehend like; when you thus cease to be finite, you become one with the Infinite. It is the reduction of your soul to its simplest Self, its Divine essence, you realize this union – this identity.*

When consciousness has altered sufficiently, we go past 'glimpses' of truth and enter the infinite realm of the true Self/One Mind where gnosis takes place. Early on, we may reach points where we think that we've gone as far as we can, that there's nothing more to change or experience. But when gnosis occurs, *it inevitably, and irrevocably, changes us* in ways that we cannot possibly anticipate. As Plotinus testified, "When after having sought the One [the soul] finds itself in Its presence...there is nothing higher, nothing more blessed than this."

This astonishing experience will surpass your wildest imaginings; it will turn your world upside down, inside out and backwards. You will no longer just 'think' that you may have experienced the Divine, there will be no doubt! Nisargadatta confirmed, "The search for Reality is the most dangerous of all undertakings, for it destroys the world in which you live." And that is the point; this world will no longer be your reality. But, as you've come to realize, this is the best possible news since the only world that can be destroyed is the one we've each crafted from illusion. Nonetheless, that change is epic. As *The Gospel of Thomas* revealed, "When one finds, one will be astonished." Outwardly, some will appear to remain exactly as they had before their ultimate adventure began. For others, very little in their life will remain the same. But either way, you'll 'know' that nothing with ever be the same.

Gnosis is not only the 'definitive experience' that's open to each of us; it's the escape route from our failed experiment with separation and specialness. It's the experience that reunites us with the Beloved. This truth was once again clearly illustrated in the parable of the prodigal son. When the young man realized his experiment in separation had failed, he both figuratively and literally, retraced his steps. First, he let go of the thoughts of separation that had carried him away and returned to the thoughts of love and oneness that would lead him home. Certainly the young man deeply regretted his mistake, but it's important to note that he didn't waste a moment more in the pig sty wallowing in regret. His second step was to take action that supported his changed thinking.

Currently, the word repent is usually associated with sin and is used to denote the sorrow we feel when we regret what we've done. But when Jesus shared the parable, the Hebrew word for repentance, *shuh*, had far more to do with actions than feelings.

It meant "to return" or "turn around," which was exactly what the prodigal son did. Gnosis does not take place simply on the basis of regret. The vital point was that the young man made the effort *on his own* to get up, turn around and head back toward home despite the pitiful condition he felt he was in. Plotinus echoed this thought when he said, "Along the same road by which it descended, the soul must retrace its steps back to the supreme Good. It must first of all return to itself."

Why didn't the father swoop in and rescue his son the moment the young man realized he had made an enormous mistake? Although it may appear to be the kinder option, if his father had stepped in at that point, or even later in the journey, his free will would have been compromised. Instead, his father gave him enough time to know, beyond doubt, that returning home was what he truly wanted and allowed for his actions to reinforce his new determination. Similarly, Ultimate Reality will not compromise our free will by interfering with our experiment but waits patiently while we let go of the little self and its thinking. Rumi made our part clear when he said:

> *Destroy your own house, destroy it now! Don't wait one more minute! Pull the whole house down! A treasure greater than Pharaoh's is hidden under it. For you can only own the treasure if you destroy your house yourself. How can you get the pay if you haven't done the work?*

It would be premature for Source to "meet us on the road" until we've reached a tipping point where we primarily think and act from the true Self and are certain there is nothing that we want more than to return home. Although this may sound daunting, if not impossible, keep in mind that while the prodigal son did "burn down the house" of the little self, he did not attempt to clean up or perfect himself before heading home. Rather, he began his return journey in the condition, and from the location, he was in. Ragged, hungry and miserable, he retraced his steps. This may sound like splitting hairs, but there is an important difference between the two. Cleaning up is physical; it is an outward act of purification that implies that who and what we are, is lacking. Spiritual practices that focus on the physical can confuse us into thinking the actions of the body, or its purity, plays a part in our return. Although the bodies we've projected have done many unloving things, we have no need to atone for them. Retracing our steps has nothing to do with the physical and Source has no interest in the illusory bodies we've projected; it's a trek that takes place strictly in consciousness.

If we find that something like meditation is helpful we can certainly use it while keeping in mind that the practice is not an end in itself and can never carry us back to Source. Instead, know that unlearning duality is what actually takes you closer and closer to Source. And while you're moving further from duality and closer to Oneness, remember that no matter what physical condition the prodigal son was in, his father never ceased watching for him. He ran out to meet his son at exactly the right time, gave him gifts that verified his continued place in the family and supported him the rest of the way home. We have every reason to trust that we too are watched for and will be met at exactly the right time.

It's important to note that the father in the parable also ignored his son's efforts to explain his plans to make amends by working as a hired servant. Why? It's impossible to work our way back to Source. Yes, the *Bible* does say "there is no profit in faith without works," that faith alone can't save us and "faith without works is dead." (James 2: 14-26) These verses are often used to support the mistaken concept that we gain salvation by piling up a record of good works. However, the real key to these passages is found at James 2:18, "But someone will say, 'You have faith and I have works.' Show me your faith apart from your works, and I by my works will show you my faith." This verse isn't promoting salvation through works as much as it is pointing to the need for consistency. If we say we want oneness but cling to separation, we're inconsistent. If say we want to experience the Divine and then systematically let go of the unloving thoughts of the little self, we're consistent. Simply put, when we become joy, peace and love, they will flow from us automatically, in both thought and deed. In the *Bible*, Jesus often chided the Pharisees, a group that exhausted themselves working for their own salvation, but completely missed the point that God was interested in "mercy and not sacrifice." (Luke 18:9-14, Matthew 9: 9-13) So, although it may be more appealing to try to purify the body and personality or rack up a long list of good deeds rather than focusing inwardly, the works, in and of themselves, cannot return us to Source.

A discussion of works wouldn't be complete without mentioning karma. Karma is generally thought of as a wheel of cause and effect. *The Bhagavad Gita* explains it this way, "every event is both a cause and an effect" and "every act or thought has consequences of a similar kind, which in turn have further consequences." Since karma is tied to reincarnation, consequences are said to be felt through many lifetimes. In karmic terms, if you murdered someone in a past life, you will be murdered in another life. Conversely, if you're dedicated to good works, your future lives will supposedly improve. As long as a karmic debt remains, it's said to be impossible to be released from the cycle of birth and death. Like the concepts of sin and judgment that are taught in the *Bible*, this system requires a scorekeeper and infers a flawed higher power that uses punishment and rewards to enforce desired behaviors.

As we've discovered, we are the ones causing our own grief, not the Divine. This is where quantum physics can release us from the fear of karma. The world we project believes in cause and effect, but in the quantum, consciousness *causes the effect*. We are not hapless victims, but the creators of our own dualistic experience. On the other hand, the saying "what goes around comes around," does have validity in the quantum world. The quantum field draws to us whatever we project from our most deeply felt beliefs and emotions. If we project hatred, we'll add to the hate experienced in our virtual reality and we'll feel its effects. Conversely, we'll experience more love when we radiate love. It may come from unexpected sources, but it will come. Simply stated, we magnetize what we project. We are not the victims of some outside entity that will even out the scoreboard, the choice is always ours. (As a quick side note to this discussion, keep in mind that the little self is not the ego, which is each body's sense of self and dies with the body. The little self is a small, isolated portion of the

One Mind, and therefore is eternal. The little self continues to project body after body as long as we choose separation and specialness. As eternal consciousness, it can carry beliefs from one lifetime to another. As the little self, we are still the ones projecting our experiences, not an entity that exists outside us.

> *He who wants to do good knocks at the gate; he who loves finds the gate open* — Rabindranath Tagore

II. Detours

> *You set out to find God, but then you keep stopping for long periods at mean-spirited roadhouses. Don't wait any longer* — Rumi

Let's step back and take some time to consider the detours the little self has constructed to waylay our return to Source. Before we reach the point where gnosis takes place, we're each faced with several revealing questions: Am I willing to release my desire for separation and the tiny portion of my consciousness that allows for it? Can I let go of the conditioned misperceptions, attachments and aversions that have kept me in separation? Am I willing to let go of my identification with the body and the personality it has acquired? Will I willingly accept my place, and my power, in the household of the Divine? Countless seekers worn down by the world, have answered these questions with a resounding YES, but have failed to continue on to gnosis and a return to Source. Why does this happen? We've discussed the fear of change, now let's look at a few more 'tripping' points.

1. Confusion

If a man does not know what port he is steering for, no wind is favorable to him — Seneca

If you don't know where you're going, any road will take you there — unknown

Most of us have been stopped at one time or another by someone asking directions. After telling you where they want to go, you do your best to direct them. But how would you feel if someone asked you for directions but had no idea where they wanted to end up? That sounds ridiculous, but countless spiritual journeys end up going round and round in circles for that very reason. It's surprising how many people who consider themselves deeply spiritual have no idea what that actually means. No matter how many maps we have or how accurate our GPS is, they won't help us if we don't have a set destination in mind, and the same is true on a spiritual basis.

The little self is thrilled if we have no end in mind, leaving it free to titillate the mind and body with whatever spiritual fad that comes along. When this happens, it becomes the excitement of the new that directs us rather than a deep desire for Divine Truth. This is an age-old phenomenon as we see from the quotes of Saadi and Rumi:

Those who are interested in the design of the jars are not thirsty — Saadi

These spiritual window-shoppers who idly ask "How much is that?" They handle a hundred items and put them down — Rumi

That is not to say that just picking any goal that sounds good to you would put you any further ahead. It would be rather like deciding you were going to visit your best friend in Seattle while buying a plane ticket to Omaha. If we realize the need for a goal, the difficulty often lies in figuring out what it should be. After our first glimpse of the truth that lies beyond this world, we were unsure of our next step. After a few missteps based on old ways of thinking, we turned to the perennial philosophy. We felt that if there was such a thing as a "valid spiritual goal," the ancient sages should have spoken of it and been in agreement as to what it was. We were not disappointed. Sages from all time periods and areas of the world have made it clear that the ultimate goal is to throw off this illusion and return to Reality, to Self, to Source:

Much as you may wander you must return ultimately to the Self; so why not abide in the Self here and now? — Ramana Maharshi

There is a returning impulse, drawing all... towards the center from whence all came. The individual soul's appetite for the Divine intellect urges them to return to their Source — Plotinus

Light and life are God...and if you learn that you are also made of Light and Life, you will return to light and life — Hermes Trismegistus

Return to your true realm of Divine freedom —
Hafiz

Use your own light to return to the Source of light... Each separate being in the universe returns to the common Source. Returning to the Source is serenity — Lao-tzu

How long will you move backwards? Come forward! Return at last to the origin of your own origin...escape that prison with its thousand traps...plunge into the vast ocean of consciousness — Rumi

Whole, he enters into the Whole. His personal Self returns to its radiant, intimate, deathless Source — Mundaka Upanishad

He who has become liberated in this life gains liberation in death and is eternally united with the Absolute Reality. Such a seer will never be reborn — Shankara

In my flowing-out I entered creation, in my breakthrough I re-enter God. Only those who have dared to let go can dare to re-enter — Meister Eckhart

Have you discovered the beginning, then, so that you are seeking the end? For where the beginning is the end will be. Blessed is one who stands at the beginning: that one will know the end and he will not taste death — The Gospel of Thomas

Remembering that this body is like froth, of the nature of a mirage, break the flower-tipped

arrows of Mara. Never again will death touch you…Freed from illusion…they have renounced the world of appearance to find Reality. They have they reached the highest — The Dhammapada (sayings of Buddha)

Your starting point is truth, and you must return to your Beginning. Much has been seen since then, but nothing has really happened. Your Self is still in peace, even though your mind is in conflict — A Course in Miracles

The infinite Mind of The All is the womb of all universes. Spirit is simply a name that men give to the highest conception of Infinite Living Mind — it means 'the Real Essence.' Don't feel insecure or afraid; we're all held firmly in the Infinite Mind of the All, & there's naught to hurt us or for us to fear. All are on the Path whose end is the All. All progress is a returning home — The Kybalion

This goal is, in itself, extremely helpful in letting go of our attachment to virtual reality. It centers us in the understanding that we are not this body and this life is no more than a shadow of the infinite possibilities that await us when we awaken to the true Self.

2. Transcendence

Unfortunately, our conditioning can easily stand in the way of accepting the goal of return. Why? Most of us have been trained to see transcendence as something outside us, the privilege of a chosen few.

When we reviewed the Nag Hammadi writings, you'll remember that it soon became clear that several of them began with a foundation of truth but then became increasingly complex, layering one misperception on top of another. And, as we discovered, most of those misperceptions focused on specialness; dividing people into groups that were considered worthy and unworthy, the few who were "called by God" and the majority who never would be. Since that time nothing has changed; the world still believes the lie that very few are worthy of being chosen. This fundamental unworthiness has been drummed into the human worldview for so long; it can feel impossible to release. Hafiz clearly understood the immense influence this lie has had on each of us when he said, "More attentive than any lover or parent is God to us, but our gauge of judgment is impaired by the world's values." Fortunately, the world is wrong.

As we've learned, the entirety of existence is One. No matter how long we choose to dream of separation, that truth can never change. And even though we've created a dream of duality, all those who have experienced the Divine instantly recognize Oneness. This Oneness testifies to the fact that in Reality, it's impossible for us to be separated from All That Is. If we accept the Oneness that the sages and quantum physics have revealed, we must decide whether that Oneness is indifferent or loving. Our own direct experience offers us a conclusive answer, but short of that, we have the testimony of the sages who have experienced the Divine. As we read in *The Gospel of Truth*, "The Divine loves all and chooses all." On the subject of Divine love, the Sufi mystics are particularly eloquent:

Be drunk in love, for love is all that exists...Be certain in the religion of love there are no believers or unbelievers. Love embraces all...You are – we all are – the beloved of the Beloved...Without love, nothing in the world would have life...God is so infinitely tender-hearted and so overflowing with grace, that if He could die for you so that duality could vanish, He would – Rumi

O, surely there is something wrong with your ideas of God if you think our Beloved would not be tender...Your unhealed wounds exist because God and love have yet to become real enough to allow you to forgive the dream...Just sit there right now. Don't do a thing, just rest. For your separation from God, from love, is the hardest work in this world...Know the true nature of the Beloved. In His loving eyes, your every thought, word and movement is always, always beautiful... We need love, because love is the soul's life, love is simply creation's greatest joy – Hafiz

The compelling combination of Oneness and Divine love act as surety that transcendence is open to all of us. As we learned from Attar's *Conference of the Birds*, it is not the Divine that leaves us standing on the doorstep; we do that to ourselves by clinging to separation:

Everything has being because of God's love. God is all love and wants to love all. God is everything that is good and the goodness that everything

possesses is God. We have always been in God's foreknowledge; known and loved without beginning...We were made for love — Julian of Norwich

Each separate being in the universe returns to the common Source. Returning to the Source is serenity — Lao-tzu

Divine love cannot deny its very Self. Divine love will be eternally true to its own being, and its being is giving all it can... God lies in wait for us with nothing so much as love — Meister Eckhart

The Lord of Love is the one Self of all — Mundaka Upanishad

God is not only true and good, he is also beautiful. He creates beauty — for the joy of it — Nisargadatta Maharaj

What kind of God would He be if the vote of millions in this world could sway Him to change the divine law of love? — Kabir

3. Gurus/Teachers/Masters

No man can reveal to you anything but that which already lies half asleep in the dawning of your knowledge — Khalil Gibran

In this world we've been taught to rely on experts. This makes sense to us since no one person can take in all of the world's knowledge or reason through it. Religion has always encouraged its adherents to hand off their spiritual responsibilities to a minister or priest who supposedly acts as a mediator between them and God. And, as long as we believe the Divine is outside us, spiritual seekers will also feel the need for a guru or teacher. However, this can be rather like expecting a doctor to cure us with pills and surgeries when we refuse to take care of ourselves. Buddha alluded to this when he said, "Does the spoon taste the soup? A fool may live all his life in the company of a master and still miss the way." Why does that happen? These quotes give us a concise answer:

Spiritual knowledge cannot be communicated from one intellect to another, but must be sought for in the spirit of God — Jacob Bohme

If you think that the Truth can be known from words, if you think that the sun and the ocean can pass through that tiny opening called the mouth, O someone should start laughing! Someone should start wildly Laughing Now! — Hafiz

When you hear that some great master has appeared...to liberate all beings, immediately clap your hands over your ears. As long as you aren't your own master...what you hear is secondhand merchandise, and not yours. The master can only bear testimony. If you have gained something within, he can't hide it, if you haven't, he can't find it for you. Why should you preserve my speech and tie up your own tongues? — Yunmen Wenyan (aka Unmon Daishi, Chinese Zen Master, 862-949)

Clearly put, there is no such thing as spiritual osmosis; it's impossible to absorb Divine knowing. On the other hand, Hazrat Inayat Khan pointed out, "One thing is true. Although the teacher cannot give the knowledge, he can kindle the light *if the oil is in the lamp.*" The italicized potion of that quote is key. When our desire for truth is real, some outside assistance may be helpful, especially when we first become aware of our spiritual nature and have no idea where to go from there. If that were not so, we certainly would not have taken the time to gather the words of the sages in this book. But if we're merely titillated by being in the presence of someone who is purported to be a guru, we might as well seek out actors and rock stars instead.

Nevertheless, Krishnamurti warns, "There are all these appalling gurus going around the world, collecting money, followers, distorting the minds of people." When we're in our spiritual infancy the little self will eagerly direct us toward the people and concepts that will keep us in thrall to separation and specialness. However, these faddish spiritual bandwagons can easily keep us traveling on one spiritual detour after another, feeling certain that everything we're seeking will be miraculously discovered around the next bend. Rumi advised, "When setting out on a journey, do not seek advice from those who have never left home." Eknath Easwaran expanded on this thought when he said:

> *The spiritual teacher must know every inch of the way, every danger and pitfall, and not from books or maps or hearsay. He must have traveled it*

himself from the foothills to the higher peaks. And
he must have managed to get back down again, to
be able to relate to students with humility and
compassion.

But this is especially difficult when we are still
unable to tell the difference between a sage and a
charlatan. Kabir adds, "The words guru, swami,
master, teacher, yogi, priest, most of those sporting
such a title are just peacocks...He is the real Guru
who can reveal the form of the formless before your
eyes; who does not make you close your doors,
and hold your breath, and renounce the world."
The important point that Kabir made is seen in the
last half of the quote. Who is that guru that Kabir
pointed to? Ramana Maharshi and Nisargadatta
Maharaj gave us the answer when they said:

The Guru cannot give you anything new which
you have not already...The Guru comes only to
say, `That God is within yourself. Dive within
and realize'. God, Guru and the Self are the
same — Ramana Maharshi

The greatest Guru is your inner self. Truly, he
is the supreme teacher. He alone can take you to
your goal and he alone meets you at the end of
the road. Confide in him and you need no outer
Guru...Words betray their hollowness. The real
cannot be described, it must be experienced —
Nisargadatta Maharaj

It is usually not in our nature to jump into uncharted
waters on our own, but in this case we are never
truly alone; you have never been separated from

your true Self. The strong desire Nisargadatta mentioned is demonstrated by our complete willingness to let go of our conditioned beliefs and allow the true Self and Source to instruct us. This can happen in numerous ways; a phrase in a book, a movie or something someone says may resonate with us. We might come to a new understanding during contemplation, but the instruction that comes through the true Self and gnosis goes past learning to knowing. This difference is so great; the two cannot be compared. Bodhidharma made this clear when he said, "A sagacious student does not depend on his teacher's words, but uses his own experience to find the truth. *The ultimate truth is beyond words.* Doctrines are words. They're not the Way." [Italics ours]

We may decide not to turn to a guru who is outside us, but do we make a guru of the brain? Buddhist teacher Edward G. Muzika addressed this issue when he said, "You can't 'figure your way out' of the conceptual prison that your mind has created. The mind cannot 'see' outside the mind. Freedom can come only when you leave the entire conceptual framework behind." And as Wu Hsin, whose name literally means "no mind," explained, "Until the boundary between inner and outer dissolves, all changes are only minor." When a student asked Wu Hsin why he could not perceive in the same way as the sage, Wu Hsin answered, "You have accepted your brain as your teacher. You listen to it and obey its instructions. Little wonder you have gone so far from your true nature."

As you've learned, the brain is an illusion and the little self, the tiny portion of consciousness that directs it, was born from the misperception that separation and specialness could work as well as oneness. The little self, and in turn the brain, wear blinders that allow them no grasp of Reality. Using the word 'mind' to refer to the little self, Ramana Maharshi pointed out, "Mind is consciousness which has put on limitations. You are originally unlimited...Later you take on limitations and become the mind." The little self and brain create a tremendously powerful closed-loop feedback circuit that supports humanity's love affair with logic, problem solving and the storage of information considered vital to maintaining control. (Note: like many other writers, Muzika used the words mind and brain interchangeably. He was not referring to consciousness, but others, like Ramana Maharshi, have used mind to mean consciousness, both the false and the true. This word has been applied in so many different ways; unless the reader takes the time to look at the context of a phrase they may be unable to discern what the writer was actually referring to.)

Scientific materialism points to the brain as your body's control center and the abode of your identity. Consciousness is considered a material brain function that must necessarily die along with the body. But the sages go beyond the material worldview and explain that the body and brain are the minions of the little self. Instead of choosing for itself, the brain sees, hears and stores what the little self wants to see, hear and store. Using every electrochemical operation at its disposal, it addicts the body to whatever makes it strong and rejects whatever weakens it. Indian teacher Meher Baba (1894-1969) recognized this truth when he stated, "Intellect is best suited to know all about duality, which is born of ignorance and is entirely ignorance."

When we realize that the little self is actually in the driver's seat, we can understand why the brain is best utilized as a useful servant rather than the despotic master it can easily become. In fact, quantum research is pointing toward a "filter hypothesis" that considers the brain analogous to the tuning mechanism on a radio receiver. We know that when we tune a radio to the station we want to listen to, we're focusing on one signal even though countless other radio stations continue to be broadcast. We no longer hear the other stations, but they are still there. The filter hypothesis describes consciousness as having unbounded, unlimited, non-local range, but the brain filters out everything else that consciousness is aware of when it 'tunes in' to the time-space channel the human form experiences. Based on his own experience of the Divine, Alan Watts testified, "To "know" Reality you cannot stand outside it and define it; you must enter into it, be it, and feel it…You must remove your own preconceived ideas of God to actually experience God." Doing that means tuning out the little self's time-space broadcast. At the end of this chapter, we'll discuss what the sages have to say about bypassing the barriers of the little self, brain and body and experience the Divine.

4. Turning the Means into the End

Crossing a body of water has often been used to symbolize the transition from spiritual sleep to awareness. Buddha used this imagery when he said, "Few are those who reach the other shore; most people keep running up and down this shore. What do I teach? Only what is necessary to take you to the other shore." In this case, a boat would stand for whatever might assist us in reaching the shore of awareness. It would seem that if something had helped us 'wake up,' we would treasure it, but Buddha had a very different idea. To illustrate the point, he told a story of four travelers who used a boat to cross a river. After crossing, they were so taken with the usefulness of the boat; they decided to keep it with them always. They agreed they could best continue their journey by carrying the boat on their heads. Suddenly, something that had been incredibly helpful turned into a burden. The boat not only blocked their sight, it weighed them down and slowed their progress to a snail's pace. Still, they loved the boat for the good it had done and they refused to leave it behind. They reasoned that it would be worth the effort to haul it with them just in case they encountered another river.

There are many 'boats' available to us: religion, 'holy scriptures,' spiritual practices, rituals and even mystical experiences. Of course the point the Buddha was making is that all these 'boats' can serve as a means, but none of them are the end. We may use maps or a GPS to guide us to our destination, but once we've arrived we put them away. If we travel the same route again, we don't pull them out and behave as if we have no knowledge of the journey. Unfortunately fear often causes us to hang on to the means we're comfortable with, sticking to it long after we've received the desired benefits and could have moved on. Going back to Buddha's travelers, we could easily imagine them hauling the boat until they became so exhausted they decided to give up the journey rather than their beloved boat. Alan Watts observed, "The happy traveler wanders and does not let himself be the slave of maps, guidebooks, and schedules, using them but not being used by them." In his book *Wake Up and Roar*, H.W. L. Poonja, also known as Papaji (1910-1997) explained that it's actually our heart condition, not a specific method, which will carry us to truth:

> *Don't worry about methods. If you are sincere and honest, and have a true desire for freedom, even wrong methods will take you there. Therefore, give rise to the desire 100 percent, and the rest will take care of itself. What you are doing is not important, the end is important. You can do anything you like. The end must be that "I have to be free." You must be sincere, serious, and honest. Then don't worry about the methods. This inside Self is consciousness itself. If you do not know the correct method, it will lead you. Where you are arriving, it already knows who is coming, and it will go out to receive you in the proper way for you. You must be honest and never mind proper methods.*

5. The Quick Fix

We live in a world of quick fixes, so it's not surprising that many expect spirituality to work the same way; read a book or two, take a class, attend a seminar or retreat and you're there. Some feel they can coast on a mystical experience or two, seeing that as proof that they've 'made it.' And a few feel sure that the Divine can be reached through drugs. The quick fix is characterized by titillation and addition, returning to Source by intense focus and subtraction. In his book *The End of Your World*, Adyashanti pulled no punches when he wrote:

> *Make no mistake about it—enlightenment is a destructive process. It has nothing to do with becoming better or being happier. Enlightenment is the crumbling away of untruth. It is seeing through the façade of pretense. It's the complete eradication of everything we imagined to be true.*

If that sounds radical, it is, but that's what's necessary. To let go of the body, its identity, conditioning, attachments, aversions and especially the control exerted by the little self, strips us of all our illusions. We can't blame Source for making things difficult for us; we're the ones that chose to go deep into the "far country," so we're the ones that need to turn around and go back. Clearly, a quick fix will never take us there. Instead, this journey demands focus and the determination that nothing will stand in our way. It would be disingenuous for us to suggest that the road of return is level and smooth; it's as rugged as we've made it. As Huang Po pointed out, "Not until your thoughts cease all their branching...will you be on the right Road to the Gate." Anyone who has tried to break a habit or change the way they think and act, experiences many ups and downs. Attempting to let go of strongly held beliefs, attachments and aversions can cause us a great deal of pain if we're also trying to cling to them. American spiritual teacher and author Gangaji (1942–) drew from personal experience when she said, "Deep inquiry is not for the faint-hearted…It's for those who are ready and willing, regardless of fears and discomforts."

In the fourth century, Ge Hong (aka Ko Hung 283–343), Taoist philosopher and alchemist, noticed an issue that remains common today:

> *To know the One is easy; the difficulty lies in cherishing it to the end…Guarding the One and keeping the mind fixed upon it demands the utmost sincerity of purpose. The thoughts must be fixed on pure spirit – the One; then will the mind reach out to the mysterious Way and the longed-for state be attained.*

Raised in an agnostic household, Christian mystic Simone Weil (1909-1943) also learned through experience that, "In purely spiritual matters, God grants all desires. Those who have less have asked for less." In spiritual matters, our willingness is rewarded, but as Rumi, Nisargadatta and Shankara remind us:

> *Half-heartedness doesn't reach into majesty—* Rumi

> *But again you must have the strong desire to find him and do nothing that will create obstacles and delays…The real is, behind and beyond words, incommunicable, directly experienced, explosive in its effect on the mind. It is easily had when nothing else is wanted—* Nisargadatta Maharaj

> *Buried treasure is not uncovered by uttering the words "come forth." You must dig, remove the stones…and make it your own—* Shankara

6. Using the World to Understand Reality

Although this point sounds like the second cousin to making the brain your guru, it's actually more about attachment to the human experience and personality. Frustrated by seekers who clung to their human identity, Nisargadatta commented:

> I am not interested in answering questions that assume the existence of an individual person who inhabits a body. I don't accept the existence of such an entity, so for me such questions are entirely hypothetical. Have your being outside this body of birth and death and all your problems will be solved. They exist because you believe yourself born to die. Undeceive yourself and be free. You are not a person.

Self-help books, seminars, webinars and retreats abound, but the 'self' they're trying to improve is usually limited to the body and personality. The little self loves this sort of detour since it can easily keep us walking it for an entire lifetime. Wu Hsin clearly understood why this attachment is such a problem, "The goal of the individual is the perpetuation and preservation of the individual. When the individual is understood as nothing other than a construct, all notions of the goal disappear." And as Rumi pointed out, "Your physical attributes, like your body, are merely borrowed. Do not set your heart on them, for they are transient and only last for an hour." Yes, many recognize the truth that we are not the body, but still have a very difficult time making that truth their reality and remain bound to the problems and worries of this world. Once again, Nisargadatta got right to the crux of the matter when he said, "You do not want to give up either worldly knowledge or so-called spiritual knowledge. And yet, through these worldly concepts, you want to understand the riddle of your existence; and that is precisely why you are not able to understand." American sage Robert Adams (1928-1997) was also very clear on the subject:

> *No matter how many times I tell you this, you're still thinking, thinking, judging, coming to conclusions, trying to work out your life. You have to let go. Totally, absolutely, completely. You have to let go so completely, that you will feel no body, no mind, no pain, nothing. That is the only time you will make progress. Do not think about this. The thoughts cannot help you. There are no thoughts that can help you realize the Self. It is only a total completely letting go, giving up.*

Keep in mind that an essential component of our experiment was 'narrowing down' our full range of consciousness, limiting our 'vision' to the time/space duality. What you are surrendering is that valueless limitation. You have never been the little self or the thousands of bodies and personalities that felt so real when you experienced them. They are the masks you've put on to play a part. You cannot use a mask to reveal the identity it's hiding any more than you can use the body to discover your Reality. Remove that mask and know who and what you've always been. You'll be amazed.

7. Building Utopia

Concerned for its own survival, the little self will also cunningly support the quest for a better world. As pure consciousness, we *had* the ability to go anywhere our imagination would take us and experience *through* all of our creations without commandeering them. And, when we return to our natural state, we'll recover that ability. So, as we've repeated over and over throughout this text, separation and specialness were the sole reasons for experiencing virtual reality in the guise of our own human creations. Although we were confident that our experiment would succeed, there must have been a seed of doubt. Why do we come to that conclusion? We chose to include an 'escape hatch' in our plans. When we begin to feel there must be something other than this world, our questioning trips a trigger that allows the whisperings of the true Self to be heard. This fits perfectly with free will, since we each have to start the 'waking up' process on our own and can slow it, stop it, or accelerate it, as we choose. The more we sincerely question and seek, the louder that inner voice becomes and the more aware we become of the true Self and One Mind. But as we've said, the very existence of the little self depends on keeping the experiment alive by doing whatever it must do to quiet the Self.

The little self's most potent and fruitful schemes have always included a strong appeal to the body. Currently there's a significant movement among the world's spiritual communities to bring about a utopia that will heal the suffering of our planet and every living thing on it. It is believed that a 'shift' in world consciousness will be inevitable when thoughts of love and oneness reach a tipping point by finally' outweighing' the hate and greed that have dominated our world. The idea that other's minds can be manipulated by the sheer force of love that surrounds them violates free will, but that fact is usually ignored. And if that were possible, it would also mean that those who want to love could be manipulated into hating if they were surrounded by enough hate. We can be grateful that the structure of consciousness doesn't support that sort of manipulation, no matter what the purpose.

We certainly understand how compelling the little self's appeal can be since we fell under the spell of utopian thinking ourselves. We felt certain there had to be a way to bring duality into harmony, to create a paradise everyone could enjoy while continuing to pursue specialness: to recognize our true nature while still coopting a body. Put like that it sounds ridiculous, but regardless of the disparity, we felt that the utopian scheme remained a noble and valuable idea. Guilt over human responsibility for the earth's acute, and perhaps fatal, pain also fueled the desire to make amends. But when we were willing to be honest with ourselves, we had to admit that this was the little self's same old scheme for yet another version of virtual reality that cannot work. How can we be so sure? The quantum holds the answer. We'll be approaching this question in a round-about manner, but the answer is on the way.

Imagine how impossible it would be to navigate the group consciousness at the foundation of this world if each of us projected and experienced it in a totally different way. While it's true that the brain's perception skews what each of us believes we're experiencing, right now we're referring to the seemingly concrete portion of virtual reality that we all experience in the same way, such as what a specific chair or table might look like, or an animal, plant or person. There could be no shared experience if everything appeared to be different for each of us. Consciousness is infinite, but without structure even it would create utter chaos. In his book *Why Materialism is Baloney*, scientist/philosopher Bernardo Kastrup explains that "the regularities and commonalities of experience across observers...are based on the idea that the flow of the contents of mind obeys certain patterns and regularities." We accept the fact that structure exists in virtual reality when we bow to the 'laws of nature.' Since we see laws, parameters and structure in everything we project, there should be no surprise in learning that the consciousness that does the projecting is also structured.

We've been referring to the 'material universe' as a virtual reality, but *everything* consciousness imagines can be thought of as virtual. As Kastrup points out, consciousness, the substrate or foundation of All That Is, is not made up of 'stuff.' *Consciousness imagines stuff, it doesn't make stuff.* You exist as a thought held in Divine consciousness, everything else exists as a thought held in the One Mind of shared consciousness. The parameters or structure that consciousness operates within allows us to share our imaginings. One of these parameters allows for consciousness to 'fix or cement' a projection so that it can be shared. For example, if I think about a table I'd like to have, draw the design and then go out to my workshop and build it, it's my conscious choices that 'cement' that thought in place. As a result of this 'cementing' everyone will see the table as I see it and be able to use it in the same way I do.

This is also how our world scenario of duality, separation and specialness came into being. When we chose to experiment with these concepts, we 'cemented' the operating parameters of the world we're experiencing. This shared projection will remain fixed in duality and will remain so as long as any consciousness desires the dualistic experience. A thought that's been cemented in this way can't be changed, but it can disappear. When you have fully accepted the fact that separation and specialness cannot work and you are no longer willing to project duality, the experiment ends for you. You'll live out the lifetime of the body you're projecting, but you'll no longer remain enmeshed in the illusion. *A Course in Miracles* refers to this state as "the happy dream" and Jesus described it as "being in the world but not of the world."

As the *Course* states, "It is impossible to see two worlds which have no overlap of any kind. Seek for the one; the other disappears. But one remains. They are the range of choice beyond which your decision cannot go. The real and the unreal are all there are to choose between, and nothing more than these." (W-pI 130:5:1-5) Jesus also taught that we cannot slave for two masters, and in this case the 'masters' are separation or oneness. Plotinus verified the impossibility of repairing the dualistic illusion when he said, "Like can only apprehend like; when you thus cease to be finite, you become one with the Infinite." And Rumi states the goal clearly, "Your task? Escape...the fires of madness, illusion, and confusion that are, and always will be, this world."

Why do we keep falling for the hoax of turning duality into a paradise over and over, no matter how much evidence mounts up proving separation won't work? For starters, the brain is geared to very selectively gather and retain information and construct beliefs that fit its expectations; or should we more accurately say the expectations of the little self? These blinders are known as cognitive dissonance and confirmation bias. In the late 1950s, psychologist Leon Festinger (1919-1989) demonstrated that the brain will shut out or explain away information that disagrees with its beliefs while favoring and reinforcing information that appears to confirm them. The more emotionally charged a belief, the stronger the dissonance or confirmation. Simply put, the little self's fear of its forgotten Reality causes the brain to cling to its familiar virtual reality. And what we know and love right now is life on earth.

Our deep love of the earth is very natural, and not just because we believe this world is our reality. We were brought into existence to join with the Divine in the joy of creation and we shared in the birth of the universe. Surprisingly, the *Bible*, at Genesis 1:26 takes note of this when it quotes God as saying, "Let *us* make man in *our image* according to *our likeness*." [Italics ours] Since this statement contradicts earlier creation accounts in Genesis, some claim that God was speaking of himself in the plural, much as a king might. But Job 38: 4 and 7 also speak of "all the sons of God" who were present and shouted joyfully when the foundations of the earth were laid. *A Course in Miracles* reminds us, "To create is to love." (T-7 I 3:3) Even though we don't remember creating this world our love for it remains, making the appeal of a healed, utopian earth extremely seductive. However, our original creation and the dualistic overlay we're projecting on it, have nothing to do with one another.

A Course in Miracles confirms, "Be confident that your creations are as safe as you are." (T-4 III 1:11) Just as we're held in Divine consciousness, our creations remain as long as they're held in our consciousness. As the *Course* goes on to explain, our experience of separation, like a dream, will evaporate when we stop projecting it, "The world is false perception. It is born of error, and it has not left its source. It will remain no longer than the thought that gave it birth is cherished." (W-pII 240:3:1-3) Although we created the time/space universe in unity and cooperation, our creation gave birth to the idea that we could experience duality as well. When we first thought of separation and specialness and began to desire them, our desire entered the quantum field and interacted with the potential for duality, bringing into form a stage where that experience could be played out. This virtual reality is no more than a warped reflection of our true creations, a screen where the story of separation and specialness is projected. Simply put, it's a mask that overlays our original creative thoughts; a dream masking a dream.

Since virtual reality can disappear only when the thought that fuels it is completely forgotten, can that ever happen? Many more have already returned to Source than we might initially imagine. Nevertheless, many find it difficult to believe that everyone will make that choice. And, as we discussed earlier, violating someone else's free will, no matter how noble the reason, is not how consciousness operates. However, there is a second, and far more probable, way for our experiment to end.

When scientists have completed their tests and verified their results, they don't continue carrying out the same experiment over and over again, Instead, they write up their conclusions, pack up their equipment and move on to something new. Even when they disprove something they had set out to prove, they don't consider their experiment a failure. Now they know what won't work and can build from there. If an experiment continually blows up in their faces, they have no alternative but to accept the outcome and move on. We came here to prove that separation and specialness could work as well, or better than, oneness. Although most of us refuse to admit it, the experiment has already failed. We've tried every form and combination of social, economic, political and religious construct possible, but eventually each has produced more problems than it has solved. Currently we cling to the belief that technology has all the answers, but we've found time and again that each new invention comes with more complications. At this point, we may well be on the brink of blowing up our experiment.

The "Doomsday Clock," a symbolic clock face maintained by scientists associated with *The Bulletin of the Atomic Scientists*, represents a countdown to possible global catastrophe. In January 2015, due to increased nuclear threats, economic upheaval, bio-weapons and climate change, the clock was moved forward two minutes and is now set at three minutes to midnight. In a 2014 LiveScience.com article entitled "Here's More Proof Earth Is in Its 6th Mass Extinction" author Laura Geggel pointed out, "Over the last century, species of vertebrates are dying out up to 114 times faster than they would have without human activity…Much of the extinction is due to human activities that lead to pollution, habitat loss, the introduction of invasive species and increased carbon emissions that drive climate change and ocean acidification." Her article shared this quote from researcher and professor of conservation ecology Gerardo Ceballos, "Our activities are causing a massive loss of species that has no precedent in the history of humanity and few precedents in the history of life on Earth…[the research] shows without any significant doubt that we are now entering the sixth great mass extinction event." As the human population explodes and that population continues to compete even more doggedly for specialness, the continued destruction of resources becomes inescapable. As eminent biologist, conservationist and author Rachel Carson (1907-1964) put it, "The question is whether any civilization can wage relentless war on life without destroying itself?" We may put it off at times, but the concrete nature of our projection will not allow us to put off the inevitable indefinitely.

As we stated earlier, if a science experiment continually blows up in the faces of researchers despite their repeated tweaking, intelligence dictates they accept the results and move on. But for many who are deeply entrenched in duality, the absolute destruction of the illusion may be the only way they'll wake up to the realization that it could never successfully compete with Oneness. This result wouldn't violate free will because it is one of the possible outcomes of the experiment we agreed to. As dire as that sounds, we must remember that the end of the experiment will resemble waking up from a nightmare. The destructive end of our experiment will no doubt feel terrifying as we project it, but as soon as we wake up we'll know that it was a dream and that the true Self remained exactly as it was when the experiment began. Considering how many novels, movies and TV shows revolve around mass destruction; this possibility must be surfacing within group sub-consciousness. We all have the choice to wake up more easily if we choose to do so now, but free will allows for either choice without loss or punishment. Jesus referred to this fact in a parable that has angered many who are attached to a belief in judgment and punishment:

For the kingdom of the heavens is like a householder who went out early in the morning to hire laborers for his vineyard. After agreeing with the laborers for a denarius a day, he sent them into his vineyard. And going out about the third hour he saw others standing idle in the market place; and to them he said, "You go into the vineyard too, and whatever is right I will give you." So they went. Going out again about the sixth hour and the ninth hour, he did the same. And about the eleventh hour he went out and found others standing; and he said to them, "Why do you stand here idle all day?" They said to him, "Because no one has hired us." He said to them, "You go into the vineyard too." And when evening came the owner of the vineyard said to his steward, "Call the laborers and pay them their wages beginning with the last, up to the first." And when those hired about the eleventh hour came, each of them

> *received a denarius. Now when the first came,
> they thought they would receive more; but each of
> them also received a denarius. And on receiving it
> they grumbled at the householder, saying, "These
> last worked only one hour, and you have made
> them equal to us who have borne the burden of
> the day and the scorching heat." But he replied to
> one of them, "Friend, I am doing you no wrong;
> did you not agree with me for a denarius? Take
> what belongs to you and go; I choose to give to
> this last as I give to you. Am I not allowed to do
> what I choose with what belongs to me? Or do
> you begrudge my generosity?* — Matthew 20:1-
> 19 Revised Standard Edition

When we desire *all* to return to Source, without exception, this parable is heart-warming. When we cling to specialness, justice tends to mean "just us" and fairness is primarily about getting what feels fair for us alone. Happily, Rumi tells us that Divine justice means "Putting each thing in its real place" and the Oneness of All That Is, is our Real place. One way or the other, we can all be assured that our return to Source is guaranteed. The question is whether we choose to wake up and return of our own accord, or be 'shook awake' by the definite and inarguable end of our experiment.

> *The only true joy on earth is to escape from the
> prison of our own false self* — Thomas Merton
> (Christian mystic and author 1915-1968)

III. The Final Fears

> *All your sufferings are from believing you know
> better than God. Such a special brand of arrogance
> as that always proves disastrous* — Hafiz

We are always asking, "What is truth?" And then crucifying the truth that stands right before our eyes — Thomas Merton

Only someone who is ready for everything...even the most incomprehensible...will himself sound the depths of his own being — Rilke

And now the task changes. It's a completely different kind of spiritual universe that you live in after you found the answer, because the task becomes facing the answer — Terrance McKenna

When we slip through the cracks of virtual reality and witness the Divine All, we realize two things:

» The mystery is infinite and magnificent beyond our most far-reaching imagination.

» It is absolutely real; so tangible in fact, that in comparison, this world loses all semblances to Reality.

No matter how ready we believe we are for this unveiling, our reaction may surprise us.

We've already mentioned Jesus' saying from the *Gospel of Thomas*, "Let one who seeks not stop seeking until one finds." Let's return to it once more but this time in a very personal context. In the Greek version of *Thomas* the verse continues this way, "When one finds, one will be astonished, and having been astonished one will reign, and having reigned, one will rest." The Coptic version contains a subtle variation, ending this way, "When one finds, one will be troubled. When one is troubled, one will marvel and will reign over all." Although each person's awakening is different, most include the six general items mentioned in these two translations: seeking, finding, being astonished/ troubled, reigning and resting.

Spiritual seeking and finding can be compared to an archeological dig. When archeologists begin excavating a new site they have an expectation of what they might find, but very few of them can be absolutely certain of what will be found hiding under the rubble. Even when they have significant historical records to back their expectation, their discoveries may range from disappointing to astounding, or even bewildering or shocking. The same is true of spiritual 'finding.' We might expect some of what we dig up on the surface, but the experience of gnosis confronts us with something the brain could not possibly have imagined and often has great difficulty adapting to.

Like the archeologist we might think that at several points during the excavation process, we've discovered all there was to find. This might be the false mind's attempt to stop further progress by convincing us we're 'there.' Or, it could mean that we need some time to assimilate and adjust to the changes we're making before digging again. Regardless, when we're not 'there' yet, some nagging questions and doubts will remain that let us know we have further to go. Since that's the case, how can we really know that we've reached the point of 'finding?'

Imagine that you have a thousand piece jigsaw puzzle, but you don't have a picture of the finished puzzle to guide you. When you've put enough pieces together that there's no doubt in your mind what the puzzle reveals, you're there, and the puzzle is solved. That doesn't mean that you can't still put in a few pieces, but those pieces merely add supporting detail; they don't alter your understanding of the picture. When Jesus said not to stop seeking until you find, he was telling us that there is a place where the picture is whole and clear. This happens during the spiritual union of gnosis when we 'become,' if even momentarily, the undeniable truth. We will continue to add details until we return to Source, but we'll hold a clear picture of what Reality is. The second clue lies in the words, "When one finds, one will be troubled."

We might also substitute words like shocked, stunned or even distressed. Why? In the *Gospel of Thomas* Jesus also promised, "I shall give you what no eye has seen, what no ear has heard, what no hand has touched, what has not arisen in the human heart." The senses long for what they can hear, taste, smell, see and touch while the brain seeks out what it can decipher, filter and store. But as we've discovered, a shift of consciousness that excludes the senses and boggles the brain, is necessary to experience the Divine. Although Jesus said we would be troubled when we find, we can also feel troubled as we seek. This is not because what we discover is actually troubling, but because it's not at all what we expected, or wanted, to find.

The sheer magnitude and magnificence of your infinite true Self can feel impossible to comprehend or accept. When this happens, remember that social conditioning, dualistic thinking and the brain's limitations couldn't possibly have prepared you for Reality. This brings to mind Chuang-Tzu's frog in the well that was unable to comprehend the existence of the ocean. Now imagine if the frog were suddenly lifted from the well and deposited on the shore. Although the frog could no longer deny the ocean's existence, that doesn't mean it would be comfortable with the truth. Why? Accepting the ocean's existence, would also mean the rejection of the frog's previous belief system, including the fact that his entire life in the well had been the aberration, not the reality. A similar loss of all that we had thought was real can pull the rug out from under us as well.

It's exciting to read about quantum research and discover that this world of matter is not our Reality. And it's mind-blowing to hear that we live in a fully conscious universe. But it can be quite troubling when you first experience your true Self in its full glory as non-local consciousness, a part of everything in existence. The brain, formerly so assured of its own supremacy and locality, reels as it is forced to assimilate the information. And, since most of us have been taught that God exists outside us, it can be troubling to cope with the truth that the Divine permeates everything in existence, and *You are That*.

Challenging as all this may be, another fear may feel even more daunting. Many are terrorized by the belief that returning to Source means being swallowed up by the Divine. Simply put, they cling to this life because they fear the loss of personal identity. But is this true? Let's begin by taking a closer look at why this concept is so frightening. In our world, a materialistic outlook reigns. We're not referring to consumerism, but rather material realism: the belief that matter is the fundamental — and the only — reality that exists. For material realists life supposedly began at an extremely simple level and became more and more complex until consciousness—a material function of the brain—evolved. Materialism contends that we have one life, and that life begins and ends with the body. The materialistic view is so ingrained, even those who claim they have a non-material soul that will go to heaven fight with everything they have to avoid the death of the body. And of course the false mind does everything in its power to reinforce the materialistic belief that we are nothing more than a 'one lifetime body.'

Oddly enough, most Western religions have developed the idea that we are the personality that's constructed during our one lifetime, and that personality becomes part of the soul that lives on. So in a way, the personality and the soul also take on a material aspect. It's no surprise that the loss of personality through brain trauma or Alzheimer's is considered catastrophic. As we've learned, the little self has built up an extremely long history of supporting, defending and identifying with countless personalities and is invested in our continued belief that we are those personalities. These misperceptions have taught us to feel certain that without our 'story' we'll lose our identity and individuality, becoming lost forever in a void of nothingness.

As we mentioned earlier in the book, some spiritual philosophies do describe Nirvana as a place where all identity is lost in Source. Other philosophies have used the word "void," which many have erroneously interpreted as nothingness. The sages, who have experienced the Divine, testify to the fact that in this case, 'nothingness' has a far different meaning than emptiness. Instead of pointing to oblivion, the term is used to symbolize the infinite potential contained within Source. Since potential remains 'unrealized' until it is realized, the ancients considered the unused potential a void. Huang Po made this clear when he wrote, "The Void is not really void, but the realm of the Real." The Divine *is* Reality, and as such, Source includes everything that exists plus the potential and energy for everything that can ever exist. As we've seen, quantum research backs this view. In *The Crest Jewel of Discrimination*, Shankara explained to a student that the void is what's left after the false mind is no longer deceiving us, but he also made it clear there is still an observer, a conscious being, aware of the Oneness that remains after the thought of duality is gone. If there truly was an empty void we all merged into, there could be no consciousness left to be aware.

We don't lose ourselves in Oneness, but rather, we finally experience the truth of who and what we have always been. And as Jesus said, this truth does set us free. Truth is always joyful, peaceful, loving and liberating, it's the false mind/little self that imprisons and limits us through fear. We live in a universe of consciousness and potential, which informs us that we also live in a universe of free will, choice and infinite creativity. Oneness means equality, the end of competition and the beginning of loving cooperation, never sameness or obliteration. In reality, every child of Source has the same talents but the infinite creative diversity that's apparent in the material universe demonstrates that each one is given the opportunity to express their talents as they will. The true Self has an identity, but that identity has nothing to do with the personalities developed by the little self. You will get a glimpse of that true Self during gnosis, but you'll have to wait until you return to Source to be completely reintegrated with the Self and rediscover exactly who you are.

As you'll remember from the section on Meister Eckhart, pantheism claims that God *is* the universe, meaning that all things are equally God, and only God. On the other hand, panentheism describes the Divine as the life-giving foundation of All That Is; a force that permeates and sustains everything in existence because everything exists within it and is part of it. You may be thinking that we just gave the same definition twice, but there are extremely important differences. Pantheism means you are the puppet and God the puppet master. Pantheism supports the belief that we were created to be *experienced through*, but all experience is the Divine's. In other words, you do not have choice or free will, in fact you are more like a tool than an individual. On the other hand, panentheism allows for beings that are one with the Divine yet are *not* the elemental foundation. In the same way, an acorn is *of* the oak tree but is not the tree it came from. It's true that acorns cannot produce anything except another oak tree; however, that tree will be a unique, individual tree while remaining essentially 'the same stuff' as the original tree. Simply put, while we will always remain *of* God; we are also unique beings that are privileged to share the Divine's life force, consciousness, free will, creativity and love.

Scientific Idealism, which concludes that conscious-ness is the irreducible foundation of everything in existence, also recognizes that within that founda-tion an infinite number of conscious viewpoints ex-ist. Bernardo Kastrup uses the metaphor of a whirlpool to demonstrate how this works. Imagine that a stream symbolize the consciousness we all share. Within that stream, some of the flow might be 'localized' by a small whirlpool. Although the whirlpool limits the water that enters and leaves its swirling motion, it is always made up of the water from the stream. No matter how tightly the whirlpool spins, it cannot become anything other than the stream. This tiny whirlpool resembles the way the little self has narrowed down the focus of consciousness so that it sees only the dualistic world it projects. Conversely, when a whirlpool widens out, it can only do so by taking in more of the stream. This happens when we access more of the One Mind by listening to the true Self. Gnosis offers an even wider scope, while a return to Source breaks up the whirlpool and we're within non-local Oneness once again. For Meister Eckhart, God was entirely beyond all and yet still completely within all, both the ground of all being and a personal God that loves us:

> *Divine love cannot deny it's very Self. Divine love will be eternally true to its own being, and its being is giving all it can…God lies in wait for us with nothing so much as love.*

Source's choice to *be* love required that other unique, individual beings exist. Obviously, love can only be appreciated, exchanged and expressed between beings that are conscious, can choose for themselves and exercise free will. When we return to Source we give up the personality shaped by the dualistic thinking of the false mind and the experiences of the body, but that that is not, and never has been, who you are. Yes, the true Self is non-local and exists throughout the stream, but this does not mean it is without personality. Each of us is a thought held in the mind of the Divine, so each of those thoughts must have variations. And, since this is a universe of choice, our own thoughts allow the true Self's personality and interests to grow and change. If that were not the case, we would not have gotten to the point of projecting our experiment. However, there are important differences between the personalities created by the little self and true Self. First, the former is a projection while the latter is a reality. And while the projected little self is bent on procuring specialness, the true Self willingly shines as one among a multitude of facets in the universal diamond. As Nisargadatta so clearly put it, "You are afraid of what you are. Your destination is the whole. But you are afraid that you will lose your identity. This is childishness."

Before we move on to the final section, we'll take a moment to go back to the "reigning" and "resting" we mentioned earlier from the *Gospel of Thomas*. What are we supposed to reign over? In the *Bible* at John 16: 33 Jesus said, "In the world you have tribulation: but be of good cheer; I have conquered the world." Most Christians interpret this verse from an apocalyptic/messianic perspective with Jesus playing the part of cosmic warrior, savior and king. From the gnostic/quantum perspective we understand that the kingdom is within each of us and we must save ourselves by waking up. No matter how much some would like to think of Jesus as a sword bearing military/political entity that literally conquers the world and establishes a theocracy on earth, what he actually conquered and reigned over was his own false self. The desire for separation and the drive for specialness no longer had a hold on him. Waking to who and what he truly was also gave Jesus the power to reign over all the illusions that had previously enslaved him.

Jesus' teachings, whether in the *Bible*'s *New Testament* or the Gnostic Gospels, are contradictory and confusing. This is not only because they reflect the confused thoughts of the writers, but they also reflect the abrupt change in Jesus' message that occurred when he 'became love.' Suddenly, in a culture focused on law and bent on vengeance, he shocked his listeners by proclaiming a God of infinite love and mercy. Rather than continuing to support earthly struggles for sovereignty, he pointed out that the kingdom is within each of us. At this point, he was resting in God. Once we reign over the little self, the struggle is over and we too can rest in the fullest sense of the word. After waking to the true Self, virtual reality becomes a game we know we've already won. We continue playing as long as the body lives, but now we play from the perspective of a detached observer. Because we know, beyond any doubt, that all is well, we rest within our own peace despite the chaos that may swirl around us. And that, dear reader, is when we pass from doing to Being.

> *Together we will disappear into the Presence beyond the veil, not to be lost but found; not to be seen but known* — A Course In Miracles

IV. Gnosis and Being

> *Mystics are those individuals who have attained conscious union with God and who can attain this union almost at will* — Joel Goldsmith (mystic and author, 1892 –1964)

The Beloved is whispering to you exactly what you need to hear and know. Who can ever explain this miracle? It simply is. Listen and you will discover it every passing moment. Listen and your whole life will become a conversation in thought and act between you and Source, directly wordlessly, now and always. It was to enjoy this conversation that you and I were created — Rumi

Yes, living in a near constant state of communion with higher consciousness/true Self/Source is not only possible, as we learned from the perennial philosophy; it's what the Divine desires. As Nisargadatta Maharaj put it, "Truth is simple and open to all. It's loving and lovable. It includes all, accepts all, purifies all." But in our world, something this simple is rarely clear and easy. Quantum physics has discovered enough to determine that this world is an illusion. It has demonstrated that you are pure consciousness, not the material body projected by consciousness. Everything in existence occurs within that consciousness, nothing outside it. Consciousness is not a product of the brain, it is not stuff, nor is it made of stuff. Consciousness is a state of being that imagines stuff. But how do we get past our dualistic focus and allow more of the stream, if you will, into our little whirlpool? From personal experience Plotinus was able to tell us:

This is not a journey for the feet; the feet bring us only from land to land; nor need you think of coach or ship to carry you away. All this order of things you must set aside and refuse to see: you must close the eyes and call instead upon another vision which is to be waked within you, a vision, the birthright of all, which few turn to see.

Plotinus is asking us to identify our birthright and claim it. What is it? The sages have one answer: Love.

Love, which created me, is what I am — A Course In Miracles

All ignorance is lack of love...In one's search for truth, the first lesson and the last is love — Hazrat Inayat Khan

Love is not a mere sentiment. It is the ultimate truth that lies at the heart of creation — Rabindranath Tagore

Love is the pursuit of the Whole — Plato

The truth of love is the truth of the universe. It is the lamp of the soul that reveals the secrets of darkness — Kabir

You are far from the end of your journey. The way is not in the sky. The way is in the heart. See how you love — Buddha

Let loving lead your soul. Make it a place to retire to, a...retreat for the deepest core of being. Then build a road from there to God — Attar

You will learn by reading, but you will understand with love — Shams i-Tabrizi

The Lord of Love is the one Self of all. Realize the Self hidden in the heart and cut asunder the knot of ignorance here and now...The Lord of Love may be known through love but not through thought. He is the goal of life. Attain this goal — Mundaka Upanishad

The Lord of Love dwells in the hearts of all. To realize him is to go beyond death — Taittiriya Upanishad

Divine laws are simpler than human ones — which is why it can take a lifetime to be able to understand them. Only Love understands...Love means...to open the eyes of inner vision — Rumi

Needless to say, we are not speaking of the pathetic emotions that masquerade as love in this world. In an attempt to understand what the brain and unmanaged emotions cannot fathom, humanity has come up with extremely strange explanations for what love is. We divide it into separate categories, give each category a label such as *eros* (physical), *agape* (selfless), *philia* (friendship), *storge* (family) etc., and attach expectations and conditions to each 'type.' And sadly, we have no difficulty believing that it's possible to pour love out on some while denying it to others because we've judged them as unworthy.

The brain quantifies love as a give and take proposition and schemes to keep its ledgers in the black. Emotional love can become so deeply mired in sticky sentimentality and romantic notions; it continually flips back and forth between agony and ecstasy. We convinced ourselves that mercy and charity allow love to look down its nose at the recipients of our largesse. We've even distorted our concept of love to the point that we've convinced ourselves there's room within love for judgment, hatred, vengeance and war. But in Reality, Source balances, and therefore transcends, all duality, so Divine love can have no opposite. *A Course In Miracles* explains, "Perfect love casts out fear, if fear exists, then there is not perfect love. But: only perfect love exists. If there is fear, it produces a state that does not exist." (T-, VI. 5:4-7)

As we've discussed, many religions explain that God's approval must be won by perfecting ourselves while at the same time they're continually reminding us of how hopelessly sinful and imperfect we actually are. But that is not what the *Course* is saying. Rather, i*t's the perfection of Divine love itself that perfects the love of anyone willing to let go of duality and BE love*. This requires us to drop our concept of love as a thing that can be given and received and instead *become love*. The vast difference between doing and being should not be too difficult to comprehend since we all understand why behaving childishly and being a child are not at all alike. How do we go about making this shift? Instead of concentrating on acts or thoughts of love, *we willingly let go of anything that is not love*. Why? As the true Self we already are a Being of Love so we have nothing to attain. We do, however, need to remove everything that obscures that Being. Nisargadatta pointed out, "When all the false self-identifications are thrown away, what remains is all-embracing love."

We begin by loving ourselves. Yes, this is another one of those extremely simple concepts that are not always easy to carry out. The difficulty was expressed by Khalil Gibran when he said, "And God said, 'Love your enemy' and I obeyed Him and loved myself." Many who believe love is a thing that can be given and received have convinced themselves it's also possible to give love to others while denying it to themselves. Some even view this denial of self-love as a virtue. When we *become* love, we can clearly see that's both ridiculous and impossible.

When we begin the process of letting go of everything that is not love, and it is a process, we quickly find that our willingness to go past duality and *be* love can evoke some very deep-seated fears. The number of fears the little self has invented would probably outnumber the grains of sand on all the world's beaches, but Divine love has an answer for each of them. Our willingness itself is enough of an invitation for Self/Source to support, assist and direct us. And, as Robert Adams wrote, "Eventually you discover that you seek love because you are love. Therefore love is not an illusion, but the Ultimate Reality."

All the words contained in this book come down to one thing: choice. Your choice is whether to continue as the little, false self or wake up to your true, Divine Self. This choice has always been before you, and it's always been yours alone. If you want to remain in illusion, continue to sleep. If you want Reality, enter the garden of gnosis:

> *Why have you accepted death when you have been given the power to enjoy immortality? Light and life are God...and if you learn that you are also made of Light and Life, you will return to light and life...Understand that what sees and hears within you is the Mind of God...The closing of my eyes became the true vision...I became God-inspired, God-Minded, and came with the Truth...Let me not be removed from Gnosis... With your grace, let me bring Light. This is the good, the aim of those who have gnosis: to become God*—Hermes Trismegistus

Index

A

Thank you!
We appreciate the time you took to read
Understanding Gnosis:
Inside *and* Outside the Gnositc Gosples

It takes a lot of courage to release the familiar and seemingly secure, to embrace the new. But there is no real security in what is no longer meaningful. There is more security in the adventurous and exciting, for in movement there is life and in change there is power--Alan Cohen

The important thing is this: to be able at any moment to sacrifice what we are for what we could become--Charles Du Bois

Add to your understanding with:

The Beginning of Fearlessness: Quantum Prodigal Son

Fearless Spirituality:
What Sages Knew and Science Discovered

The Gospel of Thomas:
Where Science Meets Spirituality

Religious or Spiritual:
How the Difference Can Affect Your Happiness

Visit the Beginning of Fearlessness/Oroborus Books website:

thebeginningoffearlessness.com

www.ingramcontent.com/pod-product-compliance
Lightning Source LLC
Chambersburg PA
CBHW030817090426
42737CB00009B/759